Francois Jean Chastellux

An Essay on Public Happiness Investigating the State of Human Nature

Nature

Volume the First

Francois Jean Chastellux

An Essay on Public Happiness Investigating the State of Human Nature
Volume the First

ISBN/EAN: 9783744743655

Printed in Europe, USA, Canada, Australia, Japan

Cover: Foto ©Thomas Meinert / pixelio.de

More available books at **www.hansebooks.com**

A N

E S S A Y

O N

PVBLIC HAPPINESS,

INVESTIGATING

THE STATE OF HVMAN NATURE,

UNDER EACH OF

ITS PARTICULAR APPEARANCES,

THROUGH THE

SEVERAL PERIODS OF HISTORY,

TO THE PRESENT TIMES.

Nil defperandum. Hor.

VOLUME THE FIRST.

L O N D O N :

Printed for T. Cadell, in the Strand.

M.DCC.LXXIV.

ADVERTISEMENT.

AN eafily difcernible inferiority will enable the learned reader to diftinguifh the notes of the Tranflator, from thofe of his ingenious Author. For this reafon, it might, perhaps, feem unneceffary to affix any particular mark to the firft; but as it may happen that by blending all the Notes indifcriminately together, a lefs attentive obferver might imagine that thofe of the original Compofer had been written by the Tranflator, a K is placed at the conclufion of the additional notes. Where remarks may prove either falfe or frivolous, it muft be a contemptible act of meannefs which could endeavour to have them afcribed to an author incapable of producing fuch. To every reader, whofe knowledge of hiftorical and literary fubjects is preferved by a tenacious memory, this humble addition of remarks muft prove abfolutely needlefs; but memory is not the perpetual atten-

dant

dant upon learning, and the fcholar, who enjoys an imagination too lively to retain a regular detail of facts, will forgive the intrufion of matters which he may, poffibly, have forgotten. To the reader, who is lefs converfant in thefe fubjects, it is prefumed that no apology can be neceffary. Senfible of the great difficulty of infufing into verfions the fpirit of the originals, it is not eafy to defcribe the diffidence and apprehenfions with which the Tranflator commits his labour to the prefs. Even now, whilft he is writing, the vanity of a fecond-hand author entirely forfakes him, and he trembles left he fhould be taxed, not only with having ennervated the force of expreffions, by running beyond the limits of a merely literal conftruction, but thrown them into interpretations abfurdly diftant from their real meaning. The nice difcernment of every fault is folely peculiar to the few, who are capable of writing with elegance and perfpicuity. As their candour hath

generally

generally rifen in proportion to their knowledge of the hardnefs of fuch a tafk, he would willingly flatter himfelf that he might caft this firft attempt before them, after having premifed, that if he had beeñ much diffatisfied with it in the clofet, he fhould never have permitted its appearance in public. If he hath done wrong, it is the refult of ignorance alone. It is not in his nature to treat with difrefpect, that clafs of readers, for whom this work is calculated.

DEDICATION.

To EDMOND JENINGS, Esquire.

Dear Sir,

AT one of our many agreeable inter-
views, you were pleafed to propofe to
me, as a relaxation from feverer ftudies,
the amufement of tranflating the work
of fome favourite author. The fatisfaction which I fhall always feel in following your advice, is the only apology that
can be made, for prefenting to you, in an
Englifh

Englifh drefs, a compofition which you underftand fo perfectly in the French drefs.

The peculiar diftinction which humbly
avoids the praife, it conftantly attempts
to merit, fhall fecure you even againft the
violence of a modern dedication. I have
been too intimate with you to be ignorant
that panegyric is as painful to you, as the
bitternefs of invective to another. But
yet you muft not be fo unconfcionable as
to fuppofe, that becaufe your memory is
too treacherous to remind you of the
favours which you have conferred, they
can poffibly have efcaped mine. Through
the engaging commerce of an honeft
friendfhip, you have unmercifully incum-
bered me with an enormous debt. I
have no method of confeffing it, but this;
and thus, inftead of being payed, you
muft become a more capital creditor
than ever. A larger fum of gratitude is
owing, in recompence for the privilege
of fubfcribing myfelf,

With inviolable efteem,

Dear Sir,

Your fincere, and affectionate friend,

THE TRANSLATOR.

CONTENTS.

CHAP.

SECTION II.

*Considerations on the lot of humanity, during
the middle ages of history.*

THE

INTRODUCTION.

AFTER the lapfe of fo many enlightened ages, in which the moft ingenious and laborious refearches of fuc-
ceffive writers appear, even in trifles, to
have tried, examined, and compleated
every fubject, I muft prefume to fix the
attention of mankind upon new objects.
If it be demanded what thefe objects are,
the anfwer is, that they are become the
moft effential to our happinefs; they
lead to enquiries into a topic, an obligation, to difcufs which, is alarming;
they point to the folution of a queftion,

where doubt alone might prove difgraceful to humanity. Shall men be always
the enemies of men? fhall beings of the
beft organization, at no period, acquire
the advantages which the vileft of the
brutes poffefs; the advantages of living
peaceably with each other? is not fociety, at leaft, fufceptible of amendment,
if not of perfection?

In whatfoever manner this important
problem may be refolved, an ample field
will lie open to reflection : the inveftigation of human nature, as merely within itfelf; the adapting of it to political
inftitutions; and the examination of it,
not by theory, but experience, applying
it to the knowledge of our errors, afcend-
ing to their fources, and labouring to di-
vert their courfe, are, all fubjects to
awaken our attention. This laft fpecies
of enquiry is that on which we now beg
leave to fix, perfuaded that the writer who
mixes fome miftakes amongft his obfervations and comparifons, may be of ufe to

him

him that follows; whilſt the examiner, that wanders wildly from his mark, not only leaves truth behind him, at a diſtance, but becomes liable to deceive others, by directing them to a wrong road.

There was a time, when every author ſeemed infected with the rage of con- cluding from particulars, to generals. Pretenſions to genius, of all pretenſions the moſt extravagant, were then exceed- ingly the mode. A leading principle ex- plained, ſome few conſequences, lightly deduced, and ſome few facts, either well or ill adjuſted to the propoſed concluſion, were ſufficient to bear away the prize due to invention and imagination. It was not poſſible for this too great facility of acquiring renown to laſt long. It aroſe from an intercourſe of ſuperficially- inſtructed writers, with readers who knew nothing. The caſe is now altered. Scarce- ly hath the reader of underſtanding, and application, opened a book, but he can eſtimate its real value. If the work be

a 2   with-

without order and connection, he criticifes the particular paffages with impartiality, and continues to read on. If it
be obfcure, he reafonably fufpects that
the author did not, abfolutely, underftand himfelf: but if it be fyftematical,
opiniative, and fallacious, he throws it
afide, and will not fuffer it to be fpoken
of. Thefe enlightened, and perhaps, too
well informed readers, unfortunately employed, even to a degree of fatiety, know
that to toil in the purfuit of truths, to
confirm, affemble, and difpofe them in
proper order, is the real employment of
the man of genius: but this employment
is, at once, flow, and gradual. The in-
ventor hath marked out his path: by walking after him, one is no longer furprized
at feeing him arrived, and the multitude,
having heared, that genius hath wings,
are unwilling to acknowledge the print of
his footfteps.

Let us leave to thefe celebrated men,
who have drawn upon themfelves praife,
                                        and

and perfecution, the tafk of pleading their
own caufe, and avenging the rights of
reafon : let us even fear left we fhould be
thought more rafh in forming; than pro-
vident in moderating this attempt : at
leaft, before we engage in obfervations
purely hiftorical, and ftudious refearches
after facts, and the principles by which
they were occafioned, let us examine for
a moment, how far a fimple fpeculation
could have made us acquainted with the
particular relations, the general tenden-
cies, and, in fhort, all the qualities which
are proper to, and characterize human
nature.   Prepared to conduct our readers
through long, and winding ways, let us
caft one glance upon the fpace which we
muft leave behind, and convince them
that thofe eafier, and more agreeable
roads, the lofs of which they may perhaps regret, are terminated only by extenfive defarts.

To fubfift, to unite itfelf, to multiply
its fpecies, is the general wifh of nature;

the great bufinefs of every animated being.
If fociety be effentially neceffary to fome
amongft thefe, ftill it is but a fecondary
want, and fubordinate to thofe which we
have taken notice of before. The vul-
ture, that lives only on its prey, that is
dreaded by every other bird, and purfued
by man, fhould daily take a different
flight. It repairs, without diftinction,
to all places where it may with eafe find
fomething to devour; its fubfiftance is
precarious and irregular : at one time, it is
in want of food, and at another, poffeffes
more than it can poffibly confume: it muft,
therefore, provide againft future neceffi-
ties: it muft hide its booty. In the night
time, it muft fix its retreat within the
fummits of the fteepeft rocks, or on the
tops of lofty trees. On the contrary, the
pigeons, and the ftarlings, which readily
procure their nourifhment, in the marfhes
and the fields, but whofe defencelefs
condition expofes them to perpetual danger, feek, in fociety, thofe means of protection,

tection, which hurt not the means of fubfiftance. Such alfo is the cuftom amongft
the quadrupeds : tigers, and wolves remain in folitude, whilft the hinds and
deer graze all together : but at a certain
time, a powerful imperious want fprings
up, and finks all others in oblivion. The
focial animal avoids the reft of his clafs,
to fix his choice on one : the defires of
love, and fhortly afterwards, the cares of
his family, occupy his attention : but, in
the fpecies, which, brutally confummates
the act of generation, and where feveral fe-
males are enjoyed by the fame male, and
feveral males unite themfelves to one female, love makes little alteration in fociety : the fexes being indifcriminately
mingled, the animals remain in herds,
nor is fociety diffolved.

The lefs compound the organization of
beings is, the more their operations bear
a refemblance to each other. The nefts
of birds, the burrows of rabbets, and the
hives of bees are common to the two

a 4   fexes.

sexes. It is the same with regard to
cuftoms, founded on fimple wants, they
are themfelves equally fimple: deriving
their origin from a neceffity peculiar to
all, they continue to be the fame amongft
all the individuals of the fame fpecies: it
is thus that nature hath furnifhed us with
the means of underftanding them all, excepting our own, tolerably well. Were we
to enter only into a phyfical enquiry, concerning the nature of man, we fhould find
that the fenfe of feeling, and the perfection
of fpeech, have fecured to him the acquifition of fuch advantages over all the other
animals, that his organization, becoming
daily more and more complete, is at length
rendered too complex to be invariable,
and too fubtile to be regular.

There is every reafon to fuppofe that
the undeviating attachment in a particular
fpecies, to one particular aliment, is lefs
the confequence of an abfolute neceffity
derived from their nature, than of the
great, or more inconfiderable difficulty
with

with which they procure their food: fome
animals fubfift equally on flefh and vege-
tables; by the chace, and in the paftures;
but man, who by the exercife of his hands,
and the peculiar privilege of fpeech, is
bleft with ability and ingenuity, can provide himfelf with every kind of fuftenance,
by hunting, fifhing, the cultivation of
the earth, and other methods. Should not
this man, then, adopt different manners
and cuftoms, in conformity to his different
means of fubfiftance? would the Efqui-
maux and the inhabitants of Greenland,
who procure their nourifhment from the
oil of fifh, eat of the aliment of the Iroquois and the Patagonians, whofe chief
food arifes from the chace? or would
all thefe imitate the Laplanders, whofe
domain is the defart, and whofe diet is
milk?

Love, or the impulfive power of mul-
tiplying the fpecies, fhould give to every
creature a more diftinguifhing charade-
riftic. In fact, women are marked, in
phyfical

phyfical order, by an effential difference:
a difference which may poffefs its influence
over the ftate of fociety, by rendering
them fit for generation at every period of
the year, and confequently ftrengthening
the bond by which they are united to
man. It fhould appear then, that amongft
our fpecies, the commerce of the fexes
might be more frequently purfued, but
not that a multitude of men and women
fhould live promifcuoufly together. Farther, all phyfical inductions feem to
prove that men and women fhould not
remain too long in couples, like birds,
and certain kinds of quadrupeds : the periods of love, geftation and delivery,
being fimilar amongft fuch animals as are
individuals of the fame fpecies, their fituations are conftantly alike, and the general order cannot be interrupted, but for
an inftant, by the competition of their
wants ; whereas, amongft mankind, defire, and the faculty of enjoying it, perpetually exifting, the union of the pairs
might

might be difturbed, whenfoever one fex
fhould find itfelf unable to anfwer to the
urgent invitations of the other fex.

It is then difficult to define what human
nature hath fixed, relative to the ftate of
fociety; but it is, at once, frivolous and
ufelefs to propofe thefe queftions: " Are
" men in a ftate of mutual and perpetual
" war ?" " are they born the friends or
" the enemies of each other?"... they are
friends, whilft lending to each other a reciprocal fupport, they can the more eafily
fatisfy their mutual wants : they are enemies, whilft circumftances eftablifhing a
competition amongft themfelves, feveral
ftrive to obtain that which one only can
enjoy. The favages who fifh fhould be
more united than the favages who hunt :
the Nomades*(a)* fhould be more infepe-
rable

(a) Several nations or people were anciently fo
called on account of their having devoted themfelves
to the care of their flocks. As the richeft paftures
were the chief objects of their fearch, they fhifted
their abode as often as they perceived one fpot to be
more fertile than another fpot. K.

rable than either. Obferve the forefts in
the fummer: at that period, each animal
is at peace and unity with the reft ; the
ftags are intermixed with hinds and fawns,
they feed, they repofe themfelves in large
herds; but, in September, upon this
lately quiet fpot, a furious war will kindle,
and all the wood refound with bellow-
ings. It hath already been obferved, that
this dreadful interval doth not exift
amongft the human fpecies, who have no
particularly fixed time for generation.
Theirs fhould only be the paffing conteft
or the momentary difpute.

This then is the refult of an attentive
ftudy of thefe important queftions. Is it
poffible to eftablifh a moral fyftem on notions at once fo frivolous and obfcure?
with fuch opinions, no reafonable travel-
ler, prepared to land upon an unknown
country, could rifque the leaft conjecture
on its legiflation or its manners. There
is nothing fo fantaftical and extraordinary
but an inftance of it may be found amongft
mankind.

mankind. And muſt we ſtill diſpute on general principles, primitive laws, and final cauſes? let us bid defiance to theſe ſublime ravings, for which nothing but genius can apologize, and reſt contented with the aſſurance that the ſtate of ſociety hath effaced even the ſlighteſt traces of what is called the ſtate of nature.

In faͨt, what are civilized men? if corrupted or amended, they are entirely new beings. They have, as it were, traded and accompliſhed an interchange of whatever might reſult from their reciprocal acquaintance. Man, before this time, ſearched out and choſe his aliments; then having ſubſiſted on them, betook himſelf to reſt: but, from henceforth, confining himſelf, at frequent intervals, within his walls, and either alone, or in company with many of his ſpecies, he neither raiſes nor prepares his food, but awaits, with confidence, its arrival, although it be not ſeldom ſent from places more diſtant than fifteen hundred miles from his abode.

There

There are other defires, the covenanting for which is lefs eafy; and thefe are the defires of love. In every profeffion which we adopt, in every labour to which we apply, woman is effentially neceffary; fometimes, indeed, the neceffity of procuring our fubfiftance, rifes in oppofition to this other, no lefs imperious neceffity. An attempt muft, therefore, be made to reconcile the two. The manufacturer, the day-labourer, the fervant, and the foldier can refide but little in the midft of their family : they take a wife, without taking a companion, nor is it poffible for them to acquire her, but by being united to her in bonds more clofe and lafting than thofe, in which, the gentleft ftate of fociety could ever have involved us. The woman, alone, and immerfed in an attention to her houfehold affairs, is not lefs difobedient to the voice of nature. At the call of intereft, maternal tendernefs muft be filent. If it be pointed out to her as a commendable

frugality,

frugality, *(b)* she muft fuffer the offsprings of this imperfect union to be difperfed about the country, and fuckled by mercenary nurfes. Scarcely have they attained to the age of cultivating an acquaintance with their relations, before they are banifhed from their paternal feats, and immured in thofe prifons, called colleges, fchools and convents. At length, when all thefe different ftrangers, who, notwithftanding, ufurp the names of father, mother, fon, and daughter, fhall have met and become united, it will be abfurdly expected that the children fhould treat their parents with an obedience and veneration equal to any which they might have felt arifing from the remembrance, that under their roof, their infant weaknefs

---

(b) It is on faving principles, that moft of the women, engaged in profitable employments, truft their children to ftrange nurfes : the care of an infant at the breaft would occupy the mother's time too much, and ftop the progrefs of her work.

nefs was protected, and their dependance on that protection amply underſtood.

We will expatiate no longer on contraſts ſo exceedingly ſtriking: poſſeſſed of too dangerous an attraction, how frequently have they occaſioned the coolnefs of difcuſſion, to degenerate into agreeable, but frivolous turns of wit! ſuffice it to remark, that they do not prove what is called the ſtate of nature, to be preferable to the ſtate of ſociety, but, only, that the ſenſe generally given to theſe expreſſions, is a very miſtaken ſenſe. If, by the ſtate of nature, the moſt brutal ſtate exiſting be ſolely underſtood, it may be ſaid to reign not more amongſt the ſavages, than in our foreſts and our fields. He who is become tired of his park, declares in favour of a walk amongſt the meadows, becauſe he loves to enjoy nature. Nevertheleſs he ſees nothing but the fruit of a long and painful work. If we regard as natural, all which is within the order of nature; all which is accomplifhed

plished in confequence of its powers and
its laws, then is there a ftate of nature
as peculiar to the city, as to the country;
to the tradefman, as to the hufbandman;
to the man that launches out into fociety,
as to him that buries himfelf in folitude. *(c)* To argue ftill farther: in every
condition is an irrefiftible attraction which
impells all beings towards the acquifition
of the beft ftate that may be poffible; and
it is here that we muft look for that phyfical revelation which is to ferve as an oracle to all the legiflators. The great error
is the conftantly withdrawing fome part
of the idea from the other parts, and
giving way to general and empty decifions.
Do we feel ourfelves fhocked at the corruption which infects the great cities?

Vol. I.   b   we

(c) That ftate in which all things are brought
about by a natural and perfect unravelling, may
be regarded as a ftate of nature: from hence it
plainly follows that political focieties are natural.
(ἐκ τέτων ἂν φανερὸν ὅτι τῶν φύσει πολισίσι) are the words
of Ariftotle, in his treatife on republics. b. I. c. 2.

we oppofe to it the ruftic manners of the
hufbandman and the fhepherd. In our
addreffes to prefent, and our eulogies on
former kings, we cite Abraham, Ifaac,
and Jacob. If a fyftem of morals be recommended to an opulent and com-
mercial nation, the Scythians and the
Spartans are brought forward as models
for its imitation. Were it not better to
purfue a different method? let every thing
that is faulty, without being at all neceffary, be prefcribed. Let alfo the nature
of thofe things, which are faulty, but yet,
in fome meafure neceffary, be examined
to the bottom; that is, let the refult of
phyfical circumftances be fo fcrupuloufly
fifted, as to accomplifh the drawing of
the beft part that can be taken. All nations cannot be under the fame government: even in the fame nation, fimilar
laws, policies, and cuftoms cannot be
adapted to the genius of every town and
every clafs of citizens; yet all have a general

neral pretenfion to the greateft advantages, which can be fecured to them.

Peace is the firft blefling which a people
fhould implore. Peace is the great fource
of all order and of all good. What efforts can they make to give permanence to
the benefits which they might enjoy, who
are continually engaged in preparations
to attack others, or to defend themfelves?
no land is cultivated, whilft the title to the
enjoyment of it is litigated in a court of
juftice. War creates a ferocity of manners. It holds out fuch objects of glory
and ambition, as the moft unpolifhed
minds may feize with little difficulty, and
thus perverts our ufeful paffions by en-
nobling our vices, and every where fub-
ftituting force in the place of juftice.
The firft ftep, therefore, towards accom-
plifhing the happinefs of mankind, fhould
be to lengthen the duration of peace, and
leffen the frequency of war. Should this
ever happen, there will be fome room to
imagine that the alteration is in fight, and

that

that its progrefs is already begun. Such
a reflection will engage us to pay a particular attention to whatfoever may relate
to this grand object. To facilitate our
obfervations, it may not, perhaps, be improper to examine, in this place, what
are the caufes of war; or rather, what
are the reafons which determine one fociety of men to attack another fociety.

The firft motive, which prefents itfelf,
is the defire of quitting a fevere, unwhole-
fome climate, for a climate more mild and
healthy; a barren land, for a more fruitful
land; an inconvenient habitation, for a
more commodious habitation. The fecond
motive is founded on a competition for feveral enjoyments, either neceffary or ufeful; fuch as the power of hunting, fifhing, and the poffeffion of mines, &c. A
third reafon may be difcovered in the ignorance and barbarity of fome yet untutored people, who, deftitute of every idea
of moderation and equity, are apt to be
eafily exafperated, and make, for flight
offences,

offences, the cruelleft reprifals. The
fourth caufe is no more than the confequence of the fame principle. It is occafioned by a ftupid credulity, on the one
hand, and the dominion of a delufive hierarchy on the other: a government, at
once, tyrannical and intolerant, impofed
upon the eafy faith of human kind, by
the juglers amongft the favages; by, the
ancient priefts of Ægypt, and of Æthi-
opia; by the Greeks, in the delivery of
thofe celebrated oracles, which the fuperftition of former times attributed to
God, and which the prefent times, have,
with equal fuperftition, imputed to the
devil. To conclude, the fifth motive, of
all others the moft powerful, and yet the
moft concealed, derives its fource from
every vice inherent to the conftitution of
the ftate. Thefe are thofe interior vices,
which may be confidered as the hidden
feed of almoft every exterior war: in like
manner, the defeéts in particular fyftems
of politics give birth to civil wars.

b 3 Were

Were we to peruſe the annals of hiſtory, we ſhould perceive how juſtly the
origin of all the wars might be referred
to one of theſe principles. If, alſo, we
ſhould at the ſame time, diſcover, from
reflection, that the activity of theſe principles is blunted and decaying, we may
reaſonably hope that the condition of humanity is ſuſceptible of amendment. On
the other hand, if an examination of the
moſt eſteemed acts of particular legiſla-
tures, ſhould convince us that all ſocieties
have formed themſelves in a ſtate of war,
having no intention, ſave that of defending themſelves at one time, and invading,
and plundering at another, the reſult will
ſtill be, that againſt the future ages, the
experience of the paſt ages can prove
nothing. Let me go ſtill farther. If the
ſole aim of all ſociety and of all legiſlation had been calculated even to procure
mankind the greateſt happineſs, its not
having been yet acquired, can be no matter of aſtoniſhment. The antiquity of
the

the world is indeed atteſted by phyſical demonſtration, but hiſtory proves that ſocieties are ſtill extremely recent; at leaſt, they are recent in moſt parts of the globe. No; fifty generations *(d)* do not contain too unlimited a time to be ſpent in the

b 4   taſk

(d) Reckoning ſixty years to the duration of man's life, fifty generations will carry us back three thouſand years; that is, into the fabulous ages. I allow that it is almoſt impoſſible for a ſucceſſion of fifty perſons to have exiſted, each of whoſe lives compleated the courſe of ſixty years: but as only the progreſs of knowledge is the matter in queſtion, we need but reckon thoſe men who died at an age ſufficiently advanced to have acquired all the experience of life. I know that it is univerſally granted that the Chineſe empire hath been eſtabliſhed more than three thouſand years; and that its forms of government (if accounts miſtake not) are the moſt perfect and happy of all thoſe of which we have any knowledge. The reſt of the world alſo muſt be far advanced. The wiſdom and ſtability, peculiar to the Chineſe government, will prevent me from taking any notice of it in the courſe of this work; and, to confeſs the truth, I do not think myſelf ſufficiently inſtructed in this point to write on it in a manner ſuitable to my wiſhes.

tafk of arriving at the perfect knowledge
of man, in his phyfical and moral ca-
pacity; of eftimating all the prejudices
and all the ridiculous ideas which owe
their birth, either to fear or hope; of
daring to attack them in thofe intrench-
ments prepared for them by force or cun-
ning; of forming a genius capable of governing; of collecting every different
circumftance which may contribute to
ftop the tyrant in an intended act of ufurpation; (an act, the perpetration of which
may be effected by talents lefs elevated
than thofe required to eftablifh order and
the happinefs of the fubject) in a word,
of deftroying every obftacle which the
diftance of places, the difficulty of arriving at them, and the varieties of linea-
ments, language, manners and opinions
had thrown up againft the reunion and
harmony of particular nations: Still let
us reft contented, that readers of a gloom-
ier caft fhould turn afide with indignation
from thefe expreffions of our hopes: al-
                                    though

though they think it doubtful that the focial world fhould ever reach perfection, yet may not this picture of the condition of humanity, through all its various revolutions, be fufficiently interefting to awaken their attention? will they efteem it an unbecoming employment, to examine the influence of every legiflation, over the happinefs of the people? if fo many authors have written the hiftory of men, will no one read, with fome pleafure, the hiftory of humanity? let us enter upon our courfe, not with the prefumption arifing from the vanity which arrogates to itfelf the merit of fuperior abilities, but with that confidence which an object, noble and unlimited, muft naturally infpire: a confidence, not regulated, alone, by honeft and difinterefted views, but aiming at the preference which is more frequently given to efteem than to celebrity and applaufe.

A N

SECTION I.

*Confiderations on the lot of Human Nature,
in the earlieſt ages of antiquity.*

A N

E S S A Y

O N

PVBLIC HAPPINESS.

C H A P. I.

Remarks on the Ægyptians, Affyrians, Medes, &c.

A Melancholy idea muft arife from the reflexion that the firft epoch with which hiftory prefents us, owes its exiftence to war. Ofiris, or Bacchus, carrying the fword within his hand, croffes the Nile, to teach the arts of agriculture to the people, whom he had re-duced into a fubjeƈtion to his laws. In fome

ages,

ages, after this period, Sefoftris, at the head
of a formidable army, marches towards the
conqueft of feveral nations, of whofe name
he, undoubtedly, was ignorant. Thefe are
the moft diftant æras of the ancient, and
refpectable Ægyptian monarchy, which, as
it was diftinguifhed by two victorious kings,
fo, confequently, was it marked by two wars
exceedingly unjuft. The moft fingular circumftance was, that neither of the conquerors feemed to defire the poffeffion of the
country, which he had overcome. After
having erected fome monuments, and exacted
tributes, they marched on, like travellers in
arms, determined to be the mafters of every
place they vifited.

No one, not difpofed to affect an univerfal
doubt of the authenticity of all ancient
hiftory, can difbelieve the exiftence of two
men, celebrated for intrepidity and underftanding, who have given rife to the accounts
which the Ægyptians delivered of their Ofiris,
and their Sefoftris: but the fabies, in which
thefe accounts are wrapped, the attributing
the invention of agriculture to Ofiris, and
the antiquity of all the traditions drawn from
Herodotus, fufficiently prove that they relate

to

to the infancy of fociety, and that they have been disfigured by time. The moft incontrovertible teftimony in the writings of Herodotus, and Diodorus Siculus, alludes to, that long interval of peace, which the Ægyptian monarchy, above all others, enjoyed after the expiration of the fabulous ages : nor can we eafily give way to fcepticifm, if we confider that thefe fame hiftorians who have not tranfmitted to us the memorials of any war, from the reign of Sefoftris, to that of Apries, have, notwithftanding, enumerated the names of thofe princes, who filled up this interval, and alfo entered largely into the feveral particulars of their lives.

If, in the beginning of this effay, it be poffible to unite the idea of an exceedingly long, and almoft conftant peace, with the idea of fo diftant and reputable a monarchy, it muft prove a very favourable omen. It is, then, clear, that whatfoever the nature of man may be, good laws, and excellent adminiftrations can fupprefs the propenfities to war. Had all the earth been peopled with nations, governed like the inhabitants of Ægypt, the problem of the poffibility of a perpetual peace might have been demonftrated

ftrated by facts, or perhaps, never propofed:
no contradiction, however, can be brought
againft the fuppofition that the world may
one day prove fufficiently enlightened, univerfally to bear a mode of government, to
which a fmaller portion of mankind had formerly fubmitted. All that relates to Ægypt
is fo well known, that it is unneceffary to tire
the learned reader with a repetition of that
matter which he hath fo often perufed in other
treatifes: I muft even imagine, that he is
ready to inform me, that, in truth, the
Ægyptians enjoyed excellent laws; but that
the relation of thofe laws to the fupport of
peace, and the defire of confirming its duration, is not eafily difcernible; that we
know but little of the real conftitution and
government of this nation, in which we obferve a king exceedingly conftrained, and tied
down to the minuteft forms;*(e)* that we have

as

(*e*) Diodorus Siculus obferves, that the employments of the kings of Ægypt were fo exactly marked,
and portioned out into diftinct divifions of time, that
they could neither eat, nor fleep; nor, even enjoy
their own wives, but at the hour appointed by the
laws; fo that their kings may be faid to have gotten
children, as our princes publifh their ordinances; by
the advice of council.

as little information concerning the perfon
who watched over the execution of thofe
laws, to which he was obliged to conform;
that, whilft we are certain that their priefts
were invefted with great powers, we cannot
determine whether they were legiflative, or
refifting powers; and, in fhort, that all is
involved in obfcurity, till we arrive at that
detail, entered into by Diodorus. To this I
the more readily agree, as it operates in favour of my argument; it cannot be expected
that I fhould give my readers an exact infight
into the nature of the government peculiar
to the Ægyptians; but fince fo many particulars are concealed from us, let us hold by
thofe we have : let us affert, with Solon,
that if their laws were not, abfolutely, the
beft exifting, at leaft, they were the beft for
them, as having proved fo very efficacious.
Our niceft examinations into this fubject will,
doubtlefs, be clouded with obfcurities; yet
we fhall find fome excellent materials: the
long duration of this monarchy, the abun-
dance of its enjoyments, and the applaufe
which it hath received from every people,
and from every age, fhould be fufficient to
confirm our moft favourable opinion of thofe

other

other circumftances, with which we cannot
pretend to be acquainted.

On the contrary, if we turn our attention
towards the Affyrians, the Babylonians, the
Medes, and the Lydians, we fhall, every
where, obferve a defpotifm, the moft abfolute, a feries of victories, the moft abfurd,
an avarice infatiably collecting riches, and an
extravagance which perverted them to the
worft purpofes.

Ninus, the firft fatal ftar that fhone in that
horizon, hath ftained the page of hiftory with
cruelty, and injuftice. He attacked, and defeated the people, fince called the Babylonians. He made their king a prifoner, and
ordered that he fhould be executed with his
children. He, then, marched againft the
Medes, put them to flight, and having taken
Pharnus, their fovereign, he not only crucified the unhappy prince, but even his wife,
and all his offspring: from thence, he turned
his arms towards Bactria, and added it to his
conquefts. Semiramis, the accomplice, the
queen, and the affaffin of this tyrant, did
juftice to the world in the deftruction of the
author of thofe cruelties which they had felt;
and in her turn committed crimes for which

fhe

fhe fhould have met an equal fate. Her ambition approached to madnefs; fhe fubdued,
fucceffively, Media, Perfia, Lybia, and Æthi-
opia; at length, as if fhe would have fubdued nature herfelf, fhe levelled mountains,
changed the courfe of rivers, and raifed,
even to the fkies, the monuments of her folly.

To thefe cruelly-heroic reigns, fucceeded
fome intervals of repofe. There were kings,
doubtlefs, worthy of our applaufe, (for tradition has not named them) who gave mankind a breathing time, and were fo fortunate
as to difcover pleafures, the enjoyment of
which, was deftructive to no one. Sardanapalus, the laft of this dynafty, too effeminate, but much lefs guilty than the
greater part of the chieftains of hiftory, hath
been treated with contempt by ancient writers,
whofe fpirit of invective hath not been loft
upon the moderns. Like Darius, Perfius, and
many other princes, his empire was torn from
him, becaufe he did not gain a battle: and
yet, he chofe death in preference to ignomi-
nious bondage: no monarchs, with their
queens, and children, were ever executed by
his command; he never made his fubjects
groan and fweat beneath the toil of piling

VOL. I.   B   ftones

ſtones the one upon the other. The moſt
pious authors have, notwithſtanding, left
Ninus and Semiramis in the peaceable poſ-
feſſion of reputation, to direct the united
force of all their ſatire upon Sardanapalus.
The Medes, having conquered Sardanapalus,
ſoon ſubdued all Perſia. They, then, attacked the new Aſſyrian empire, founded
by Belus; but whilſt they were, obſtinately,
purſuing this war, they were aſſaulted, in
their turn, by the Cimmerian Scythians; and
after having been conſtrained to divide the
empire between them, they got rid of their
inconvenient gueſts, deſtroying them by an
act of treachery, of all others, the moſt un-
manly.

The next in turn is Cyrus. Hiſtory doth
not declare, preciſely, on what occaſion the
war was kindled between this celebrated conqueror, and a prince, whoſe mingled lot of
good, and ill fortune, hath rendered him no
leſs remarkable. I mean Crœſus, king of
Lydia; a name in the mouths of many, who
are ignorant of his hiſtory. It is equally
difficult to aſſign the real cauſes to all the
other wars which Cyrus waged, and which,
in the end, made him the ſovereign of Aſia.

So

So different are the recitals of Herodotus,
and Zenophon, that every competent reader,
obferving, on the one hand, fuch fabulous
puerilities, and on the other, a moral treatife,
thrown into fcenes of action, feems, as it
were, reduced to a kind of choice between
the Orlando of Ariofto, and the Telemachus
of Fenelon. Let us, therefore, content ourfelves with believing, that there exifted, in
former times, a conqueror named Cyrus,
who fubdued Afia, and founded the Perfian
empire.(f)

B 2   A fuf-

_____

(f) Mr. Rollin is far from having thrown much
light on the obfcurity of thefe diftant ages. He begins
by relating, with all the gravity of hiftory, the little
romantic details with which Xenophon has judged
proper to adorn his cyropœdia. It muft, however, be
confeffed that the infinuation that, poffibly, not a
word of truth is in all this, frequently efcapes him : neverthelefs, he continues to take the account of all the
principal facts as far down as the battle of Thymbria,
from Zenophon. Then, fhifting round to the teftimony of Herodotus, he will have it that Cyrus engages
in a frefh battle near Sardis, where he makes him
have recourfe once more to the ftratagem of oppofing
camels, to the cavalry, without perceiving that all this
is but the fame ftory, varioufly related by two different authors. He goes farther, not to lofe the hiftory
of

A fufficient number of facts hath already
been advanced in a work not hiftorical: let
us, now, pafs on to thofe fuggeftions which
muft naturally arife; and firft, it may be obferved

---

of Crœfus, who, on the funeral pile, invokes Solon,
he fuppofes that this fame Cyrus, whom he hath held
out as a model to kings, had condemned his enemy,
to be burnt alive: and this he advances without
deigning to make the fmalleft apology for this extravagant inequality in the character of his hero. I cannot deny myfelf the liberty of making one more obfervation. He had a greater advantage in printing his
work forty years ago, when the language met with
indulgence, than he could have expected now. Here
follows an example of Mr. Rollin's ftile: fpeaking of
Gobrias, the Affyrian general, he fays: " le roi mort
depuis peu qui en connoiffoit tout le merite, et le cou-
fideroit extrémement, avoit refolû de donner fa fille
en marriage a fon fils." I believe that every thinking
reader will be offended with this grammatical inceft,
which fo religious a man as Mr. Rollin, has made the king
of Affyria commit; either the prince chofe to marry his
own daughter, to his own fon; or the daughter of
Gobrias, to the fon of Gobrias. In fome lines lower,
Mr. Rollin talks of a citadel in which this fame Gobrias lodged: (logefit)—lodge in a citadel! the ancient hiftory, and the Romifh hiftory, which are, on
many accounts, valuable productions, furnifh faults
ftill more difgufting than thefe.

Having given, with the cold fidelity of a tranflator,
the verbal conftruction of this note, the author muft
pardon

ferved that as hiftory hath not tranfmitted to
us any accounts of the government of the
people, of whom we have been treating, we
can only form a judgement from the appearances of facts.   Thefe appearances acquaint
us that the government was abfolutely military, and defpotic; and(g) it is well known

B 3   that

---

pardon me for thinking fome parts of it, inconfiftent
with his natural fpirit of liberality. The moft eminent
in the learned world have nothing about their characters fo facred, as to exempt them from a detection of
their errors: but genius hath a title to refpect, and
the difcovery of its miftakes, can never be too deli-
cately expofed. It is impoffible to perufe the French
fentence, and the remarks on it, without a fmile; yet
it will not be, in either cafe, a fmile of approbation.
The meaning of Rollin is eafily underftood, and this
facetious expofition, was beneath the wit that made it.
The other charge is, indeed, of more confequence,
and requires an abler advocate than I am, to confute
it. The freedom with which our author criticifes the
ftile of Rollin, will not eafily difpofe him, to believe
that the fincerity of Atterbury was equal to his complaifance. A paffage in the letter which that exile
wrote to Rollin, runs thus: fi Gallicè fciffet Xenophon,
non aliis illum in eo argumento quod tractas verbis
ufurum, non alio prorfus more fcripturum judicem." K.

(g) It would be uncandid to attempt, in this place,
to conceal the eulogies which Herodotus, and Zenophon have beftowed upon the ancient Perfians. It is
even

that a prince, ruling with unlimited authority, muſt have acquired that authority
by the means of ſuch an army as he could
not have been maſter of, unleſs that he had
waged war. We ſhall not, therefore, he-
ſitate to aſſign the vices of government, and
the ignorance of political, and moral principles, as the cauſes of thoſe wars, to which
we have, already alluded. And, here, the
irruption of thoſe Scythians who came from
the Boſphorus, is well worthy of our notice.
It may be ſeen, for the firſt time, how theſe
inhabitants of the North, ſpread themſelves
through the moſt fertile countries, and triumphed over the moſt warlike nations. What
is ſtill more extraordinary, they made the
                                        ſame

------

even neceſſary to confeſs, that (if Herodotus may be
believed) this people wcre leſs barbarous than ourſelves, as they never puniſhed the firſt crime with
death; and as the legiſlature had enacted no penalty
againſt parricide, from the principle, that inſanity
alone could drive a man to the perpetration of ſuch
an act : but, excluſive of the impoſſibility that, merely,
good civil laws can be ſufficient to conſtitute a good
form of government, it is evident that the manners
of the Perſians were more calculated to render the people
warlike, and victorious, than to inſpire them with a
love of agriculture, and all the arts of peace.

fame treaty with the Medes, into which they
entered afterwards with the Roman emperors;
that is to fay, they ftipulated with the ancient
poffeffors, for the enjoyment of a joint part-
nerfhip in their lands, and for that fingular
manner of reigning with others, in quality
of guefts.(h) It is clear then that this fpecies of war refers to our firft principle: the
defire of quitting a rigorous climate, for a
more mild climate.

(h) Confult the remarks of l'Abbé du Bos, on the
French monarchy, in which this ingenious author
proves, that the Franks, and the Lombards, who fettled
in Gaul, Spain, and Italy, gave out that they were
the guefts (hofpites) of the Romans, and that their
chief ftiled himfelf king of the Franks, and Lombards,
but not king of the Gauls, and of Italy.

B 4   CHAP.

C H A P. II.

*The means of estimating the happiness of man-
kind, and more particularly, the happiness of
the people existing during the first ages of
antiquity.*

OUR investigation of the first epochas of
history must prove exceedingly useless, if,
from the multitude of events with which it
presents us, we were unable to draw some
general facts; facts infinitely more certain
than those which have been so sedulously
transmitted to us, and which, like grains
of dust, could have no weight, unless united
in a single mass. The facts, to which we allude, are those important ones, which historians have almost constantly neglected, as if
willing

willing to treat of every thing, excepting
that which was inconteftably true. It is not
abfolutely certain that Cyrus, at the head of
one hundred thoufand Perfians, gained a victory over five hundred thoufand Affyrians,
Ægyptians, &c. or that Ninus built a city
more than twenty-eight miles in length ; but
it is certain, on the one hand, that an army
well difciplined, and commanded by a warlike king, triumphed over an ignorant, and
undifciplined multitude; and, on the other
hand, that a nation of flaves, almoft deprived of fenfe, by the impofition of a gall-
ing yoke, were condemned to labour in obedience to the caprice of a mad, and arbitrary
tyrant.

Can we, amongft all the fpeculations to
which hiftory may give occafion, difcover
one more excellent and more entitled to our
attention, than that the great object of which
is the happinefs of human nature ? many
authors have, diligently, examined, how far
one nation furpaffed another, in religion, in
temperance, and in valour : but no one hath
attempted to difcover which nation was the
happieft. Were the Ægyptians, in this
refpect, fuperior to the Medes; the Medes

to the Greeks, and the Greeks to the Romans? thefe are points, to determine which, but little pains have yet been taken. If any one hath ventured to difcufs the fubject, his conclufions hath been drawn from vague, and infufficient principles.

One great, and common error, amidft a multitude of other errors, is the confounding the people with the government. The people are fuppofed to be happy, whenfoever the government profpers: inftead of keeping in view the good of individuals, nothing is confidered but the growth, and duration of empires, as if the public profperity, and the general felicity, were two infeparable matters. For this, the Cynic was, facetioufly, told that he fhould have changed the maxim, " falus populi fuprema lex efto," into " falus gubernantium fuprema lex efto." I fhall have more occafions than one to complain againft thefe prejudices: but, for the prefent, I fhall confine myfelf to thofe reflections which have been fuggefted to me by the facts under examination. I fhall begin by an affertion that I do not think that any nation hath been happy, becaufe it may have erected immenfe pyramids, or magnificent palaces. On the contrary,

contrary, I prefume that thefe fuperb edifices, and vaft monuments, indicated the poor condition, and limited abilities of the people who affifted in the raifing of them. As this truth refults from very extenfive principles, I cannot difpenfe with the neceffity of explaining them. They belong to the fcience of Economicks; a fcience equally difficult, and obfcure; to define it, hath been the bufinefs of multitudes; but to agree in thofe definitions, the lot of few. Thefe principles will, then, have fome merit, fhould they prove true, and clear: and I dare flatter myfelf, that, in fpite of the quantity of writings, which have appeared on this fubject, they will not be deftitute of novelty. It is, indeed, a cold, and dry difcuffion; but I fhould be guilty of injuftice to the age in which I live, and to my readers, were I to feel an inclination to avoid it.

In every attempt to eftimate the happinefs, or the mifery of the people, the impofts with which they were laden, have been almoft the fole objects of confideration. No eftimation hath been made of the rigour of thefe impofts, but from the mode in which they were levied; that is, according to their nearer,

or

or more diftant approach to the form of a
tribute, and fuch a one, alfo, as the con-
tributor was compelled to take from his private purfe, and give to his fovereign. Now,
it feems to me, that there is a more extenfive,
and fure method of eftimating the condition
of the fubject, as it may bear fome relation
to the prince, in cafes where the weight of
the tax preffes upon the firft ; as thus :

Firft : how many days in the year, or hours·
in the day, can a man work, without either
incommoding himfelf, or becoming unhappy ?
one may perceive, at the firft glance, that
this queftion refers to the nature of the climate ; to the conftitution, and to the ftrength
of men ; to their education, to their aliments ;
&c. &c. all, cafes, which may be eafily refolved.

Secondly, how many days muft a man
work in the year, or, how many hours muft
he work in the day, to procure for himfelf
that which is neceffary to his prefervation,
and his eafe ? having refolved thefe queftions,
it will be no difficult matter to determine
how many days in the year, or how many
hours in the day, may remain for this man to
difpofe of : that is to fay, how many may be
demanded

of him, without robbing him either of the means of fubfiftance, or of welfare: fo that, now, the whole matter refts upon an examination, whether the performance of that duty, which the fovereign exacts from him, be within, or beyond the time, which each man can fpare from his abfolutely neceffary avocations.

In the interim, to draw from this expofition, all its refulting confequences, we muft imagine that every part of the labour, exercifed throughout the ftate, is equally divided amongft a fet of individuals. I would fuppofe, for inftance, that every man being obliged to build, furnifh, and maintain an houfe; to procure, and drefs his victuals; to equip himfelf with cloathing, &c. &c. muft, confequently be, at once, a mafon, a tiler, a cultivator of the ground, a cook, a weaver, a taylor, a fhoe-maker, &c. &c. After this, it will be neceffary to calculate either the number of days in the year, or of hours in the day, which muft be fet apart for this employment: and then, it muft be determined what time he hath left upon his hands, to be difpofed of, in the fervice of his fovereign. Thus, fhall we be led to a juft

decifion

decifion on the happinefs, or the mifery of the people.

Such as have exercifed their thoughts on thefe economical matters, will, foon, perceive that it is this remaining time, which will, whenever it fhall be thus employed, produce (either for the fovereign, or that perfon who may poffefs the right of managing it) the *net revenue*, which hath given birth to fo many difputes. They will, alfo, be convinced that, if the demands of the fovereign become too exceffive, the refult will, immediately, be, that the fubject, condemned to diminifh the number of thofe hours, which he had deftined to his own proper ufes, muft behold the fruits of all his induftry, and culture, fallen to decay; in fhort, this fame fubject, thus lofing the neceffaries of his life, muft either defert or perifh.

Let us, now, endeavour to lead the queftion back, by degrees, to the propofed object. Let us examine, for inftance, what conclufions, in fupport of the power, and the happinefs of the Ægyptians, may be drawn from our knowledge of thofe immenfe monuments, for the raifing of which, they have been fo celebrated. This matter may be

feen

feen in feveral different lights : firft, the population of Ægypt having been extenfive,
it may have happened that the avocations
from the other ufual, and neceffary labours,
to thofe of affifting in the ftructure of thefe
vaft edifices, were not of fuch material confequence, becaufe the work was fubdivided
amongft all the individuals, who, by turns,
relieved each other.

Secondly, thefe fame buildings might have
occafioned the employment of all that time,
which remained to be difpofed of.

Thirdly, the population not having been
fufficiently confiderable, the portion of leifure
time became too fmall, and occafioned a
breaking in upon the time that fhould have
been otherwife employed.

In the fourth place, poffibly, the population was not confiderable, but, at the fame
time, the wants of individuals were fo limited, that they were unemployed enough to
labour, without inconvenience, in the fervice
of their fovereign.

It, now, remains to determine, under
which of thefe four predicaments the Ægyptians fall. And, perhaps, this tafk is not fo
difficult as one might, at firft, imagine it to
be,

be, confidering the great diftance at which
thefe objects are removed from us. We
know that the inundations of the Nile diminifhed, and reduced, almoft to nothing,
the labours neceffary to cultivation. The
Ægyptians, therefore, were always fure of
enjoying plentiful harvefts at a fmall expence.
On the other hand, we have no reafon to fuppofe that thefe people were very refined, and
extravagant, in the ornaments of their perfons, the fetting out of their tables, and
other fimilar expences. It will not, therefore, be impoffible to prove that each individual was employed but few days in the
year, or few hours in the day, in procuring
his neceffary conveniencies. Indeed, a fair
calculation might be made: it is a problem,
which, being refolved by algebraical com-
putations, will eafily afcertain the numerical
proportions.

One very important circumftance, is, that
this will, naturally, lead us to a definition of
luxury, and its effects. We may, at prefent
call it, all the employment of time which
breaks in upon that, of which particulars,
and the ftate, have a real want. According
to this principle, it would be an equal luxury,

were

were a nation, either, to apparel themfelves with a ftuff, which exacted, from each individual, an hour of labour, every day, or to drefs the hair in a manner which, daily, took up the fame fpace of time: but thefe two articles can only be confidered as acts of luxury, in proportion to their encroachments upon that time, which cannot eafily be fpared from more neceffary avocations.

And, here, I may be afked what poffibi-lity there is, of afcertaining the quantity of labour which each individual fhould referve for his own ufe? Were it to happen that one particular perfon fhould be uneafy, unlefs he could be clad in velvet, would you efteem it neceffary that fuch a portion of time fhould be employed in the raifing of filk-worms, and the manufactory of velvets? perhaps fo. And, why not, if that were poffible? but the fact is, that a fimilar inftance cannot arife. I fhall, therefore, have no occafion to anfwer this objection, being able to advance a general principle; and this principle is, that the wants of particulars, fhould be limited by the wants of the ftate; that is, that private convenience fhould only follow public fecurity, and that a certain enjoyment is preferable to an extended enjoyment. I will add, that it is this confideration, which fixes limits to eafe, and to luxury; fo that luxury may, equally invade the province of the fubject, and the province of the fovereign; and (not to mention the pomp of courts) is found as' frequently amidft too numerous armies, as in the exceffes of too magnificent an apparel: in fhort, if the Sybarites were too luxurious in their paffion for effeminacy, the Spartans were equally involved in too extravagant a thirft of glory, and ambition.

It is an indifputable point, (or, at leaft, there is room to think it, in this philofophical age, an acknowledged truth) that the firft object of all governments, fhould be to render the people happy. On every occafion where (plans having been concerted to aggrandize the government) the fubjects become conftrained to facrifice a part of either thofe days in the year, or thofe hours in the day, fo neceffary to be employed towards their own private advantage, unpardonable exceffes, and abfolute abufes will, naturally, creep in. On the other hand, if a foft, and enervated people fhould refufe to furnifh the ftate with fuch a portion of labour as may be
neceffary

neceſſary to maintain the public fecurity, they
will expofe themfelves, by fo negligent a
provifion, an eafy prey to the firſt power that
may think proper to attack them : and this is
a misfortune which they quickly muſt experience. But, how often may circumſtances
float between thefe two extremes, without
ever meeting ? it is this which multiplies, in
fo great a degree, the nature, and complexion
of either the mifery, or the profperity, vifible amongſt different nations, and in different
ages.

We fhall give but a fmall number of inſtances of the various modes in which thefe
caufes may act. An ignorant, and flothful
people, knowing neither their faculties, nor
their wants, may remain in fo annihilating a
fituation, as not even to employ, in proper
ufes, as much time as might be neceſſary to
eſtablifh them in the poſſeſſion of a peaceful
and advantageous life. It may, alfo, happen,
that the government, exacting from this
people, a certain portion of labour, may ac-
cuſtom them to activity, and induſtry ; and
then, the fovereign, by augmenting the
number of days in the year, or of hours in
the day, which he might exact from the fub-

ject,

ject, would augment, in a fimilar proportion, the time which this fubject would employ to his own advantage.

On the other hand, were a people to exift, who, enjoying a mild, and fruitful climate, and contented with the benefits of nature, feel no uneafinefs of defire, we fhould pronounce this repofe to be one of their chief effentials ; and ill-concerted muft be that policy, which could wifh to add any thing either to the labour which they had referved for private ufes, or that labour which they had deftined for the fervice of the ftate.

After all, it may arrive that the ftate may exact too much from the people, without haftening on a national decay : but the bad confequences of this excefs are ftill exifting; and if the fubject be not robbed of that which is neceffary to fupport life, at leaft, he is plundered of the means of making that life agreeable.

May we not, now, infer that the firft cafe is naturally applicable to the inhabitants of the temperate climates, and even to the northern nations? that the fecond cafe extends to the fouthern nations, fuch as the Italians, the Greeks, and the Afiatics? and that the

third

third cafe refers to almoft every warlike nation, inhabiting the centre of Europe.

Another truth refulting from our principles, and which we have already fhewn, is,
that no *net revenue* exifts, unlefs it be at all
thofe times, whenfoever individuals are obliged to work fo long in the fervice of the
ftate, as to break in upon thofe hours which
they intended to have appropriated to their
own private ufes. In Ægypt, for inftance,
all the *net revenue* belonged to the king, to
the priefts, and to the foldiers; for it is remarkable, that, amongft this people, there
were, ftrictly fpeaking, no owners of lands.
The labourers, like the artifans, formed a
clafs of mercenaries; or rather, the firft were
reduced to the rank of farmers, as they were
only the mere cultivators of thofe lands,
which belonged to the three great proprietaries of ftate.

That the *net revenue* of the Ægyptians
was exceedingly confiderable, will not admit
of any doubt; particularly, if we reflect on
the great number of priefts which this nation
entertained, and the enormous fums which their
kings lavifhed on buildings : exclufive of all
this, they had, conftantly, on foot, an army of

C 3   four

four hundred thoufand men, which will appear the more extravagant, when we recollect that Diodorus Siculus eftimates the population of Ægypt, in the moft flourifhing times, at a rate no higher than the number of feven millions of inhabitants.*(i)*

We cannot very well determine whether or no the Ægyptians had occafion for fuch a multitude of troops. It appears, only, that this nation was neither engaged in broils, nor in victories, and, therefore, there is every reafon to fuppofe that fo numerous a militia. was neceffary to its prefervation. As to the quantity of priefts, which it fupported, we can ftile it nothing but an immoderate fuperfluity. It was the luxury of ignorance,

of

(i) I prefume that a fmall contradiction is in this paffage of Diodorus, for, at the fame time that he only allows feven millions of inhabitants to Egypt, he fays, that this kingdom contains a very great number of villages, and more than eighteen thoufand towns. Now, were we to fuppofe that each town was peopled with only a thoufand men, the number of inhabitants would amount to eighteen millions. After this chapter had been written, I met with the fame obfervation in a differtation by Mr. Hume, on the population of ancient nations. I fhall, hereafter, have more occafions than one, to avail myfelf of this excellent work.

of all other luxuries the moſt detrimental, becauſe equally incapable of exciting induſtry, and producing one agreeable enjoyment.

Let us, now, endeavour to form an eſtimate of the happineſs which the Ægyptians might have enjoyed, if, inſtead of furniſhing a ſubſiſtance for ſo many prieſts, and ſoldiers, they had employed all their leiſure time in procuring the commodities of life: the concluſion will, too evidently, prove, that war, and ſuperſtition, have always been the greateſt obſtacles to the happineſs of nations.

It follows alſo, from what we have advanced, that if a nation exiſted, which, without being poor, produced no *net revenue*, ſuch a nation would be the happieſt in the world: its individuals would employ all their leiſure time in continually adding to their proſperity. But I ſhall be aſked, how this nation could be thus happy, if it employed in labour the greateſt part of its leiſure time: to this I anſwer, that there are particular kinds of labour which add to our welfare: for inſtance, had men no cloathing, did they repoſe in the open air, they would be very happy by employing a part of their time, in building of houſes, and making of habits:

or

or in other words, it would be extremely
fortunate for the taylors that there were mafons, and for the mafons that there were
taylors. In like manner, the individuals,
whofe only food had been bread, whofe only
liquor had been water, might rejoice over
their increafe of labour, if it furnifhed them
with the hopes of, one day, eating meat, and
drinking wine.

 Thefe principles are fo true, that, were
we to read hiftory attentively, we fhould be
perpetually induced to apply them. We
fhall perceive that, previous to the knowledge of the arts of procuring conveniencies,
which declaimers call, the arts of luxury, in
the times, when unpolifhed, or (if it be a
more proper phrafe) frugal nations, covered
with only a fimple cloak, fubfifted on milk,
barley, and lupines :(k) at this period, I fay,

we

(k) A fpecies of common bean, much in ufe, amongft
the ancients.

Protogenes, drawing the picture of Jalyfus, is faid
to have taken no other nourifhment than this pulfe,
mixed with water, left the fire of his imagination,
might be damped by the luxury of his food. The
truth of this account is immaterial, but the leffon of
tem-

we fhall perceive, that when population was fenfibly increafed, the only remedy known, and in ufe, was the drawing of lots to determine which of the individuals fhould go and feek his livelihood elfewhere.(*l*) In fact, how could this fuperabundant population, thefe new ramifications of families, induce the firft proprietaries of lands to redouble their labour towards furnifhing the means of their fubfiftance? It is certain that this could not have happened, unlefs thefe individuals laboured, on their parts, in works capable of exciting the inclinations of the firft inhabitants.

This, I believe, is the earlieft origin of colonies. Let us prefent to our imagination an unpolifhed people, confifting of ten thoufand

---

temperance, which it contains, is not unworthy of the painters notice : without fome exercife of this uncommon vertue, even the hand of Reynolds might err, and all the glowing expreffion of Weft, become lifelefs, and infipid. K.

(*l*) This policy was very oppofite to the policy of Sir William Petty, who wifhed that, for the advantage of Britain, the inhabitants of Scotland and Ireland might be tranfported into England ; and that, after this, thefe two kingdoms might be fwallowed up by an inundation.

fand individuals, who, without any great
effort of either care, or labour, cultivate the
ground which extends over their domain.
Let us fuppofe, farther, that, inftead of an
increafe in the population, at the rate of five
thoufand fouls, the fame number of artifans
fhould land, at once, in this country, and,
feverally, propofe to furnifh habits, fhoes,
wine, and various utenfils, in exchange for a
certain quantity of productions cultivated by
the firft colonifts: can it be doubted that
thefe individuals, excited by the defire of obtaining the conveniencies of life, would redouble their labour to augment their harvefts,
and, of courfe, the means of exchange?
thus, the enjoyment of one convenience would
lead to the acquifition of another; new defires would follow clofe upon the laft; and
the original fimplicity of drefs, would, at
length, break out into an attire as full of ornaments, as the wardrobe of a theatre.

Such would have been the progrefs of our
commerce with America, if, inftead of deftroying the unfortunate inhabitants of that
extenfive country, we had been fatisfied with
civilizing their manners. To thefe reflections,
we may add the obfervation, that more co-

lonies might have been founded by republics, than by monarchies. A fovereign will never be at a lofs to find objects of labour, fuffi-cient to employ the whole flower of his people : whereas republics neither erect py-ramids, nor plume themfelves on having planted trees on eminencies that touch the clouds. It even feldom happens that they carry on thofe ufeful, but expenfive works, the accomplifhment of which, muft be the joint refult of power, and unanimity. Had Rome been free at that period when fhe counted fourfcore thoufand inhabitants, fhe might, perhaps, have founded a colony, in-ftead of building the famous aqueduct, ce-lebrated by the name, " Cloaca magna." It is certain that Tarquin could not have exe-cuted fo great an undertaking, unlefs he had compelled that clafs of citizens, referved for the employments of Agriculture and trade, to work fo much more than they would have done, if all the individuals engaged in this enterprize had been difperfed amongft the artifans and the hufbandmen. (m)

Let

(m) It hath been a matter of aftonifhment to many that Rome, at that æra, not only in her infant ftate, but

Let us, therefore, conclude this digreſſion, which is already much too long, by obſerving the impoſſibility of eſtimating the happineſs of the people, in the firſt ages of antiquity, by either the frugality of ſome, or the extravagance of others. Their vertue can no more be proved from the great ſimplicity of their

---

but engaged in war, could have conſtructed, in ſo ſhort a time, this immenſe aqueduct. I have been equally ſurprized at it; but we may eaſily reſolve this problem, on our own principles. According to Livy, and Dionyſius Halicarnaſſeus, the inhabitants of Rome, during the reign of Tarquin, were, in number, eighty thouſand. Recollect the ſimplicity, and frugality of the ancient Romans, and, then, calculate the number of days in the year, or hours in the day, which an individual was obliged to employ for his own particular uſes. Another method may be, to examine how ſmall a number of individuals was needful to provide for the neceſſities of the reſt. A paſſage from Dionyſius is a ſtill ſtronger confirmation of this opinion. Romulus, having conquered the Antemnates, and the Ceninians, ſent three thouſand to Rome, and thought it ſufficient to replace this number with ſix hundred men. Hence, it appears that ſix hundred men could cultivate as great a quantity of land, as might be requiſite to furniſh a ſubſiſtance for three thouſand. In the colony of Cayenne, the Negroes do not board with their maſters: theſe laſt permit them to employ every Saturday in the fortnight, in the cultivation of thoſe fields from whence they derive their food.

their manners, than their felicity from the profufion of their mignificence. Through every period, ignorance, defpotifm, war, and fuperftition, have, by turns, plundered mankind of the advantages with which nature had prefented them.

CHAP.

C H A P. III.

On the middle æra of antiquity, and, principally,
the Grecian æra.

THE subject of this chapter might induce me to lead off, with Milton, and hail
the light which I, at length, discover, after
having wandered so long in darkness.*(n)*   If
I must, still, call in history to my assistance;
if it be expected that I should continue to
produce a relation of past events, in support
of the principles which I have established, it
will not be necessary to consult either the
childish stories of Herodotus, or the fabulous
                                                    traditions

---

(n) " Hail, holy light! offspring of heaven. &c."
                          Paradise lost, book 3.

traditions of the poets. I am now armed
with the authority of the moft refpectable
authors. I can cite thofe celebrated writers
to whom the prefent refined age looks up as
models. Thucydides, Xenophon, Diodorus,
and Paufanias, at once enlightening each
other, have fufficiently paved the way to the
difcovery of truth. It is now certain that,
whatfoever variations of patriotic zeal, a fuperftitious imagination, and, perhaps, too
pofitive a ftile, might have infufed into their
writings, the characters of Darius, Xerxes,
Themiftocles, and Ariftides, will defcend to
pofterity, as accurately marked, and as eafily
diftinguifhable, as the characters of Charles
the Fifth, Guftavus, De Witt, and Barnevelt.
As foon as we approach the Median war, but
more particularly, the war of Peloponnefus,
the veil of antiquity feems to withdraw itfelf,
and the light of hiftory beams, all at once, over
the paft ages. At the very name of Greece,
enthufiafm becomes awake, and prefents to
our ideas a picture of vertue, courage, dif-
intereftednefs, and aufterity of manners, united with perfection throughout the arts; all
the delicacy of tafte, and all the refinements
of pleafure: fo capable is admiration of join-

ing

ing fuch oppofite extremes ! As for us,
having propofed to ourfelves, when we undertook this work, no other object but the
, welfare of humanity, we fhall reft contented
with referring all to this fingle confideration :
it is on this, only, that we fhall ground our
commendations, and our cenfures.

Some citizens are affociated, in deference
to the advice of a brave and enterprizing
man.(o) Shortly afterwards magnificent buildings arife, the feas are covered with innumerable fleets, and the great King is infulted,
attacked, and repulfed.   Many rich and flourifhing iflands, together with a very confiderable extent of coafts, are made tributary :
Athens, the amiable, the fplendid Athens,
rifes upon the ruins of barbarifm, and its formidable ramparts feem only deftined to afford
a fanctuary to genius and the arts. .

On the other fide, an individual, whofe
ardour was vehement, whofe difcernment
was profound, and, whofe difpofition was
auftere, conceives a project to reform the
government of his country.   Animated with
a fpirit

a fpirit of patriotifm, he contrives and executes the extroardinary plan of immortalizing this enthufiafm, by perpetuating it, from race to race. The haughty Sparta erects her brazen front againft all Greece, and takes up arms, with a determination to quit them no more.

What memorable exploits have fignalized the infancy of thefe republics! Marathon, Platea, Salamina, and the Micelæ, announced their future grandeur. In vain, did feventeen hundred thoufand men land in Greece: there remain two cities: but what do I fay? there remains only one: for Athens is annihilated, or exifts but on the waves. Xerxes is, notwithftanding, put to flight, and purfued even to another continent.

What valuable and facred bonds muft have united thefe republics, which had been equal fharers in enterprizes fo glorious! Tyranny muft difappear from every quarter; an inviolable affociation muft connect all the members of Greece, to thefe two revered heads, and peace muft flourifh amidft the defenders of liberty.

It is, here, that we are obliged to change our language, and caft a fecond glance upon

the fame objects. Shall we not, on a clofer
examination, perceive in the republic of
Athens, an ill-difpofed populace, vain, frivolous, ambitious, jealous, interefted, incapable of marking out a proper conduct for
themfelves, and grudging their chiefs that
fortune which they fhared with them : full
of fagacity in their difcuffions, but deprived
of it, when it is neceffary to determine: bigotted to an idle eloquence, always ready to
abandon the depths of argument, for empty
forms, and give the found of words a preference to reafon : unjuft to their allies, ungrateful to their chiefs, and cruel to their
enemies ? . . . On the other fide, if we turn
our examination upon the Spartans, and fcru-
tinize them more attentively, inftead of perceiving the celebrated mafterpiece of morality, and politics, we fhall be at a lofs how
to defcribe them. Are they a nation? yet they
cultivate no land; they defpife its produce,
and claim a merit from difpenfing with it, as
much as poffible. Are they a fociety? yet
the ties of families, of marriage, of parent-
age, of love, and of friendfhip are entirely
unknown to them. The bonds which join
the women to their hufbands, are precarious,

and

and uncertain: the children do not belong
to their own fathers: nature is fentenced to
be filent. Only one imperious voice is heard.
The *country* expects, claims, and poffeffes
every thing; and yet it neither gives, nor
offers, nor promifes any thing. What then
is Sparta? an army always under arms; if it
be not, rather, one vaft monaftery. In fact,
when we obferve, on the one hand, their
continual exercifes, their mock fights, and
their abfolute renunciation of arts, agriculture, and commerce; and, on the other
hand, their fevere difciplines, their macera-
tions, their refectories, and their public ceremonies, we fhall be inclined to fuppofe
ourfelves, at one moment, in the fortrefs of
of Spandaw, and at another, in the convents
of the Camaldulians.*(p)* What heart, un-

D 2 lefs

(p) The Camaldulians form a religious order, inftituted by St. Romauld, and take their name from a
fmall plain, called Camaldali, on the mount Apennine,
in the ftate of Florence. At firft, the cells of thefe
devotees were feparate, nor did they ever meet but at
the hour of public prayer. They, annually, obferved
an inviolable filence, either during Lent, or the fpace
of one hundred days. Twice only in the week, they
quitted their fare of bread and water, to feaft on herbs.
Their

lefs it were defended by the three-fold fhield of erudition, but would fhudder with as much terror, at the recital of the Lacede-monian manners, as at that of the feverities, practifed by the Fakirs,(q) and Jammaboes?(r) Already,

---

Their aufterities have been lately mitigated by new regulations, and as this hermitage is now becoming rich, perhaps its inhabitants may foften, by degrees, into fomething like men of the world. The founders of thefe fects were equally ignorant of human nature, and its all-bounteous Lord. Whatever fuperftition, and the extravagancies of religion may advance, it is certain that the creature, who flies without reluctance from fociety, is more than contemptible; and it is pro-bable, that to the Creator, the rational enjoyment of every thing which he hath given us, is not the leaft ac-ceptable act of thankfgiving. K.

(q) The mortifications of thefe oriental Monks ex-ceed all belief. Some cut their bodies with knives; others remain, a whole life-time, in one pofture. It hath been faid that the number of Fakirs in India, amounts to more than two millions. K.

(r) "The Jammaboes are Japonefe hermits, divided into two orders; the order of Tofanfa, and the order of Fonfanfa. The Jammaboes of the firft order are obliged to climb up the dangerous fides of the moun-tain Fikoofan, once, in the courfe of each year. It is ridiculoufly, and perhaps artfully afferted, that fuch as afcend it, in a ftate of impurity, are feized with madnefs. The Jammaboes of the fecond order, have, alfo, their mountain, to whofe top they muft, annually
clamber;

Already, I feem to hear many voices raifed againft me, and oppofing to my obfervations, the power, and the duration of this republic. They dwell, alfo, on the circumftances of its having triumphed, firft, over the Perfians, and afterwards, over all the Greeks. It is true, that they do not inform me, that the Athenians alone decided the fuccefs of the Median war, by the victory at Marathon,(s) a victory, of which a vain pretext, extreme-ly fufpicious on a fimilar occafion, deprived the Lacedemonians. They do not add, that they were, by turns, vanquifhed by all the people of Greece; and even by thofe the· leaft celebrated; to begin, for inftance, with the

D 3

Meffinians,

---

clamber; and here too, the rafh adventurer muft ex-pect to be dafhed to pieces, if not free from all conta-mination. Their food confifts of herbs, and water; they practife the moft fevere aufterities, and impu-dently boaft that they are great adepts in magic: the multitude, too ftupid to detect the tricks of thefe re-ligious juglers, have contributed not a little to fupport their pretenfions, to the power of working mira-cles." K.

(s) It may be objected that this victory was no in-terruption to the fecond expedition of the Perfians: but would the Greeks have gained the battle of Pla-tæa, if they had not felt that confidence which their firft fuccefs infpired?

Meffinians, and end with the Thebans.*(t)*
They are cautious of confeffing, that it was
with the fuccours and the treafure of the
Perfians, that they accomplished the conqueft
of the Athenians, their ancient allies. But
when it fhall have been proved, that Sparta
was indebted to its conftitution alone, for all
its fplendor, and length of exiftence, will it

follow

(t) The war waged by the Lacedemonians, againft
the Ilotes, and the Meffinians lafted more than ten
years, with equal advantages to each party. Neverthelefs, the Meffinians were not Monks of the reformed
order of Lycurgus. Thucydides (b. 1.) relates that the
Ilotes having fled to Ithomus, the Lacedemonians were
compelled to avail themfelves of the affiftance of the
Athenians before they could take this place. In the
famous war of Peloponnefus, the Spartans were defeated at the fame time, on land, and at fea, by Alcibi-
ades. On another occafion, forty-feven of their gallies were at firft compelled to fheer off, and afterwards
difperfed by Phormio, the Athenian, who commanded
only twenty gallies. In like manner, Thrafibulus
overcame Callicratidas who commanded the Spartan
fleet. No one is ignorant of their total defeat at
Leuctra, and Mantinea; and that if Epaminondas had
furvived his laft victory, Sparta had been ruined. Do
they who magnify fo greatly the advantages which the
Spartans gained over the Athenians, towards the
conclufion of the Peloponnefian war, recollect, that in

the

follow that fuch a conftitution could have
merited the approbation of an enlightened
and philofophical age ? if it hath not rendered men either more vertuous, or (what is
much the fame) more happy : if it hath not
confirmed the felicity, either of Sparta her-
D 4 felf,

---

the courfe of this war, the former adopted the humiliating expedient of fending embaffadors to the latter
to fue for peace. And that even one of thefe embaffadors had the meannefs to confefs, that nothing but
a fubfidy from the king of Perfia, enabled his countrymen to carry on the war. (See Diod. Sic.) It evidently appears, that the fuccefs of Sparta, in the war
of Peloponnefus, may be attributed to thefe three
caufes: the plague at Athens, the expedition to Sicily,
and the affiftance of the Perfians. Now I fee no af-
finity between thefe three caufes, and the refectories
of Lycurgus. The injuftice which reigned in the policy of Sparta, was a circumftance fo well known amongft
the Greeks, that Polybius, endeavouring to paint the
Etolians in the moft odious light, as guilty of in-
fractions in their treaties, compares them to the Lacedemonians ; he quotes, on this occafion, two incidents,
by which they may be better known. Phebidas (fays he)
having made his entry, treacheroufly, into the city of
Thebes, and become poffeffed of it, the Lacedemo-
nions punifhed the author of the confpiracy, but left
a garrifon in the place. After having proclaimed that
they reftored all the Grecian cities to their liberty,
they appointed over them, every one of the governors
whom they had before fettled, there.

felf, or of her neighbours, fhall we be ftill
fo blind as to lavifh upon it fuch enthufiaftic
admiration, and that on the mere credit of
Xenophon and Plutarch? If it be alledged
that the Spartans were happy, in fpite of their
poverty, and feverity of manners, it may be
anfwered, that the inclination which the
greater part of their magiftrates felt, to poffefs riches, and honours, is a proof that they
only defpifed them, in proportion to their
being ignorant of them. Obferve a Paufa-
fanias(*u*) felling his country to the tyrant,

over

(*u*) The prefents, and the promifes of the king of
Perfia were irrefiftable temptations to Paufanias, already difgufted at the behaviour of the allies. Not fatisfied with having betrayed the *Lacedemonian* interefts,
he afpired to the fovereignty of *Greece*. The *Ephori,*
jealous of his ambitious projects, recalled him. Convincing proofs were as yet wanting againft a man,
whofe conduct was violently tainted by the breath of
fufpicion. At length, the *Spartans* were relieved from
this fufpence, by the evidence of a flave, who produced
a letter which he had received from *Paufanias*, with
orders to deliver it to *Artabazes.* The criminal, thus
detected, took refuge in the temple of *Minerva.* The
door was blocked up, whilft his mother, a female *Brutus*,
affifted in the punifhment of an unworthy fon, and
brought the firft ftone, to prevent his flight: in this
confinement, Paufanias was ftarved to death. K.

over whom he had lately triumphed; and selling it, even in the very moment, when he was intoxicated with succefs at Platea. Behold a Lyfander bargaining with the governors of the Perfian provinces, for the fate of Sparta, and of Athens: a Gylippus,(x) who robs his general, and, at once, reveals to his countrymen, the treafure and the theft. Such were thefe citizens; at home, humble and fubmiffive; abroad, arrogant, ambitious and tyrannical; in thefe refpects, like bold, intriguing monks, who, after having over-thrown provinces, and even whole ftates, perceive themfelves compelled to retire again within their cloifters, where, in filent indignation, they bend beneath the laws of obedience and aufterity.

What

(x) *Lyfander*, who had received prefents, in return for promifes, which he never intended to perform, entrufted to *Gylippus*, the care of conveying to *Sparta*, the treafures which had been collected, during the campaign, and which amounted to fifteen hundred talents, exclufive of the crowns of gold, given by the different cities. Gylippus unripped the facks, at the bottom, ftole three hundred talents, and then, having very dexteroufly fown up the openings, concluded that it muft be difficult to detect him; he was miftaken: the written accounts of the enclofed money were concealed within each fack, and betrayed his treachery. To avoid death, he fled into exile. K.

What hath been already advanced, may
ferve to afcertain the vertue of the Lacedemonians. On this occafion, one might fafely
appeal to their admirers, who have never yet
been able to difguife from us, that inhumanity fo confpicuous and univerfal amongft this
people, and of which no other country furnifhed an example.

۱ We wifh that it were poffible to conceal
the exiftence of a government, fo ferocious,
as to have judged it proper to have treated
men, as they would have treated favage
animals, whom it might be neceffary to deftroy, as often as they multiplied too faft.
As we practice the hunting of ftags, and
wild boars, fo, the Spartans fent their young
men to the chace of the Ilotes. When thefe
unfortunate wretches became fufficiently numerous to give uneafinefs to their mafters,
all kinds of ambufcades were placed to en-
fnare them; their affailants concealed themfelves, at one time, behind the thickets, and
at another time, taking the advantage of the
night, they traverfed the country, and mur-
dered every individual whom they met, incapable of defending himfelf. What renders
this cuftom ftill more horrid, is, that it was

not

not the mere refult of an act of momentary fury, but of formal habit, and bore the name of *"Kruptia"* from the Greek word Κρυπτω, to hide ones felf. At the relation of fuch fhocking circumftances, the pen drops from my hand; but my indignation is lefs directed againft the Spartans, than againft thofe authors who have, coldly, tranfmitted to us, the detail of thefe execrable facts, and, complaifantly, expatiated on the praifes of the barbarous people, who committed them. Hence, I have been induced to think that hiftory, thus written, may become too dangerous to be perufed by youth, in general, and by young princes, in particular. It feems a kind of high treafon againft humanity, to mention fuch atrocious facts, without invoking pofterity to turn from them, with horror.

After fuch inftances, it would be needlefs to dwell upon the bafe, and groundlefs jealoufy, which, towards the clofe of the Median war, provoked the Spartans to hinder the Athenians from building their walls; or to relate the fnares prepared for the immortal Themiftocles; the maffacre of the Athenian Greeks, or the allies of Athens, at the open-

ing

ing of the Peloponnefian war; and their ad-
vifing the people of Syracufe to put to the
fword all that Athenian army, which had
been forced to furrender themfelves prifoners.

Such was the virtue of Sparta; and fuch
was the morality of that republic, which became an example to Greece, and which hath
been fo often propofed as an example to our
corrupted ages. O philofophy! O reafon!
O humanity! fhall the man of learning, and
the politician, at no period, be introduced to
your acquaintance?

It were to be wifhed, at leaft, that the conduct of the other Grecians, had been contraft-
ed with the conduct of the Lacedemonians:
but it cannot be denied that humanity was a
vertue to which thefe people, in general, were
ftrangers. In vain did learning, and the arts
arrive to fix their abode at Athens. The decrees iffued againft Mitylene, and the inhabitants of Sicyon, are fuch monuments of
cruelty, as fufficiently prove the fuperiority
of our modern philofophy, over that which
could accomodate itfelf to fuch abominations.
It is beyond difpute that their articles of war
permitted the putting of prifoners to death.
The Corynthians, the Corcyrians, and the

other

other people of Greece, to be lefs celebrated,
were not lefs cruel than the Spartans, and
Athenians.(y) In fhort, we are obliged to
confefs that what is called the fine age of
Greece, was a fcene of torture, and punifhment, inflicted on humanity.

Let us, now, haften to obviate the difagreeable conclufions, which may be drawn
from fuch a confeffion. Is it poffible, then,
(it will be faid) that this æra, enlarged on
with fuch expreffions of horror, can be any
other, than the æra of the fine arts, and polite literature?(z) If, as the human underftanding became enlightened, the depravity
of the heart increafed, what hope have we
from

_____

(y) At the beginning of the war of Epidaurus, the
Corcyrians, after an advantage gained over their allies,
the Corynthians, put all fuch prifoners, as had not
been born in Greece, to the fword.

(z) I have been fo unfafhionable as to reject the expreffion "belles lettres" which hath been naturalized in
our tongue as early as in the time of Addifon, if not
earlier. *The exactnefs of the other, is to admit of fomething
like difcourfe, efpecially in what regards the belles lettres.*
.... *Tatler.* Perhaps, I have not rendered the original
into a term equally fignificant, but I fee, with indignation our excellent language, too often deviating towards a Gallic phrafeology, and that I might avoid it,
have ufed every freedom of conftruction allowable in
the fidelity of tranflation. K.

from the prefent and the future ages? what
relation then doth the progrefs of the mind,
bear to the augmentation of public happinefs?

Here, a croud of anfwers pour in, at once,
upon me: I am puzzled, either how to chufe,
or in what manner to digeft them. Let me,
however, begin by afferting that the human
underftanding proceeds at a flow, and gradual pace. Its infancy is employed in the
cultivation of painting, fculpture, and architecture, which we may call the agreeable
arts; and in the ftudy, and profeffion of poetry, and mufic, which we may ftile an exertion of frivolous talents. A tafte for difcuffion follows at fome diftance, and is attended by a fubtilty of reafoning, a fpirit of
controverfy, and a Logomachia ;(a) till, all
opinions becoming equally falfe, and equally
fpecious, reafon, fatigued with floating in un-
certainty, embraces the fide of doubt, and
ex-

(a) Thefe dialectical fubtilties are, facetioufly, ri-
diculed by Lucian, who, after having obferved that
the Sophifts fupported their opinions fo well, that they
were perpetually crying out either yes, or no, as they
affirmed, or denied, adds that they may be compared to
fleepers, in a carriage, whofe wavering heads feem,
by turns, to nod in contradiction, and with affent.

experiment, and thus forms, by little, and little, the true, and (if one may fo call it) the laft philofophy.

I, now, apply this principle, and examine what progrefs philofophy, and politics have made amongft the Greeks. A judgement may be formed of philofophy, by adopting two methods: the firft method is to examine it, as in itfelf; and the fecond method is to obferve the alterations which it hath produced in the manners of the people.

It is well known that, before the time of Socrates, philofophy had abfolutely neglected morality, to indulge itfelf in the empty fyftems of cofmogony, and theogony;*(b) (c)*
and

(b) Socrates boafted of having occafioned philofophy to defcend from Heaven, where fhe had been confined, and give him her hand that he might lead her back to earth. It muft be confeffed that, then at leaft, fhe fat out upon an idle journey. She might, certainly, have been more ufeful, not only when fituated in Heaven, where fhe might have difcovered the planetary fyftem; but when above the furface of the earth, where, by dint of obfervation, fhe might doubtlefs, have acquired a knowledge of fome phyfical truths, more ufeful to men, than all the morality of Plato: and, here, it may be remarked, that more errors than might be, at firft, fufpected, derived their
fource

and that, even, when the fcholaftic tafte was
veering round to the ftudy of morality, this
fcience ftill retained much of its predominant
fpirit, nor ever became fixed upon a folid bafis.
But were we to judge of caufes, by their effects, could we ftile that people philofophical,
whofe individuals were addicted to the moft
extravagant fuperftition ; (d) who were not
cruel

---

fource from an ignorance of phyfics ; and that it is
impoffible but that, in the long run, a good phyfical
fyftem muft introduce a good philofophical fyftem.

(c) The Greeks were engaged in feveral wars, on
a religious account, before the war of Peloponnefus.
One of thefe wars, and the Perfian war, undertaken by
Philip of Macedon, pointed to much the fame objects.

(d) It is exceedingly ridiculous to obferve Sparta,
and Athens, at the beginning of the Peloponnefian
war, ready to conteft, even with violence, for the firft
rank, and the government of Greece, and opening
their debates with mutual, and childifh reproaches,
on account of pretended acts of profanation. Efchines,
in his harangue againft Ctefipho, relates, alfo, that,
in the time of Solon, the Acrogallides, and the Sy-
rians, having profaned the Delphic temple, the oracle
directed that a war fhould be waged againft thefe
people, that they fhould be reduced to flavery ; and
that their lands fhould be confecrated to Apollo,
Diana, Latona, and Minerva : by the advice of Solon,
all this was executed.

cruel to their enemies, alone, but ftill more
fo to thofe whom fortune had thrown within
their power ; and who, infenfible to the benefits of nature, and all their proper ufes,
placed their whole happinefs in glory, and
their whole glory in war ? no, if wifdom be the
art of living in felicity; and if (as its name im-
ports) philofophy be, truly, the love of wifdom, then, the Greeks never were philofophers.

Nothing, now, remains but the fcience of
politics : to ftrip thefe celebrated republicans
of their pretenfions to this fcience, doth not,
at the firft glance, appear an eafy tafk.   Yet,
even under the poffibility of being accufed of
having rifqued a rafh opinion, we fhall not
fcruple to advance, that their knowledge of
politics was exceedingly imperfect, and much
like that which they had formed of morality,
and philofophy.   It will not be difficult to
prove this, whether we confider their fyftem
of politics, in its general relation to the nations amongft themfelves, or in its more diftinct relation to the particular government of
each people.   The firft point of view prefents to us, the Greeks, rafh, and inconfide-
rate ; relinquifhing the project of a neceffary
confederacy, almoft as foon as they had form-

ed it; eſtabliſhing a ſpirit of tyranny, and
uſurpation, in the two chief republics, without fixing any equal balance of power, in the
reſt : Sparta, and Athens, ambitious without
principle, confining all their politics, the one,
within the forcible eſtabliſhment of an Oligarchy,(e) and the other, within a no leſs
violently conducted introduction of Democracy ; the firſt, in ſhort, ſo forgetful of
juſtice, and her real intereſts, as to have re-
courſe to the king of Perſia, and, thus, avail
herſelf of an enemy to injure her allies. If
we, next, examine that interior ſyſtem of politics, which determines on the form of the

go-

(e) Sparta not contented with having eſtabliſhed Oligarchy, in preference to Democracy, hath incurred
the indelible, and infamous reproach, entailed on all
advocates for tyranny. Witneſs the thirty tyrants of
Athens, and the protection which ſhe granted to Dionyſius the tyrant againſt the people of Syracuſe. It
muſt be added that we are far from being the ſole ac-
cuſers of this republick, for having promulgated the
firſt principles of a policy ſo pernicious to humanity.
Salluſt hath long ſince given us the example. " Poſtea
vero quam in Aſiâ Cyrus, in Græciâ Lacedemonii,
atque Athenienſes cœpere urbes atque nationes ſubigere,
libidinem dominandi cauſam belli habere, maximam
gloriam in maximo imperio putare, &c.... in Catil.

government, we shall perceive that, here, as
in all other things, the Greeks manifested a
greater share of spirit, than reason. And yet,
whatever liberties we may have taken with
the Spartans, we cannot, possibly, pronounce
the name of Lycurgus, without offering a
tribute of admiration to the sagacity of his
mind, and the extent of his genius. It is
not to be denied, but that his laws were conceived in an uncommon depth of thought,
and that a very singular unity pervaded every
part of his plan. But was his project a rea-
sonable project? I pass over in silence,
that particular idea of making, entirely,
a people of soldiers, and I allow that the
Spartans should have been as regularly
brought up to the profession of arms, as
Emilius, to that of a carpenter ; but if, to
fix the maintenance of liberty, defensive
wars, only, were undertaken, would it not
have followed that sooner, or later, having
neither walls, nor strong holds, they must
have been as effectually subdued, as they
concluded themselves to be, after the battle
of Leuctra? If their courage, and discipline
ensured to them no decisive advantages, there
must have arisen an absolute certainty, that,

with the nature of their conquests, their spirit must have, also, varied; and that, by degrees, they must have assumed the manners, and the vices of the people, whom they had subdued ?(f) might they not, also, have foreseen, that, at some future period, the new improvements in the military art, would render money as necessary as valor towards the support of war. Was it natural, in this case,

---

(f) I shall have more occasions than one to remark, that, a state of ease, and tranquility, a rich system of agriculture, and an active industry, are the goals to which every state directs its course: for this reason, I have ventured to compare the greater part of our legislators, to those sensible persons, who, having met a troop of men, upon the road, gave them the most excellent directions in what manner to conduct themselves on their way ; but as they had made no provisions either against their arrival, or to accomplish their establishment, this multitude, having reached the end of their journey, perceive themselves entirely disconcerted, and equally unable either to fix their residence, or to return.

Such, perhaps, at present, is the fate of the English colonies. In this respect, Locke was the wisest, and Lycurgus the most rash of all the legislators. The former stipulated that his laws for the province of Pensylvania, should only remain in force during one hundred years ; and the latter is said to have sacrificed his life in the attempt to render his decrees immortal.

cafe, for Lycurgus to fuppofe that his republic fhould receive their pay, as foldiers,
from thofe tyrants who were the enemies of
Greece? In other refpects, fhould not the
great difference between the feverity of the
difcipline at Sparta, and the eafe enjoyed at
the camp; the infignificance of thefe kings,
in times of peace, and their unlimited confequence during the war, have operated as
reafons for involving the republic in difficult
and dangerous battles, threatening to terminate in either their deftruction, or their
flavery? if it be objected to me, that the
laws of Lycurgus preferved their force,
through a term of more than fix hundred
years, my reply is, that the neighbours of
Sparta were for a very long fpace of time, ill
inftructed, and badly governed; nor is this
inftance more fingular than that inftance fo
evident amongft the Iroquois, and feveral
other American nations, who have long exifted under the fame laws. The really flourifhing ftate of Athens began not till after the
clofe of the Median war, and from this
epoch, to the battle of Leuctra, little more
than one hundred years are fuppofed to have
elapfed. The Thebans, who imagined that,

by the fuccefs of this action, they fhould have deftroyed the Spartans, to all intents, and purpofes, had been diftinguifhed at the opening of the former wars of Greece, only, by the contempt which they had drawn upon themfelves, in the Median war. The battle of Mantinea, and the univerfal conqueft of Greece, by Philip, and Alexander his fuccef- for, may be comprized almoft within the fpace of twenty years; fo that the event ra- ther condemns, than juftifies the conftitu- tion of the Lacedemonians: and here, indeed, the event fell, as it might have been ex- pected to fall, on individuals whofe confti- tution was calculated to ftartle their nature, but not to convince their underftanding.(g)

It is unneceffary to take any great pains, to prove that the government of Athens was corrupt. Every one hath read the works of Demofthenes, and Thucydides; two cele- brated

---

(g) It may be proper to obferve what Polybius (b. 6.) hath remarked concerning the republics of Sparta, and of Rome. Ite proves, that the laws of Lycurgus were but ill fuited to the aggrandizement of the republic, however they might appear to tend, all, to that point; whereas the Romans might have en- creafed their grandeur, by adhering, merely, to the principles

brated Athenians, who have, with fuch accuracy, tranfmitted to us a picture of the manners of their country, and who have equally, excelled ; Demofthenes by the force, and Thucydides by the truth of his colourings.

It appears, in general, that the government of Athens was never in any very great repute. What, in fact, fignified the fenate compofed of four hundred perfons, and that mixture of Ariftocracy, and Democracy, which eftablifhed diftinctions in properties, without reducing them to the ftandard of their influence over public affairs ? for, in the laft refource, every thing was referred to a populace, whom they could affemble, and harangue without form, and without precaution.

There will be no occafion to mention the other ftates of Greece. It is fufficient

E 4   to

principles of their conftitution. Thus, only, can we judge of ancient governments: if, folely, their power, and not the happinefs of individuals, became the object of their views, they muft be condemned, as often as they appear to have referved to themfelves, a principle, which contradicted the end, which they had intended to accomplifh.

to obferve that their government was reduced either to a tyrannical oligarchy, or to
a tumultuous democracy, each of which degenerated into two factions; the faction of
the great, and the faction of the inferior ranks
of people ; the faction of the populace, and
the faction of the opulent.

Were we not apprehenfive of anticipating
the reflections which we muft referve for the
conclufion of the work, it would be no unpleafing tafk, to reft a little over the com-
parifon of modern republics, to the antient
republics. What fubjects, for admiration,
fhould we not difcover in that wifdom which
prefides over the federal governments of
Switzerland, and of Holland ! how muft we
applaud their permanence, and, particularly,
the heroifm which founded them ! an heroifm, at once, calculated to excite intereft,
and admiration, fince it nourifhes, and protects the moft natural fentiments ; the love
of our properties, the defire of living with
our wives, of educating our children, of
cultivating our fields, and of worfhipping
our God with fuch a mode of homage, as
may be the moft pleafing, and the moft
fuitable.

But

But the admirers of antiquity will fay : We freely permit you to lead us, from argument to argument, until the Greeks fhall have been ftripped of thofe two advantages, the poffeffion of which hath hitherto, particularly, redounded to their repuation : what fophiftry, however, can be fufficiently fpecious to perfuade us, that this people excelled not in poetry, eloquence, painting, and architecture ?   If you cannot deprive them of the credit of having enjoyed thefe accomplifhments, are you firmly rooted in the belief that they have not equally excelled in thofe other particulars, a fuppofed defect in which hath drawn from you this thoughtlefs condemnation ?

This argument would, doubtlefs, carry fome weight with it, were it to be judged of, only, at firft fight : but it will fall, at once, on the affignment of the reafon, why the perfection of the fine arts ought to have preceded, at a confiderable diftance, the accomplifhments of the rational fciences.   This object might, of itfelf, furnifh matter fufficient for a differtation, but, in this place, it is only neceffary to obferve ; firft, that the lefs inftructed the people are, the more

the

the imagination is liable to become poetical ; and that, probably, a multitude of barbarous nations have only wanted a fine language, and more celebrity, to have been capable of tranſmitting to us, poetical compoſitions, like thoſe of the Greeks : witneſs the poems in the Erſe language,(b) thoſe of the Scandinavians, &c. Secondly that it is exceedingly natural that eloquence ſhould flouriſh in the midſt of a people governed by orators. In faɛt, this art was ſo dependant on the particular nature of the government, that it was driven forward to its perfeɛtion, at Athens, and abſolutely unknown at Sparta. Thirdly, that the exceſſive ſuperſtition of the Greeks, having induced them to build ſeveral temples, and to ſpare no expence in theſe particulars, the architeɛture of the outward

(b) Let the philoſophical literati ſolve this problem. Why do the poems in the Erſe language breathe the nobleſt, and ſublimeſt ſentiments ; the ſentiments of love, glory, honour, a veneration of anceſtry, patriotiſm, &c. whereas the ſentiments ſcattered up, and down the Iliad, are baſe, and vile : ſuch, for inſtance, are, the deſire of plunder, the low ambition of enjoying the beſt ſhare at a feaſt, the exaſperated violence of paſſion, tranſporting itſelf into aɛts of barbarous, and cowardly revenge, &c ?

ward decorations ought, in courfe, to have
made a great progrefs amongft them : I fay,
the architecture of the outward decorations,
for it is not perceptible that they have approached to our modern architects, in the
workmanfhip within, which is a proof that
their progrefs, in architecture, was owing to
their rage of raifing temples. As to fculpture, it is well known that the athletic exercifes were, of themfelves, fufficient to form
able ftatuaries. Men, deftined to appear
naked in public, could not avoid an attention to and practice of the fineft poftures ;
nor want the faculty of difcerning when they
were either more, or lefs graceful. In their
public games, where wreftling, the pugilatus,
the pancratium, &c. (i) were performed,
every attitude was to be ftudied, and all the
combinations of elegance, and ftrength, particularly marked. What a fchool was here
for

(i) The pugilatus of the antients was frequently attended with confequences more fatal, than the confequences arifing from the bruifing matches, fo peculiar
to my fellow countrymen. The latter, contented with
the exercife of the naked fift, have, in general, not
only furvived the battle, but preferved their features,
and

for painters, and fculptors! the moderns have only faces to infpire art, and, I had almoft added, fentiments. Let us, alfo, fee what has been done for them. What painters, what refemblances in bufts, bracelets, fnuff-boxes, &c! Imagine, then, what the Grecian fculptors ought to have been; the fculptors, for whom, the face was only a fubordinate, and fecondary object.

Now, let the reader pafs his judgment: convinced that we are, at once, incapable of admiring too warmly, or cenfuring too feverely, the productions of antiquity, we fhall fubmit to his decifions, without reluctance.

The only favor which we would require at his hands, is, that he would not fuppofe thefe

and their limbs. If the celebrated heroes, Slack and Broughton, had introduced the ceftus, in their memorable conteft, one combatant, at leaft, and, probably, each of them, muft have died a martyr to the innovation. When this formidable gauntlet was in ufe, the clofing up an eye, or the breaking a jaw-bone were, only, calamities of courfe: if the Athletæ of old were neither killed at a blow, nor left dying on the fand, it was efteemed a fingular inftance of great fkill, or greater good fortune. The pancratium was a medley of wreftling, and boxing, in which every kind of attempt to get the better, was fair. K.

thefe reflections foreign to our undertaking ;
but recollect that as the progrefs of the human mind, in its relation to morality, and
politics, was the object of our examination,
the fixing our attention upon this celebrated
people, became the more important, as it
furnifhed us, at the firft glance, with the
following melancholy truth : that the progrefs of the human mind hath, in no fhape,
redounded to the advantage of the people.
How very neceffary was it, then, for us,
who build all our hopes upon the advancement of reafon, and philofophy, to enter
into an examination of thofe facts, which
feem fo violently to oppofe our principles ?

We are not deftitute of apprehenfions,
when we reflect upon the manner in which
we have fpoken of the Greeks. Our fears
not only forbode the difpleafure of fome eminent literati, whofe refpect for antiquity may
be unlimited ; but the poffibility of being
taxed with having adopted that modern falfe
glare of wit, to which, the cavils of criticifm are better fuited, than inftruction. We
can neverthelefs, affert, that if letters and
arts had been the only topics in queftion, we
fhould have rendered ourfelves much more
liable

liable to have been cenfured as enthufiafts, than as fatyrifts. We are, in this place, impatient to declare what we may, perhaps, at fome future time, have occafion to repeat: and this is, that we cannot too much wonder at the falfe road (if the expreffion be allowable) which we are, daily, purfuing in our ftudies; quitting the path which would conduct us to the fources of our knowledge, to tread on the path which directs us to a crowd of exceedingly imperfect imitators; the reader muft perceive that the preference given to the Latin,, in prejudice to the Grecian literature, is, here, alluded to. What time do we not employ in learning a mixed, and half barbarous language, inftead of acquiring one fo accurate, and fo metaphyfical, that it may be confidered as, of itfelf, an introduction to all the fciences! how furprized muft Cicero be (that Cicero, who not only profecuted his ftudies in Greece, but collected an immenfe library, confifting, entirely, of Greek books) were he to revifit the world, and perceive our youths learning his mother tongue, in preference to the language of his tutors!

CHAP.

CHAP. IV.

The condition of humanity amongst the Greeks; its situation in those countries which were known during this second epoch.

WERE we to confine our search to such objects, as might administer comfort to humanity, in its depressed situation, our advances through the different periods of history, would prove useless. Far from perceiving mankind to be enlightened with ideas of their real interests, we observe an universal encrease of confusion, and disorder. Even Egypt, that happy, and renowned country, on which we have fixed our attention, with so much pleasure, became subject to the laws of a stranger, and bore, with

Asia,

Afia, a fhare in the misfortune of exifting
under the moft cruel defpotifm.   Greece
feems to have been divided into fo large
a number of different ftates, for no other
reafon, than that it might (if the expreffion
be allowable) ftretch the furface of war, and
calamity ; for it is worthy of obfervation,
that the divifion of fovereignties multiplies
difafters through the land.   We can, boldly,
affirm that each of the little republics of
Greece,   underwent,   during   a   period   of
fifty years, feveral revolutions to which one
half of its citizens became the victims;
that each, throughout the fame fpace of
time, faw its territories ravaged by wars; in
fhort, that no individual of thefe unhappy
towns had run the common courfe of life,
without detefting the hour, in which he had
received it.(*k*)

I am not certain that fufficient attention
hath been paid to this vice, fo inherent in
little ftates.   Mr. Rouffeau hath remarked,
that

___

(*k*) Diodorus Siculus (b. 15.) mentions a revolution effected at Argos, in the hundred and fecond
olympiad, when, after feveral acts of barbarity, per-
petrated by each party, the prevailing party ordered
twelve hundred citizens to be led to execution.

that wherever the citizens become fo numerous, as to render it neceffary, that the government fhould be lodged in a representa-
tive body, there can exift no true liberty. (*l*)
I am, neverthelefs, of opinion, that there
will be no fubftantial, and lafting liberty,
and, in particular, no happinefs, but amongft
individuals, where every thing is tranfacted
by a reprefentative body.   Obferve this
little republic, where each citizen is, as it
were, all, becaufe the ftate is nothing; where,
at one moment, he affumes the gown, and
at another, his military armour: a fhallow
politician, an incapable judge, and an undifciplined foldier; continually, either a prey
to faction, or expofed to the rage of war:
where as an extenfive fociety, in which every
individual is united to each other, by the
fame interefts, and the fame laws, derives its
peaceful fituation from the prudent partici-
pation of its labours.   In fuch a fociety, the
foldier is not engaged in pleading the caufe
of the oppreffed; nor is the magiftrate employed in defending the ramparts.   The la-
bourer, unmolefted, purfues the cultivation

F

of

(*l*) See the focial contract.

of his ground, whilft the judge watches over
the political welfare of the ftate, and the
warrior repels its invaders: and if the laft
appear to bear, entirely, the public burden,
he is amply indemnified by falaries, and
honours. In fuch a fociety, peace wears a
hundred additional charms, and war throws
off a hundred of its horrors. The extent of
the domain, and the precautions taken to
prevent all accefs to it, like a centrifugal
force, inceffantly, drive back the war to the
frontiers; and in the fame manner, as the
interior affairs are tranfacted by a reprefentative body, a fimilar body is invefted with
the power of prolonging, or determining
the operations of the war. At the opening
of the Peloponnefian war, when Athens
wanted to raife fuch an army, as might with-
ftand the attacks of her enemies, the militia
of the city was, of neceffity, compofed of
old men, and boys. All the citizens, including thofe, before, fcattered up and down
the lands of Attica, were compelled to confine themfelves within the town: and from
this circumftance arofe that remarkable contagion, to which one half of the people fell
a facrifice. Every place, then, may be faid

to

to have felt, at once, the greateſt miſeries of war. . . . Whilſt France was engaged in the wars of 1733, 1741, and 1757, no more, at any time, than the hundredth part of her inhabitants, were ſharers in the danger. Extenſive provinces, ſtill, enjoyed the calmeſt ſerenity, and even millions of labourers, knew not in what part of the world the armies were engaged.

To theſe advantages, we may add that ſweetneſs of manners, and thoſe comforts of life, which the people can ſcarcely retain, but by the means of regular troops ; that is to ſay, thoſe repreſentatives of the nation, who are intruſted with the care of conducting the war. If it be too truly proved, by the experience of all ages, that the greateſt misfortune which can happen to a people, is to be ſubdued, it is certain that an endeavour to acquire a ſuperiority over every neighbouring ſtate can not be too ſteadily purſued. It is no leſs evident that this point can never be attained to, but by a military education, ſo that every citizen, to be a ſoldier, during one ſingle day of his life, is obliged to embrace the profeſſion of arms, from his birth. Hence, aroſe the neceſſity of adopting, in

every

every age, military manners, alone. What
muft have been the deftiny of men who
paffed their whole lives, as if every day had
been the eve of a battle! the cuftom of
maintaining a ftanding army, became the
fole remedy againft this inconvenience. By
the means of this arrangement, wherever it
fhall have become general, the people may
be happy, without being ennervated, and
foftened, becaufe a proper difcipline is kept
up in armies, where the principles of honour
and courage may maintain themfelves, in a
certain degree of accumulation, without
which their vigour, and influence, would be
but fmall.(m)

We have already feen that defpotifm had
not only driven happinefs from the bofom of
Afia, but expelled it from a part of Africa:
Greece, during her moft refined æra, was but
a theatre of bloody revolutions. Hiftory,
then, prefents us with no more objects for
our reflections, fave the Phenicians, and the
Carthaginians. The firft have been little
noticed, except in matters relating to their
commerce, and their colonies. There is every
appear-

(m) Majores noftri bella gefferunt, noftributa depen-
dimus, ne bella patiamur. PAUL. OROS. HIST.

appearance, to confirm us in the opinion, that this active people, equally engaged in the practice, and promotion of industry, conducted themselves on principles, superior to the principles of the Greeks: but their vicinity to the Perfians, whilst it, continually, tied them down to an exceffively great dependance, prevented them from giving any certain stability to their government.

Whatfoever commendations Ariftotle may have lavifhed upon the laws of the Carthaginians, we cannot believe that a people, whofe avarice was fo infatiable, whofe fyftem of politics was fo jealous, and fo cruel, and whofe religion was fo fuperftitious, and atrocious, could poffibly have known true happinefs. The imagination ftarts back, with horror, from thofe human facrifices, at the celebration of which, the barbarous mothers threw, with their own hands, their children into the flames. A philofopher, one day, reading that paffage in Genefis, wherein it is written, " that God created man in his own image," immediately obferved, that man had, with no fparing hand, returned the image to God again..... A judgment may, generally, be formed of a people, by their

F 3   mode

mode of worſhip: if it be ſimple and
modeſt, then are they active, and induſtrious; if it be full of ſolemnity and pomp,
then are they vain and frivolous; if it be
melancholy and auſtere, then are they fierce,
violent, and obſtinate.

We ſhall take no notice of the Scythians,
the Indians, and the Chineſe, as we have no
ground-work, but in conjectures, and fabulous relations. We are, only, ſenſible that
the life which the Scythians led, bore a
ſtriking reſemblance to the life of the ſavages.
Diodorus Siculus mentions the Indians, with
particular approbation, but as he adds the
deſcription of an iſland, which never exiſted,
and other circumſtances, of which, ſome are
incredible, and ſome have been proved falſe,
it is evident that, to make his hiſtory appear
complete, he was not at all nice in the
choice of thoſe materials, of which he has
availed himſelf.

We muſt, therefore, be contented to conclude this chapter, with a refleſtion, which,
though extremely natural, ſeems to have
been overlooked by the partiſans of antiquity.
It is, that ſlavery, alone, was ſufficient to
render the condition of humanity, in general,

a hundred

a hundred times worfe, than it is at prefent.
In faɛt, it would be but to little purpofe to
tell a philofopher that, the thirty thoufand
individuals, who fhared a country (Laconia
for inftance) betwixt the n, were very ftrong,
brave, fierce, and accuftomed, during their
lives, folely, to the exercife of arms, in
battle; were this philofopher to difcover that,
thefe thirty thoufand individuals had reduced
more than fix hundred thoufand of their fel-
low-creatures, to a condition, a hundred
times worfe than the condition of beafts of
burden, he would turn his eyes afide from
this people and regard them, for the future,
only, as the fcourge, and difgrace of humanity. I prefume that it is no exaggeration,
to advance that, reckoning the towns and
country, the proportion which the number
of freemen might be fuppofed to bear to the
number of flaves, may be fixed, in Greece,
at fomething lefs than the rate of one to
four.(n) And what, for the moft part, were
thefe flaves? free men, educated in plenty,
and profperity, who, having been made pri-

F 4   foners,

(n) At the battle of Platæa, each Spartan was accompanied by feven of the Ilotes.

foners, either in battle, or by the Corfairs, were, at length, fold for the benefit of the conquerors. Every one knows how far the rights of the mafter over his flaves extended. The proftitution of the two fexes was one confequence of that power.(o) Let us, for a moment, imagine what muft, in our days, be the condition either of an officer, or of a magiftrate, who, reduced to the vileft drudg-eries, felt the moments of his labour doubly embittered, by perceiving his wife, and children, obliged to facrifice their perfons to the debaucheries of an infolent mafter. It is fcarcely to be fuppofed, that a perfon could, now, be found, either brave enough, or bafe enough to fupport himfelf under fuch a fate. All this, however, frequently hap-pened amongft the antients, and, particu-larly, amongft the Greeks. I muft be per-mitted to urge the difference between flaves, bought from amongft the individuals of fome poor, and half favage nations, and thofe whom the fortune of war had reduced to this fhocking condition : and, with confufion,

let

(o) I cannot recollect the author who hath obferved that " impudicitia in ingenuo crimen eft, in fervo ne-ceffitas, in liberto officium."

let it be admitted, that our age is not yet,
totally, exempt from the reproaches, which
we have thrown upon antiquity. Although we cannot fufficiently lament that
adherence to this practice, which avarice,
ftill, maintains amongft the people of the
Weft, and which barbarity, and ignorance
have eftablifhed in the Eaft, yet we muft
obferve; firft, that flavery is no longer
known, amongft the Chriftians, except it be
in the colonies : fecondly, that the flaves are
all drawn from an extremely favage, and
brutal nation, and that even the natives come
to bargain with our traders, for the fale of
their own countrymen. Thirdly, that though
reafon and philofophy proclaim the neceffity
of treating the flave, like an European,
(" quamvis ille niger, quamvis tu candidus
effes") it is notwithftanding true, that the great
difparity between thefe unhappy wretches,
and ourfelves, is but little calculated to
excite in us, the fine feelings of humanity,
and ferves to nourifh thofe cruel prejudices,
which occafion them to remain in a ftate of
oppreffion. Fourthly, that if thefe flaves
have been treated with a moft inexcufable
barbarity, experience hath, yet, frequently,

proved

proved that no tendernefs, no benefits could erafe from the minds of thefe individuals, their bafe, ungrateful, and cruel characterif-tics : that there is every reafon to believe that, if even the flaves belonging to the colo-nies, had been Europeans, they would, al-ready, have intruded themfelves into the poffeffion of the rights of citizens, in like manner as the villains of our feodal govern-ment, recovered, by little and little, their civil liberty : in fhort, that the number of flaves, in our time, is much lefs confiderable, fince it is limited to the fugar colonies alone ; and that amongft more than a hundred mil-lions of Chriftians, exifting at prefent, we cannot, affuredly, reckon a million of flaves ; whereas, that, to a million of Greeks, there were more than three millions of thefe unfor-tunate human creatures.(p)

                                        C H A P.

(p) If the reader be curious to know the fentiments of the anciens, refpecting flavery, let him read the third, fourth, fifth, and fixth chapters of the politics of Ariftotle. He will there find, that " fervitude is both juft, and unjuft, that it is fometimes natural, without being legal, and legal, without being natural ; that it is the order of nature, that the leaft perfect fhould ferve the moft perfect; thus, the animals fhould ferve man ; and women obey their hufbands: that in the
                                            cafe,

CHAP. V.

Reflections on the Romans.

IT is to be prefumed, that the reader, already informed of the object which we have in view, doth not expect to find in our refearches, a fcrupulous adherence to chronological order. Having been, once, introduced

---

cafe, where force alone, hath reduced the people to captivity, flavery is juft, without being fo, in an abfolute fenfe, becaufe, although it be a fuperiority of vertue, that confirms the authority, it is never in the order of nature, that noble people can be reduced to flavery : but that if there be noble nations, there are other nations on the contrary, ignoble ; that amongft the Barbarians, their nobles are only fuch, as confidered, relatively, with their fellow-citizens ; whereas there are

nations

duced amongſt the Greeks, it became impoſſible for us to take leave of them, till we had
fixed an eager attention, on thoſe many
wonderful particulars, which have attracted
the admiration of every age, and whoſe real
value, it was ſo neceſſary to eſtimate, we
have ventured to declare, that what ſeemed
fine, was not, on that account, always good;
and, conſidering antiquity, as we have conſidered the characters exhibited upon its
theatre,

---

nations which are noble every where." Here is certainly enough to prove in what hands the ſacred rights
of humanity were, formerly, depoſed. But a circumſtance ſtill more ridiculous, than barbarous, is, that
Ariſtotle, propoſing to take a family, for the model of
political ſocieties, diſcovers that this primitive family
is, eſſentially, compoſed of three parts, the firſt of
which includes the maſter, and the ſlave; as if nature
had, in the beginning, formed two beings of different
kinds, the one to be the maſter, and the other to be
the ſlave. It is unneceſſary to add, that the other two
integral parts of ſociety are, the huſband and the
wife; and the father, and the children.

The fine, and benevolent ſentiment of Alcidamus,
as preſerved in the Scholiaſt, upon the rhetoric of
Ariſtotle, is a glorious contraſt to the latter part of the
preceding quotation. Ἐλευθερυς ἀϕηκε παιlας θεός; ε᾽δενα
δυλον ἡ ϕύσις πεποίηκεν. "God ſent all men forth
free, nor hath nature made any individual a ſlave."
The

theatre, we have plucked the mafk from Agamemnon, to difcover the flave, who reprefented a king of kings. We muft, now, refume our labour, and attempt a tafk at leaft as difficult as the former.

Whilft the Greeks were bufied in the improvement of their laws, the conftruction of their temples, and the difcipline of their armies, Italy foftered in her bofom a people deftined to deftroy her government, to pull down her buildings, and triumph over her troops.

The defign of nature, and the will of its great author, have been fo exceedingly perverted, that to fuppofe the world could, ever, enjoy a ftate of univerfal freedom, might feem the wild fuggeftion of infanity. Even the cultivation of our colonies, abroad, might have been conducted by the labour of fervants, as free as the reftraint of falutary laws could permit them to be; and, perhaps, it would, on enquiry, be found, that, however impolitic a general enfranchifement of the flaves, in our Eaftern and Weftern Indies, might prove, yet the neceffity of a code of laws, to reftrain the barbarity of mafters, and overfeers, fhould engage the attention of the Britifh legiflature. That it will, is exceedingly doubtful. It were natural to imagine that, whilft the patriot, vehemently harangues the fenate, in favour of the liberty of an Englifhman, he would wifh to extend that liberty, if poffible, to all his diftant dependants: but the living, and the dead, have furnifhed us with contrary inftances. K.

troops. As Demosthenes, his ambition
struggling against his nature, disdained to
mount the rostrum, until a long and indefatigable practice had convinced him, that
his oratory must prove succesful; so Rome,
whose origin was barbarous, whose beginning
was abject, and whose progress was slow,
was employed, during four whole ages, in
learning the art of conquering, and of governing. Surely, no study hath a stronger
claim to the attention of the philosopher,
than that study which endeavours to investigate the principles, which could raise a
simple city, to such a heighth; or, to speak
more properly, to that excess of glory, and
prosperity: But known events are not, always, in proportion to known causes; and
it frequently happens that political writers
imitate the ancient astronomers, who, tolerably well, described, and even announced,
the particular phænomena, but imputed them
to absurd causes. Yet, were it certain, that
we had discovered the real sources of the Roman grandeur, of what advantage could such
an acquisition be to us, who wish not to
know in what manner a state is aggrandized;
but, merely, whether by being rendered
                                        great

great it is become more happy. Such a difcovery would bè, in our eyes, no better than
a large, magnificent road, which could not
conduct us to the place, whither we defire
to go.

If the Roman government can be faid to
merit the approbation of pofterity, it is not,
becaufe its individuals, confined within the
circumference of their city, either made a
preparation to defend it, or formed their
fyftems of civil policy : but it is, certainly,
becaufe Rome, beginning to rule in Italy, at
length reduced thofe fine countries to a fubmiffion to her principles, and her difcipline,
at leaft, if not to her laws: it is, becaufe,
having extended her influence over all the
Mediterranean, fhe added Sicily, Sardinia,
and Spain to her empire ; and, chiefly, it is
becaufe that in the moment, when fhe became the miftrefs of Africa, fhe arrivèd at
the privilege of giving laws to Afia. 'Now,
if, in thefe oftentatious æras, mankind were
more free, and unmolefted ; if tyranny was
abolifhed ; if the rights of peace were more
facred, and the laws of war more humane ;
if the fields were better cultivated, and if
commerce multiplied the links, in the great
political

political chain, which united nations to each
other ; then, let us affent to the admiration
of every paft age, nor ceafe to ftudy the form
of government, peculiar to a people, who,
beginning to labour at the acquifition of their
own happinefs, perceived themfelves by the
fole perfection of their public adminiftration,
and the fingle energy attached to their conftitution, in a condition to prefcribe laws to
barbarifm, to hold ambition in chains, and,
in fhort, to teach the reft of the univerfe, to
whom they had been, at once, the bene-
factors, and the models to afpire to an affi-
milation with themfelves. But, if nothing
like this hath happened ; if the Romans,
far from triumphing by the afcendancy of
their vertue, were indebted for their prevalence, folely, to crimes, and entirely eftablifhed themfelves upon the ruins of the
world, who fhall hinder us from loading them
with cenfures, as fevere as thofe, which we
have paffed upon the Greeks ; the Greeks,
who were as brave, as heroic, and more
amiable than the Romans ?

Perhaps, we˙ have, at length, found an
opportunity of being reconciled even to the
admirers of Greece ; for the learned world is
divided

divided into two parties, one of which confifts of advocates for the Greeks, and the
other, of advocates for the Romans. It
muft, in general, be confeffed that the opinion of thefe laft appears to be the too hafty
fruit of erudition, or rather, the firft production of an imperfect ftudy. The modern
ages have been, indeed, fufficiently fingular,
whilft they contented themfelves with propo-
fing, as models, thofe, who were, in every
department, flow and feeble imitators; but,
by an aftonifhing caprice, it hath fallen out,
that the more profufely Rome in her glory
hath been loaden with efteem, and veneration,
the more have her encomiafts been conftrained to difparage her original condition.
Plutarch was the firft writer, who maintained
that the founders of this queen of the world,
were only robbers, and outlaws. This idea
hath been eagerly embraced by certain fyftematical literati, (q) who being perfuaded that

VOL. I.   G   the

(q) Giam-Baptifta Vico hath endeavoured to fupport this opinion, in a work entitled " principi di
fcienza nuova intorno alla commune nature delle nazioni." This was followed by a fimilar publication
from Mr. Duni, (" Origine, e progreffi del cittadino,
e del

the Roman government had no mixture of democracy, in the infancy of its conftitution, have imagined it impoffible to reprefent the fubjects of Romulus, in too difgraceful a light. They, confidently, affert that this new-born colony was peopled, folely, by va- gabonds, and individuals difowned by all; that from amongft thefe, their legiflator chofe the moft eminent, that is to fay, fuch as were

originally,

---

e del governo, civile di Roma,") whofe fentiments are adopted by Mr. l'Abbé Bignon, in his " hiftoire cri- tique du gouvernement Romain." Although we do not think ourfelves obliged to admit the principles of thefe authors, in their utmoft latitude, yet we cannot mention the learning, and penetration, which they have difcovered in their writings, without the higheft applaufe. We would, in this place, willingly, at- tempt to give the reader an idea of thofe reafons, which they have advanced, in fupport of their argu- ment; but were it even poffible for us to undertake this tafk, without wandering too far from our fubject, we fhould, notwithftanding, be of opinion, that it would be better to recommend a thorough perufal of their works, the matter of which would make ample reparation for the pains of having examined it. It will fuffice, then, to obferve, that the argument from whence our authors draw the greateft advantage, is, the difference which the privilege of taking the au- guries, eftablifhed amongft the citizens. Mr. Duni has fully proved, that only the auguries could confti-

tute

originially, free men, (ingenuos) and whofe
fathers were known; that it was from thefe,
that he felected the fenators, and with the
fenators, only, that he divided the authority;
and that the people (Plebs) or in other words,
the commons, were, only, compofed of
clients, or bondmen attached to their chiefs;
or elfe, of a troop of fugitives, whom the
protection offered by Romulus, had collected
together.

G 2

If

· tute a marriage in that form, which the Romans called
nuptiæ; whilft the union of perfons of different fexes
was, amongft the Plebeians, nothing but a kind of cohabitation, underftood by the word, connubium. All
thefe obfervations are juft, and ingenious; but the
great error lies in their having been perverted. As to
the Plebeians not marrying, in the face of the church,
does it, therefore, follow that their marriages, their
fucceffions, and their inheritances, were no more regulated than thofe of the Negroes, belonging to our
colonies, are, at prefent? does it, alfo, follow that
the people had no fhare in the government? if, on the
contrary, it be certain, that the Plebeian families,
like thofe of the Patricians, perpetuated themfelves by
inheritage; if the rewards acquired by fervices in war;
if diftinctions, names, and properties were preferved
from race to race, then did not the people, however
deprived of the privilege of taking the auguries, form
a body politic, and a part of the republic? befides,

it

If Livy, and Dionyſius Halicarnaſſius, ſhould prove equally full in their evidence againſt this paradox, our learned authors would not ſcruple to rejeƈt their teſtimony. *" Theſe writers have pretended, to aſſert what they were ignorant of. A profound night co-*
vered

---

it doth not appear that the free Romans, at any time, married ſlaves: and if the ſimple connúbium had been ſo abjeƈt, and ſo brutal an union of the two ſexes, how could the Patricians have ſubmitted to an intermarriage with mere Plebeians? it is, nevertheleſs, certain that theſe marriages were cuſtomary, previous to the law of the twelve tables, and ſince it is not evident that this uſage was, at that time, forbidden, as being a recent innovation, there is every reaſon to ſuppoſe that it exiſted, even before the people had tribunes, that is, when their condition was the moſt abjeƈt, and unfor-tunate.

It appears, then, that our authors, with all their abilities, and intelligence, were deceived, by extending their principles too far. In this reſpeƈt, they are, certainly, very excuſable. There would be but little erudition amongſt the men of genius, if a taſte for pa-radoxes were not, ſometimes, to come to their aſſiſ-tance. The writer of imagination ſuffers himſelf to be captivated by an idea: he ſeizes on it with ardour, and having once pierced into it, employs all his talents to ſupport it: he reads, examines, and compiles; how much muſt learning be obliged to him, when, thus, made the inſtrument of freeing him from the yoke of pedantry!

vered the firſt ages of Rome, and it is raſhneſs
to attempt to penetrate through its obſcurity :"
and yet our modern critics, have found no
difficulty in effecting, what theſe two celebrated antients could not accompliſh. It is a
fact, that in ſpite of their having excepted
againſt their depoſitions, they condeſcended
to avail themſelves of them, whenſoever they
appeared to ſuit their purpoſes. For example, after a peremptory condemnation of the
opinions, given by Dionyſius, relative to the
Roman government, they, nevertheleſs, confidently preſent us with citations, taken from
paſſages, in thoſe numerous harangues, with
which that author thought proper to adorn
his works ; as if what he had, viſibly, in-
vented, could have had any weight, when
thrown into the ſcale, againſt what he related,
and as if he had not known, much better than
another, the conſequences of theſe pretended
contradictions. As we do not perceive ourſelves concerned in this diſcuſſion, we ſhall,
therefore, reſt contented with making the
following obſervations.

First, ſuppoſing it to be even certain, that
hiſtory hath not tranſmitted to us, any authentic traditions, reſpecting the firſt ages of

Rome, this circumftance would, then, furnifh
the moderns with a pretext for believing,
that they could advance better reafons, and
conjectures, towards the elucidation of this
fubject, than the Romans themfelves have
ever given.(r)

Secondly, were it, as fome have ingenioufly infinuated, a fact, that hiftorians have
been more fcrupulous in their detail of events,
in proportion to the diftance of thofe ages,
the tranfactions of which they wrote, it would
not follow, from thence, that they deferved
lefs confidence than their predeceffors; for
the art of criticifm and inveftigation is peculiar to enlightened æras; nor is it the pro-
fpective glafs, but the illuminating torch,
which

(r) It is exceedingly to be lamented that the accounts
of the eftablifhment of nations, of all other accounts in
the hiftorical department, the moft interefting, and
the moft inftructive, fhould be fo univerfally defective.
A want of authentic memorials is not peculiar to the
firft ages of Rome. The annals of Britain are, perhaps, equally involved in obfcurity, and equally
wrapped in fables. The improbability that the two
firft kings of Rome fhould have been, accidentally,
called by names, allufive to their future actions, hath
often been remarked. Every one knows that the words
Romulus, and Rome, are taken from a Greek expreffion, fignifying force; and that the name, Numa, is
derived from the fame language, and means law. K.

which is fo neceſſary to the ſtudy of hiſtory. Who, for inſtance, can doubt, that the preſent times poſſeſs a more competent knowledge of the reigns of the firſt race of our kings, than thoſe times in which Froeſ-ſart exiſted ? Who, alſo, can doubt that Di-onyſius Halicarnaſſius had, after twenty years of aſſiduous labour, conceived better notions . of the Roman hiſtory than Fabius Pictor.

Thirdly, all the hiſtorians, and all tradi-tions inform us, that Romulus conducted to Rome, a colony of Albans : now, we have not the leaſt proof, that the people of Alba ſtood, at any time, in that diſgraceful light, in which the Romans of that age, were painted. On the contrary, if conjectures may be admitted, there is every reaſon to be-lieve that this people became eſtabliſhed under Amulius, becauſe every monarch, de-ſirous of being abſolute, rather protects the people, than the great.

Fourthly, antiquity furniſhes us with many examples of the prodigious difference, which ſubſiſted between the freeman,(s) and the

G 4   ſlave ;

(s) Dionyſius Halicarnaſſius obſerves, that Servius Tullius ſhared the conquered lands amongſt the citizens, who,

flave; but it produces no inftance of that middle order, that race of bondmen, intended to have been brought to Rome, in the retinue of the Patricians. Every flave had a mafter, and his only abode was the houfe, to which he belonged. He could not, therefore, form, with others, a clafs apart, however abject that clafs might be fuppofed to be.

Fifthly, the Sabines having united themfelves to the Romans, by a free covenant, and

---

who, having nothing belonging to them, were obliged to work with their own hands; fo that, after this difpofition, the individuals amongft the Romans, confifted only of proprietaries, and flaves. Now the fame author, willing to juftify Servius Tullius, for having made a great number of thefe laft free, enters into a long detail, that he may inform us, under what predicament the flaves ftood amongft the Romans. He remarks, that they were all compofed, either of fuch as were made prifoners in war; thofe fold towards the increafe of the public revenue; or, even, the flaves of the enemy, who always made a part of the plunder: from hence, refult two important circumftances : firft, that, amongft the Romans, war was the fole fource of flavery; and next, that that race which confifted of the vaffals, and dependants of the great, (as defcribed by fome authors) never exifted at Rome. There are, alfo, other paffages fo decifive, that one would wonder at

their

and formed, as it were, an identical part of the people, it is to be prefumed that the con- dition of the Roman populace was not either more bafe, or more unfortunate than that condition under which they exifted in their original country ; fince they did not ftipulate, for the enjoyment of any privilege, or diftinc- tion : and in this, they were imitated by the people of Alba, who, joining themfelves to the Romans, though, indeed, lefs willingly than the others, yet never remonftrated againft that abject fituation into which they
must

---

their having efcaped the attention of our critics. Such is that of Livy, who, relating the tumults, which pre- ceded the retreat of the people, to the facred mount, expreffes himfelf thus : Civitas fecum ipfa difcors in- teftino inter Patres, Plebemque flagrabat odio"... and a little farther on ; " magno natu quidam cum omnium majorum fuorum infignibus fe in forum pro- jecit." Now, what could this citizen of great birth, who fhewed the wounds which he had received in combat, and the blows by which he had been bruifed, in his ftate of flavery amongft the Patricians ; whofe misfortunes not only interefted all the people in his fa- vour, but made them take arms againft the great, pof- fibly be, but a Plebeian ? Thus, about the two hun- dredth and fixtieth year from the foundation of Rome, there was a Plebeian, whom Livy, the violent Partizan of ariftocracy, diftinguifhed as a man of elevated birth.

muſt (were ſome authors to be credited) have, certainly, been thrown.

Sixthly, all writers not only agree in acknow-ledging, that the people enjoyed the privilege of electing kings, creating magiſtrates, enacting laws, and determining either on peace, or war ; but Dionyſius Halicarnaſſius, ſtill more poſitively aſſerts, that when Horatius had ſtabbed his ſiſter, the power of paſſing judgment on this atrocious crime was referred to the people.

Here, is matter ſufficient to convince us, how reaſonably the Roman government was, hitherto, ſuppoſed to have been intermixed with monarchy, ariſtocracy, and democracy. Now, what claim hath this complicated, this modified government to our eſteem ? doth it furniſh us with any conſtitutional plan ? In fine, what was it, in its firſt principles ? let us not ſcruple to call it a ſimple polity, the interior arrangement of a city. I intreat the reader to pay ſome attention to theſe words; in my opinion, they not only contain a new idea, but caſt a great light upon the ſyſtem of politics.

Upon

Upon the fyftem of politics!(*t*) the expreffion which hath juft dropped from my
pen, may ferve to prove the truth of what I
am going to unfold. It is that all the governments of antiquity, except the great antient
monarchies, the origin of which we are ignorant of, owe their birth to a town, to a
city. A little reflection would convince us,
that it could not have been otherwife. In
fact, men were not known under the name
of a people, but when they equally enjoyed
the fame laws, adhered to general cuftoms,
and felt thofe mutual dependancies, which
united them, and, as it were, attefted their
identity. Now, mankind ftood in no need
of laws, and conventions, except when great
numbers were affembled in a fmall fpace.
The more individuals are diffeminated over
the furface of the earth, the more are they
occupied in procuring their fubfiftance, either
by the chace, or the cultivation of the ground;
the lefs, alfo, do they want a legiflation. On
the other hand, the more they are united,
the more the circumftances which draw them

to

(*t*) Πολιτικη, regendæ civitatis fcientia, from πολις,
a city.

to each other, are multiplied ; and the more
are they conftrained to have recourfe to treaties, and conventions. The refult, therefore,
is that the firft want of every fociety, muft
have been the want of a polity ; and that all
governments began by being no more than a
fimple polity. In this inftance it, particularly,
appears that language ferves to explain facts,
and not, that facts ferve to explain the language. Πολιτεια, amongft the Greeks, and civitas, amongft the Romans, fignified, originally,
only the government of a city, although
they were, afterwards, fuppofed to mean
every thing, which appertained to an adminiftration, in general : and, in the prefent
times, by the word, polity, may be underftood, the government of men, in oppofition
to the term, adminiftration, which, rather,
fignifies the government of properties.

It will, perhaps, be objected to me, that
war is the firft fource of authority, and confequently, of government ; to which I fhall
anfwer, that fuppofing the war to have been
long, and the army numerous, the government of this army muft ftill have appertained
to a polity ; and that if the war had been
fpeedily concluded, a quiet fociety, and the
poffi-

poffibility that men might live together without being molefted, would have proved the
firft object of the conqueror, and the firft
fruits of peace. In thefe two cafes, a polity
would have been eftablifhed, either in the
camp, or in a newly-rifing city. Were thefe
confiderations to be extended to the animal
creation, it would, in like manner, appear,
that the fociety of wild beafts, which, inde-
pendent upon each other, eafily procure
their fubfiftance, is the moft imperfect fociety
of all; and that the fineft examples of a regular polity, difcernible in the works of nature, are found amidft the hillocks of ants,
and the hives of bees. Every thing, therefore, concurs to prove that the firft conventions were made for a multitude, and that
they were confined, as it were, to the laws of
juxta-pofition.

Far from fuppofing that it is neceffary,
ftill more extenfively, to unfold thefe truths,
we apprehend that they would appear too
fimple and trivial, if we did not prefs forward
towards a demonftration of their importance,
and fix the attention on thofe contradictions,
which reign amidft the firft principles of all
go-

government, and the ends which all government fhould have in view.

What, in fact, are human creatures, upon
the earth? They are children at the breaft,
obliged to prefs the bofom, from which they
muft receive their nourifhment. What are
human creatures in cities? They are tranf-
planted plants; improvident, and uncertain
beings; and like that multitude of micro-
fcopic animals, which fluctuating from fide to
fide, and, inceffantly, precipitating themfelves upon each other, feem to have been
created, only, that they might preferve themfelves in motion.

Let it not be doubted that agriculture
fhould be the firft object of legiflators, and
property, the leading principle of agriculture.
Nature granting nothing but to reiterated
follicitations, her firft benefits were bought,
and the firft expences, whether of money, or
labour, ought to have eftablifhed the firft
right of property. The perfection of cultivation would not have failed to have introduced plenty, and variety of productions,
from whence muft have arifen commerce,
and from commerce, muft have proceeded
riches. Then, the neceffity of public markets,
and

and the convenience, refulting from places fituated by the banks of rivers, or by the fhore of the fea, muft have given rife to cities : but thefe, regarded as the laft produét, or the fimple confequence of an.agragarian government, muft have received from it, their manners, and their laws. Such peaceable cultivators could not, poffibly, have neglected an eftablifhment of the full influence of their falutary principles. Thefe men, attached, by intereft and habit, to the foil, would have made their own prefervation the bafis of their politics; and, perhaps, the word glory, would not have been known in any language; but the contrary to this hath been the cafe.

Whether the firft inhabitants of the earth, perceived themfelves placed by nature, in thofe advantageous fituations, where her gifts were more abundant, and lefs neceffary; whether force, poffeffing, from the beginning, more means of exerting itfelf, foon, knew the method of prevailing over labour; or, whether the progrefs of population hath been, always, more rapid, than the progrefs of induftry; we cannot difcover that ftates have been indebted for their origin to cultivators;

on

on the contrary, they feem to have been founded by robbers, and vagabonds ; hence, it hath happened, that cities were the firft rudiments of nations ; and that the political government hath ferved as the chief principle in the conftitution of ftates.

This we have already obferved : the origin of antient monarchies is unknown to us ; but, let us, without fearching, with an ufelefs attention, into the obfcurity of the times, dwell, for a moment, on the progrefs of population, in that part of the world, which during fo long a period gave either laws or examples to the whole earth.

Whether, or no, Danaus, Pelafgus, Inachus, and Pelops were the firft founders of the Grecian cities, it is, neverthelefs, certain that Greece was peopled by colonies, which came from Afia, or from Egypt ; and it is equally true, that all the great cities of Greece, and Sicily, iffued from Sparta, Athens, Corinth, Argos, &c. Now, if the progrefs of this population be traced, as many republics, as cities, will appear to have arifen from it. And, if ever any of thefe eftablifhments became united, and feemed to form a political fyftem, it was ef-
feČted

feted by a fimple federal union, like the union of the Amphictyons, the Etrufcans, and
the people of Latium. On the other hand,
if thefe rich mines of the human fpecies, if
thefe vaft oriental monarchies, funk under
the efforts of the newly-rifing republics, what
could have remained upon the earth, except
the veftiges of that fingle government, which
the conquerors obeyed? Corinth gave birth to
Syracufe; Tyre to Carthage; Troy to Alba;
and Alba to Rome. To thefe famous names,
add the names of Sparta, and of Athens, and
you will have enumerated the principal ac-
tors on the great theatre of the world.

Let the refpectable philofophers, who labour to difengage mankind from fuch frivolous amufements, fuch idle fpeculations,
and attach them to thofe two important objects, their fubfiftance, and their happinefs,
no longer wonder if the plan of a government,
founded upon agriculture, and territorial property, fhould prove an abfolutely new idea,
exifting only in opinion, or on paper. Would
they account for our ignorance of fo interefting a matter, let them recollect thofe innumerable errors, which were committed by
that political fyftem of government, which

VOL. I.   H   became

became the irreconcileable enemy of property. They will, there, perceive perpetual convulfions, censures, reformations, divisions of land, distributions of corn, arbitrary taxes, and, in short, all property hazarded in every one of these political quarrels. They will, then, eafily obferve, that at all times, when alterations in the conftitution of the ftate, and the fortunes of individuals, were, necef-farily, involved together, quarrels, and fedi-tions grew more frequent; and that, on the contrary, whilft factions mutually difputed concerning their privileges, and dignities, it was much eafier to appeafe them, than if they had, at the fame time, attacked the properties of each other.

If a municipal adminiftration, and fimple forms of polity, had conftituted the firft go-vernments of every ftate, there could, cer-tainly, be no reafon to expect that its origin should account for its progrefs. Thus, it would be needlefs to feek, in the infancy of ftates, the feeds of their future grandeur ; and particularly, to amufe ourfelves with the vain hopes of finding upon fome little hill, furrounded by walls, the principles of an uni-verfal monarchy.

A young

A young, ambitious man, fatigued with waiting till he might fucceed his grand-father, and, perhaps, apprehenfive that his legitimacy might be difputed, propofes to found a new eftablifhment. He, eafily obtains affiftance, and even fucceeds in the art of enticing away fome of his countrymen. A convenient fpot is chofen, contiguous to which, dwellings are built, that the inhabitants may be nearer at hand, in cafes of mutual affiftance; the circumference is drawn, and furrounded by ramparts, and ditches. Scarcely is this eftablifhment formed, but an attention is paid to the interior arrangements: it is not poffible for the founder, whofe affociates were collected together, folely, by the hopes of liberty and equality, to rife, all at once, into the rank of mafter; yet, at the fame time, the leading part which he took in the plan, and the execution of it, gives him a particular pre-eminence, and conftitutes him the chief of this rifing ftate. The fathers of families, and the moft refponfible men, compofe a council, whofe province is the difcuffion of every fubject; but the decifion of the moft important fubjects is fubmitted to the general affembly of all the

colonifts.

colonifts. They, foon, turn their thoughts towards putting themfelves in a ftate of defence, and, even, concert meafures whereby they might be enabled to attack their neighbours. The new inhabitants are divided into different bodies; companies of foot, and troops of horfe are formed, and this city militia ferves as the model to their army. The defire of acquiring additional forces, prevents them from being over-fcrupulous in their reception of recruits. An afylum is .opened to all adventurers, and, efpecially to fugitive flaves: fuch a circumftance was, then, of the utmoft importance, and promifed to be the fource of an extenfive population: But as this admiffion of ftrangers, of all denominations, introduced colonifts, folely of one fex, a projeft is conceived, highly expreffive of the morals of fuch citizens. The women, belonging to the neighbouring ftate, are carried off, in defiance of all the laws of hofpitality. To recover them, the infulted people betake themfelves to arms: in the very moment, whilft they are profecuting their revenge, they fuffer themfelves to be difarmed; the two nations are united by a treaty, folemnly

confirmed,

confirmed, and (what is still more extraordinary) religiously obferved. The city encreafes, and its polity becomes more perfect. A king, acting in the character of a lawgiver, fucceeds a warlike prince; he, also, in his turn, gives place to military monarchs. The nation grows warlike, but is furrounded by ftates of the fame character, and every decifive advantage which it gains, feems, entirely, owing to the conduct of its chiefs : Such an advantage depends on fortune, and cannot, yet, be the effect of the political conftitution, &c. &c.

Thus far, the confideration of the progrefs of the Roman republic, would be to little purpofe. I know but of two caufes, which may be affigned : the one is due to chance, which will, conftantly, have great weight in all human affairs and thefe inftances of chance, are, the capacities of the kings, and the length of their reigns : the other caufe belongs more to polity, and is that principle of population, eftablifhed by Romulus, and adopted by his fucceffors; a principle which induced the Romans to inftitute a law, enacting, that the vanquifhed, inftead of being reduced to captivity (at that time the cuftom)

should

fhould be all tranfported to their city. This is the real fource of the greatnefs of Rome. It was this, which, in the fpace of two hundred and fifty years, after its foundation, occafioned the number of its inhabitants to mount up to one hundred and thirty thou- fand citizens.(*u*) As to its government, what idea can we conceive of that, when we perceive the people bafe enough to groan fo long, and patiently, beneath the yoke of fuch a tyrant as Tarquinius Superbus? In- deed, if the Roman youth had not been wearied out by a toilfome, and protracted war; and if a moft horrid tragedy had not happened, opportunely, to roufe the fpirit of the people, Rome muft have become, what Syracufe was, the fport of tyrants, and the theatre of revolutions.

But their kings were expelled, and liberty fat in their places... Liberty!... what liberty? Tyranny did but exchange hands, paffing from kings to the great. The people bewail their earlieft captivity; they complain, and are not heard; reduced, at length, to an
excefs

(*u*) Or, according to the calculation of Dionyfius Halicarnaffius, one hundred, and forty thoufand fouls.

excefs of defpair, in the violence of their woes, alone, they find the courage neceffary to make them terminate. The eftablifhment of the office of Tribune confirms the effect of the Valerian law. The people receive new life; and fcarcely have they ceafed from fearing, before they become formidable. Here, the complexion of the times undergoes an univerfal change; and the hiftory of the Roman government is, from henceforth, a detail of the progrefs of Democracy. The Plebeians are, by marriages, confounded with the nobles, and Rome, practically democratical, is no longer ariftocratical, except in fpeculation; for it is remarkable that the Roman polity was never proportioned to the conftitution of the government; fo that the people, when ftripped of their privileges, preferved their influence, by the terror which they infpired, and the nobility, when deprived of their original rights, were indebted, for their confequence, to popular refpect.(w)

I would, now, afk thefe fubtle politicians, who fee every thing in Rome, as Malle-

branche

(w) During the fecond Punic war, moft of the dignities were held by the Patricians.

branche faw every thing in God, what æra,
what moment of this perpetual fluctuation,
they would feize on, to take from the Roman
government, a pattern, which every other nation ought to follow ?   They may, perhaps,
be fomewhat embarraffed by this queftion,
and yet, they may contrive to elude it.
This will be their anfwer.   " We allow that
the conftitution of the Roman republic never
had any properly fixed principles ; but you
cannot deny that its polity enjoyed, at
leaft, an equal advantage.   That fpirit
of difcipline, that perfection in the art
of war, that fyftem, to which power, and
encreafing grandeur were attached, fufficiently plead in favour of the principal
fprings in the machine of government.
Such great effects, muft have proceeded
from powerful caufes."

Here, I muft beg to be indulged with the
infinuation of a doubt, the temerity of ad-
vancing which (if doubting can be temerity)
I fhall not endeavour to conceal.   The Romans, indeed, as their own hiftorians affirm,
triumphed over their neighbours, almoft as
frequently as they fought ; but to form a
judgment concerning thefe great advantages,

let

let us recollect that they waged war, during
a space of time, nearly approaching to four,
hundred years, ere they reduced to submission, the single city of Veii:(x) and let us
wait, before we estimate this superiority of
the Romans, until we shall have read, in the
works of the historians of the Volscians, the
Æqui, the Samnites, and the Etruscans, the
same facts which Livy hath related : yet even
this, is unnecessary : for that very author,
somewhere, confesses, that, for a long space
of time, the Volsci were, at least, as success-
ful as the Romans. We will not, in this
place, call forth the too well known histories
of Porsenna, Coriolanus, and Brennus, the
Gaul; but shall rest contented with remarking
that if Horatius Cocles had, unfortunately,
fallen, when he received the wound on his
knee; if the mother of Coriolanus had died,
some years sooner; and if Manlius Capito-
linus had slept one quarter of an hour more,
the

(x) It appears that, after a siege of ten years, the
Romans accomplished their reduction, solely, by the
error, which this city committed, in choosing a king,
and abandoning her alliance with the Latins; a defection which they could never forgive.

the miftrefs of the world had been entirely overthrown.

I cannot avoid fixing the attention of the reader, for a moment, upon this object. Let him judge, with me, how frivolous the common place obfervations, fo frequently repeated, by thofe authors, who have written concerning the Romans, muft, unavoidably, prove. What is more common than to find it afferted, that the fpirit of conqueft was the foul of their government? The fpirit of conqueft, amongft men who fuffered three hundred and fixty years to roll away, without bethinking themfelves of attempting a fiege! the fpirit of conqueft, amongft a people, whofe wars were only wars of reprifals, or of plunder! the fpirit of conqueft, amongft individuals, who never imagined that, to fubdue their enemies, they fhould have feized their military fortreffes! We need not quit the ftreets of Rome, to difcover the fecret fprings in their machine of government: let us direct our refearches, folely, into the diffenfions betwixt the people, and the great; thefe diffenfions conftitute the fources of all thofe events which excite our furprize. At firft, the great dreading the

people,

people, when animated by their Tribunes,
conceived the expedient of fending them to
war: but as the foldiers were obliged to
furnifh themfelves with fubfiftance, at their
own expence, it was not convenient to make
long campaigns.   It was, therefore, only for
à time that they were diverted by war, from
an attention to public affairs, and, that time
being elapfed, they returned from battle,
more burdened, and more mutinous, than
they had ever been.   A projeɛt was, then,
concerted to prolong the war, and to lay
fieges.   To effeɛt this, it became neceffary
to adopt the refolution of giving pay to the
troops.   The Patricians entered, heartily, into
the facrifice of their contingent, and fent it,
of their own accord, to the public treafury :
But the Tribunes were not fo eafily duped.
They tore the mafk off from this falfe generofity, and expofed the fnare, concealed under
this apparent beneficence.

What is the refult of all this ? it is, that it
occafions, in our opinion, a reaɛtion of effeɛts upon caufes, and of caufes upon effeɛts :
that is, for inftance, we are induced to judge
of the conftitution of a government, from
fome fplendid circumftances, which excite

our

our refpect; and, on the other hand, full of
this idea, we place moft of the events, in the
fame point of view, from which we beheld
the principal events. Now, I confider human reafon, as armed with two inftruments,
and thefe are contemplation,(y) and experiment. Thefe, only, can enable it to pierce
through the chaos of opinions, in fearch of
truth; but if, inftead of perfecting them,
it were to hurry on, through the concurrent
ufe of each, the confequence muft be, that,
clafhing inceffantly, the one againft the
other, they would be impaired, before they
could affift it.

It is aftonifhing, that mankind fhould have
been almoft conftantly miftaken in the ufe
of thefe two inftruments. The phyfical fyftem
hath been fubmitted to contemplation, and
the political fyftem to experiment. The laws
of nature have been founded on ingenious,
but extravagant conjectures; the laws of fociety have been founded on particular facts.
The cruelties of a tyrant occafioned the ex-
tirpation of monarchy; an unfortunate fuccefs,
an error of councils, effected the difmiffion
                                          of

(y) Theory, which is derived from the Greek word
Σεωρια, fignifies, only, contemplation.

of democracy ; an abufe, either of power, or
of riches, threw a difcredit over ariftocracy;
a crime committed on the perfon of a female,
exceedingly beloved, eftablifhed a violent feverity in the infliction of punifhments; a
reprifal, dictated by paffion, fixed the rights
of war. Thus, men, gueffing at the events
of future days, by the circumftances which
had arifen in the courfe of the preceding
days, have blunted the inftrument of experiment, and, entirely, abandoned the inftrument of meditation.

How different fhould have been the path,
marked out for the exertion, and progrefs of
the human underftanding ! aftronomy, Phyfics, and natural hiftory, have, as it were,
been lavifh of thofe given problems, which
they have prefented, for our difcuffion. All
that remained for us, was to adjuft the equa-
tion, to arrange, and to number; a fecond
ftudy, then, courted our refearches, and
that was Zoology, or the knowledge of
living creatures, either in their kinds, or fe-
parately, the which ftudy conducted us to
the philofophy of phyfics, that is, the art
of preferving mankind, in the moft perfect
ftate of welfare, poffibly attainable, by equally
em-

employing phyfical, and moral means: I
fay, moral means, for who doubts whether,
or no, morality be a branch of phyfics?
Here the quantity of facts was immenfe, but
the inconvenience arifing from variety coun-
terballanced the advantage, refulting from
multiplicity. In this cafe, experiment muft
have been attended with timidity, and whilft
expectation was involved in doubts, the
practice, or the fcience thrown into action,
could not have been employed, except with
much referve. To thefe ftudies, naturally
fucceeded the ftudies of government, that is,
of political bodies; of thofe organized ag-
gregations, which under the name of empires, or republics, prefent to us a new order
of moral beings. Now, who doth not, at
the firft fight, perceive that thefe political bodies, in number extremely fmall, and full of
varieties, or anomalies, are, of all the objects
of our refearches, thofe objects which, more
than any others, elude the light of experiment?

From thefe reflections, which we do but
juft hint to the reader, a new fyftem of fcience, hitherto unknown, feems, all at once,
to fpring up. The examination of nature,
and

and of her fixed, immutable, and neceffary laws, fhould be the firft foundation of all knowledge, the initium fapientiæ. From thefe primary notions of nature, one might proceed to her principal productions, and, at length, to her circumfcribed, and individuated operations. Andrologia, or the knowledge of man in general, would ferve as the bafis to medicine, natural hiftory, and morality; and thefe would give birth to politics, which would prove but the refult of all the others. It is, then, that an abfolute Phyfiocratia would arife, a government founded on the powers of nature, and the energy of her action.

In a lefs enlightened age, and at a period, when the human mind might not be fo much accuftomed, as it is at prefent, to the moft fubftantial nourifhment, it would be neceffary to apologize for this philofophical digreffion, and, particularly, for that concife, and abftracted form, into which I have thrown thefe reflections : but I am not ignorant, that knowledge is, in our days, become fo diffufive, that authors can, fcarcely, make any other pretenfions to a fuperiority over their readers, except thofe pretenfions which may

may have arifen from the labour of having meditated, longer than them, upon the fub-jects concerning which they may have written. I, even, perceive that nothing can be more grateful to the compofer of a work than to imagine himfelf placed near a man of genius, who, rapidly, feizes all his thoughts, whofe attention animates him, whofe looks encourage him, and at whofe fide he finds frefh vigour imparted to his abilities, and additional certainty infufed into his conceptions. In this confidence, I flatter myfelf, that I may difpenfe with expatiating on the refult of what hath been advanced; and proving farther, that, on the one hand, the principles of polity, adopted by mankind, have never refted upon a folid bafis; and that, on the other hand, it is very neceffary that there fhould be a fufficient number of facts, attendant on this fcience, to reduce it to experiment, or, in other words, to the doctrine of example.

To return to the Romans: it may be proper to recollect what hath been already ob-ferved, concerning that error, which leads us to judge of facts, rather according to our anterior prepoffeffions, than by an examination of thofe facts, as within themfelves. We

shall,

fhall, then, quickly perceive to what extremes the vanity of the Romans, the adulation of the Greeks, and the enthufiaftic admiration of pofterity, have ftretched themfelves, to give a kind of bold, and fingular relief to the infancy of the republic. Thus, when Servius Tullius had been elevated from a ftate of flavery, to the royal dignity, it was afferted, that a celeftial flame had formerly been obferved to defcend upon his cradle.

This difpofition appears no where, fo ftriking, as in the opinion conceived of the Roman art of war. Not contented with having beftowed on it the applaufe which it deferves, its encomiafts would fain perfuade us to forget that it did not reach its laft degree of perfeftion, till the time of the Scipios: and they would willingly call, that military knowledge, which the Romans derived at length, folely, from the frequency of mifconduft and bad fuccefs, the neceffary confequence arifing from the wifdom of their government.(z)

VOL. I.   I   I am

(z) As I am precluded, by the fubject of this work, from entering into a long detail, concerning the
Roman

I am aftonifhed that no perfon hath, as yet, been induced to compare the quantity of battles, which Livy makes the Romans gain, with the fmall number of real fucceffes, which they acquired, during the fpace of four hundred

---

Roman art of war, I fhall only produce one, from amongft the many errors committed, on thefe occafions.

Becaufe it hath been obferved, that the Romans, towards the time of the Punic wars, formed themfelves into fuch a difpofition of battle, as to have occafioned the ranging of the infantry, in chequers, or fquares, confifting of three files, with the cavalry, on the wings; it was, therefore, imagined that they, always, drew up their army in this order. I am, however, enabled to prove, that, during the four firft ages of the republic, the cavalry was conftantly ftationed, as a body of referve. From amidft a multitude of facts, tending to confirm this opinion, I fhall reft contented with a felection of thefe facts which follow. Livy, mentioning a great battle, between Fabius and the Samnites, afferts, that this conful ordered his cavalry to charge, but that they threw their own troops, and the forces of the enemy, into equal diforder. Equites ducibus tribunis antè figna evecti, haud multò plus hoftibus, quam fuis præbuerunt tumultus. Now, thefe equites ante figna evecti, who occafioned fo much confufion amongft their own infantry, and the infantry of the enemy, could, furely, be no other, than a body of referve, rufhing on to the charge, through the intervals of their foot.

hundred years. I am ftill more furprized,
that no doubt is entertained concerning the
authenticity of the hiftory, when the hiftorian is obferved to be fo very exact, as never
to omit the detail of a fingle action : there
are fufficient opportunities of comparing this

I 2   fcru-

---

foot. I omit the defcription of a number of battles,
during which the conful is fuppofed to have ordered his
cavalry to fall back into the rear, in order to charge the
enemy, in flank ; a kind of attack, which muft have
proved unavoidable, in the very beginning of the action, had the cavalry been ftationed on the wings;
and which, alfo, could never have been executed, if
the cavalry of the enemy, had obferved the fame difpofition : but let me remark that the four hundredth, and
fortieth year, from the foundation of Rome, is the
period, at which Livy fixes the firft introduction of this
difpofition of battle, fo often practifed afterwards.
Treating of the Samnites, his words are : Itaque in
aciem procedunt, equitibus in cornua divifis. Doth
not the particular attention with which the author de-
fcribes this difpofition, fufficiently prove that, it was,
hitherto, almoft without a precedent ? The following
paffage informs us, that the infantry did not march on
to the attack, in chequers, or fquares ; and is an additional confirmation of the opinion, which we have
advanced, infinuating that the cavalry was ftationed, as
a body of referve. The dictator, Marcus Valerius,
coming up to the affiftance of an advanced guard,
marched in the following order. Prima incedebant
                                        figna

ſcrupulous attention, with the attention employed in tranſmitting to us all the harangues; and of remarking, in particular, a certain uniformity in the deſcriptions, which gives the intelligent reader occaſion to ſuſpect,

 ·   that

ſigna legionum, ne quid occultum, aut repentinum hoſtis timeret, ſed reliquerat intervalla inter ordines peditum, quâ ſatis laxo ſpatio, equi permitti poſſent. By this, it may be perceived that on the one hand, the legion did not, conſtantly, leave intervals, for then the hiſtorian would have been ſatisfied, with ſaying, that they had been augmented : and that on the other hand, the cavalry was not ſtationed at the wings; for had that been the caſe, in this particular inſtance, ſo new a diſpoſition would have excited the attention of the enemy, and have taught them to expect a rapid, and unexpected aſſault, (quid repentinum) what aſtoniſhes me the moſt, is, that no perſon hath been led to make theſe obſervations by a conviction, that they were abſolutely neceſſary, to effect an explanation of certain paſſages, which muſt, without it, have appeared abſurd. It hath been obſerved that the Roman cavalry ſometimes attacked the enemy in flank, and, at other times, in the rear; and thus gained a deciſive victory : they, ſometimes, alſo, alighted, to renew the fight, on foot. Now, it is ridiculous to aſſert, that the Romans, having no ſkill in horſemanſhip, frequently gave the preference to an attack on foot, becauſe it is well known, that the deciſion of the battle was, often, owing to their having charged on horſeback. The fact, then, was ſimply this. When the enemy had kept their

                                                                              flanks

that the variety of the different orders of
battle, was confined to the tactics of the author, and not to the poffibilities of war.
What! after fo many battles gained, by the
left, the right, and the center divifions;

I 3 after

---

flanks too clofe, to apprehend their being broken into,
and when the firft attack of their infantry had made
the Roman foot give way, the confuls, perceiving that
they had neither time, nor opportunity, to make a diverfion againft the wings, failed not to order the horfe-
men to alight, and, at the fame time, directing the ma-
niple to open, they led on this body of referve, (ante
figna) that is, in the front of the troops.

As to the Roman art of war, in general, the beft
judgment which I can prefume to pafs on it, after the
moft mature examination, is this: during almoft five
ages, Rome did not much outftrip her neighbours in
the acquifition of advantages. Her infantry were never
diftinguifhed by their fuperiority, and in moft of her
fuccefsful wars, the victory was owing to the good
order, and intrepidity, with which the cavalry charged.
I am convinced that this truth is but little known; but
could I perfuade the military men to read Livy, with
attention, I flatter myfelf that they would agree with
me. As to the reft, the Romans had no idea of continuing the war by campaigns, and fo ignorant were
they of ftratagems of any kind, that when Hannibal
employed them, and when his Numidian cavalry gained
advantages over the cavalry of the Romans, the latter
were

after three hundred and fixty years, paffed in war, is Veü not yet taken ! Veü fuftains a fiege of ten years : (let it be obferved how fufpicious the refemblance is, between this account, and the account of the fiege of Troy). At the end of this period, the taking of Veü is effected, folely, by the fuperior genius of one man. And what man ? the deliverer, the reformer of his country, the immortal Furius Camillus ! what fhall I fay of the Samnites, who fupported a war againft Rome, during a fpace of forty years ? or of the Gauls, who almoft conftantly triumphed over the Romans, however hiftorians may have laboured to difguife, and even to alter

the

---

were involved in a feries of defeats, which, as they increafed, were attended by additional circumftances of humiliation.

To conclude ; it doth not appear, that the Roman authors, who wrote the annals of thofe times in which the republic ftill exifted, and before flattery had arifen to its full heighth, did, at any period, fairly make out their pretenfions to thofe exceffive praifes, which were afterwards lavifhed on their nation. Witnefs that confeffion of Salluft. — Sciebam. . . . facundia Græcos, gloria belli Gallos, ante Romanis fuiffe. . . . . (Bellum Catil.)

the narrative of facts?(*n*) but it will be objected to me, that Rome, at length, became
the miftrefs of the world; and I fhall be
afked what proofs can remain to account for
her prodigious fuccefs, if her fyftem of government, and her art of war be thus attached.

To this objection I anfwer, firft, that he
who takes the dimenfions of an edifice, doth
not, on that account, pretend that he can
pull it down; and if I have imagined, that
an enthufiaftic admiration hath attributed too
much merit to the polity of the Romans, I
am not the lefs induced to revere a thoufand
admirable circumftances, which have been
handed down to us, as examples worthy of
our imitation. Secondly, I muft remark, that
whilft men, endued with the moft profound
learning, and the moft lively genius, have

I 4   facrificed

(*a*) It is apparent that the account of the arrival of
Furius Camillus, when the Romans were on the point
of treating for their ranfom, is no more than the fabulous invention of either pride, or flattery. The Chevalier Folard hath fully refuted it, in his commentaries on Polybius, notwithftanding that he hath paffed
by the teftimony of Diodorus Siculus, fo directly oppofite not only to the affertions of Livy, and Plutarch,
but, alfo to the authority of Tacitus, who puts this
fentence into the mouth of Claudius. " Capti a Gallis fumus."…. V. Tacit. Annal. lib. 11.

facrificed all their attention to the tafk, o
finding in Rome herfelf, the fource of her
grandeur, they have too much neglected the
inveftigation of thofe exterior caufes, which
contributed to that grandeur ; as if, in determining on the power of a lever, it were not
neceffary to go to the extreme point, and afcertain its refiftance. It is an omiffion, of
which I accufe the celebrated Machiavel, and
the illuftrious Montefquieu, above all others,
(b) becaufe the former, and the latter could
not have avoided infufing into their obfervations all the fire of their genius, and all the
fagacity of their underftanding: fince they
have neglected this object, let us endeavour

to

(b) Machiavel, in the compofition of his admirable
difcourfes, concerning the firft decad of Livy, doth
not feem to have endeavoured to unravel the fyftem of
the aggrandizement of the Roman republic. Neither
hath the prefident Montefquieu fuppofed this to be a
new and neceffary tafk: doth his work, then, correfpond with its title ? the reflections which he allows himfelf to make on the five firft ages of the republic
fcarcely take up fixty duodecimo pages ; I muft confefs,
that, whatfoever genius may diftinguifh thefe reflections,
they feem fo vague, and fo detached, that they refemble
marginal notes, written on the fame work, of which
Machiavel was the commentator.

to throw some light upon it, and first, let us consider Italy, as within herself.

Nothing could have been more favourable to the establishment of any state whatsoever, than the posture of Italy, at the demise of Tarquinius Superbus, that is, at the period, when the Roman republic began to acquire a certain stability. In fact, matters were so arranged, that the neighbouring inland nations, although sufficiently warlike to exercise the courage of the Romans, were, notwithstanding, as yet, too barbarous and too unpolished, to avail themselves of the means of reducing them to submission; whilst the people inhabiting the countries nearer to the shores of the sea, were, at once, affluent and refined, but too effeminate and ennervated, to render themselves formidable. Thus Italy found herself divided into indigenous nations, still retaining their barbarism, and Grecian colonies, amongst which, commerce and industry had, already, introduced luxury and corruption. The Romans, having become the conquerors of the nearest neighbouring nations, should, at the same time, have vanquished all Italy. The weakness of Capua, and the pusillanimity of the people of Tarentum,

tum, may, eafily, be recollected; but it
fhould, alfo, be remembered that, if Pyrrhus
lefs inconftant, lefs vague in his projects, or
rather more immediately interefted in the liberty of Italy, had vigoroufly pufhed on the
war, perhaps, Fabricius had been the laft
hero of whom Rome could have boafted.
Rome, having once rendered herfelf the miftrefs of Italy, what was wanting to make her
the miftrefs of the whole world, but to conceive it poffible that fhe might be miftrefs?
Carthage taught her to perceive it, and feemed
to enter into competition with her, only to
enable her to know her own power. In fact,
what ftate had the Romans to fear? was it
Sicily, divided into feveral fmall republics,
and governed by feveral petty tyrants?
Could the Illyrians, a defpicable people,
whofe whole lives were fpent in acts of piracy,
be the objects of their apprehenfions? or,
could even Macedonia herfelf alarm them,
when engaged in all the Grecian quarrels,
and rendered, in her turn, the theatre of revolutions? all the forces of Europe had paffed into Afia, and the military power became,
lately, fixed there, as if that region had been
its native refidence.

Car-

Carthage, then, was all that remained in the Weft: but, what, within itfelf, was this power of Carthage? it was like the power which the Englifh enjoy, at prefent, in America, and in India; that is, a power, which, having been eftablifhed, by an afpiring and victorious commerce, at once, extended itfelf along the coafts, and caufed its influence to be felt, through all the inland parts: there is, however, this difference; the power of the Englifh pointed, at leaft, to a refpectable object, a kind of vice, where its whole force concentrated; whilft Carthage, like thofe polypuffes, the vague exiftence of which, lofes in energy, what it acquires in the fuperficies, feemed more jealoufly employed in extending than in fortifying her poffeffions. The Numidian kings, fuch as Syphax, and Mafiniffa; the people of Spain, fuch as the Celtiberians and the Lufitanians, the inhabitants of Sardinia, and of Corfica, were to Carthage, what the Morattoes, and the Indians are, in this age, to the Englifh eftablifhments, and, particularly, what the Mexicans would have been to the Spaniards, if thefe laft, contented with trading amongft them, had not cruelly refolved on their deftruction. Now, thefe

powers,

powers, thus eſtabliſhed by commerce, find it more neceſſary to attack, than to prepare for a defence. Some ſea-ports, ſome forti-fied factories, and, chiefly, the ſuperiority which valour and induſtry acquire over the ignorance of a cowardly, and ſtupid people, are the only means to be employed in enforc-ing the obedience of ſo many tributary, or allied nations. In the moment of having re-courſe to arms, and declaring war, it is eaſy to obtain ſuccours, which may follow in the train ; but when the enemies, recovered from their firſt fright, ſhall have thought of making diverſions, then all the advantage will begin to paſs over to their ſide. They have only one plan of attack, but theſe other powers muſt concert a thouſand methods of defence. The proſpect of the vaſt extent of their domains, far from inſpiring them with confidence, ſerves only to multiply their fears, and as a ſingle ſacrifice is thought a preſage of bad ſucceſs, the deſire of preſerv-ing every thing, induces them to divide their forces. Theſe timid precautions diffuſe a languor over the operations of war. The allied nations which, before, ſeemed to atteſt their authority, ſoon become ſuſpected in

their

their turn. Inſtead of ſending them againſt the enemy, it is neceſſary to watch over their motions ; and it is thus, that a republic which ſeemed the ſovereign of Africa, of Spain, and of Sardinia, concluded every thing, with having for its enemies, the Africans, the Spaniards, and the Sardinians.

From this picture, it is eaſy to judge whether the Romans, who aggrandized themſelves only by repelling the attacks of their neighbours, and who were, in fact, rather raiſed to a relief, than aggrandized, ought to enjoy an advantage over the Carthaginians. Placed in the centre of Italy, of which they had rendered themſelves the maſters, their fleet might eaſily command the two ſeas, and their armies might quickly march to every part, in which the enemy ſhould have dared to appear.(c) Beſides, in the firſt Punic war, the Romans were but auxiliaries, and ſince Syracuſe, under Gelo, under Dionyſius, and under Agathocles, could ſo effectually,
and

(c) Strabo imagined that the ſituation of Rome had contributed much to the aggrandizement of the republic : he reaſoned like a geographer. Monteſquieu diſcovers all theſe cauſes in the nature of their government : he reaſons like a civilian.

and fo often refift the force of Carthage;
nay, could even reduce her almoft to the
brink of deftruction, it is not aftonifhing that,
with fuch an ally, Rome gained fome victories. Had the life of Hiero been prolonged,
he, undoubtedly, would have contrived an
expedient, that might have ballanced the
power of thefe two formidable enemies, and
have applied himfelf to the tafk of delivering
Sicily, from the inconvenience of being burdened with any foreign troops. Indeed, the
accomplifhment of fuch an enterprize, muft
have been attended with fome difficulty, as
this ifland contained a number of different
fmall ftates, divided in their interefts, and
jealous of each other. But Hiero was protected by the Romans : there can be nothing
more dangerous, than to receive protection
from an ambitious power; the fpecious pretext with which fuch a power invefts itfelf,
anticipates that firft effort, of which every
nation, jealous of its liberties, is always fufceptible.

Whilft the Romans, like a wreftler, who
had the victory, without being fatigued by
the conteft, were happy in the undifturbed
enjoyment of their own power, the empire
of

of Carthage was fhaken, even to the foundations.   A war amongft the Mercenaries, a
hundred times more terrible than the war of
the Romans, occafions the blood to flow in
rivulets, and fcatters confufion around the
government; it was, then, that Rome, in
oppofition to the faith of treaties, nay, in
oppofition to that decency which would be
maintained, in our times, even during the
very exertion of an act of ufurpation, took
poffeffion of Sardinia, and thus, rendered
herfelf the miftrefs of the Mediterranean.

The fecond Punic war quickly blazed
forth, and here it·is, that the Romans begin
to fhew themfelves in their   true colours.
Whatfoever title to our admiration, they
may have pretended to poffefs, they are
going to lofe it, in the courfe of fome few
years.   A fingle man tore off the mafk ; it
was not even Carthage ; it was Hannibal
alone, who contended with this powerful republic ! what an aftonifhing feries of defeats!
what accumulated inftances of weaknefs in
her councils, and· cowardice in her com-
bats!

Yet Rome did not fink.... true.... but
doth it follow that the Romans produced examples

amples of an admirable firmnefs, and con-
ftancy ; that Fabius was one of the greateft
generals of antiquity ; and that Rome, at
length, prevailed, by the ftrength of her
conftitution, and by her fole afcendancy over
Carthage ? This queftion hath, often, been
decided in the affirmative, and we cannot
treat of it, here, without giving too much
into common-place quotations, with which
the reader muft have been, frequently, fatigued.   We rather chufe to hazard fome reflections upon the plan, concerted by Hannibal ; and we muft confefs that it appears to
be the moft rafh, and extravagant plan, that
ever entered into the human mind : not, indeed, that we prefume to blame thefe daring
diverfions : but what is the object of a diverfion ? it is to give a terrible and unexpected
ftroke.   Thus Agathocles, leaving Syracufe
befieged, prefented himfelf, at once, before
the walls of Carthage : but the rapidity neceffary to thefe operations, requires that they
fhould be conducted by fea ; that their firft
fuccefs fhould be eafy, and that the terror
into which the enemy might be thrown,
fhould be fudden and unforefeen.

On

On thefe principles, let us form a judgment concerning the conduct of Hannibal.
Could there have been a longer, a more laborious, or a more loathfome expedition, than
that expedition in which it became neceffary
to crofs the Alps, and the Pyrenean mountains, whilft the foldiers felt fatigue, difeafe,
and mifery, as the preludes to a bloody war?
To what were his firft fucceffes owing? to
the treachery of fome peafants, to the helplefs
fituation of the mountaineers, and ftill more,
to the ignorance and mifconduct of the Roman generals, who neither defended the paffage of the Rhone, nor the defiles of the
Alps.   I pafs over, in filence, thofe unexpected victories near Sicinum, and on the
banks of the river Trebia; but what fhall be
faid of the march of Annibal, through the
moraffes of Clufium; of the folly of the Roman generals who, at laft, gave his army
time to reinforce themfelves, and who came
to an engagement, at Thrafymene, in the
very moment, when they ought to have been
fatisfied with keeping them at bay, and reducing them to the perplexing neceffity of entering into Winter quarters?   What! if
Frederick the Great, hath been, once in his

life-time, accufed of temerity, becaufe the
fiege of Olmutz was drawn out to a confiderable length, and this alfo, when the efforts
of the Auftrians, to retake the field, were incredible; fhall Hannibal be juftified, for
having undertaken an enterprize, which muft
have proved his ruin, if attended by a fingle
misfortune, and to which, victory herfelf
could have infured no fuccefs?

It will, perhaps, be objected to me, that,
if fortune favoured this celebrated Carthaginian, at the beginning of his expedition,
fhe, foon afterwards, manifefted her incon-
ftancy, when the fenate of Carthage refufed
to fend into Italy the neceffary fupplies, towards the continuation of the war: to which
I anfwer, firft, that Hannibal, before it became likely, that he fhould receive any fuccours from Africa, had furmounted the
greateft difficulties, attending his enterprize,
and, of courfe, already fubmitted to all thofe
events, of which, if a fingle event had proved
unfavourable, he muft have been irretriev-
ably loft. Secondly, that all his credit, at
Carthage, was limited to a faction; and that
he fhould have known, that when a republic is divided into two factions, the faction
which

which acquires its advantages abroad, is liable to lose its influence at home, because great successes attract envy, and remove, at the same time, that dread which, alone, can maintain order in a divided state. No circumstance, therefore, was more easily to be foreseen, than the fall of the Barcinian faction ; nor could any thing be more inconsiderate, than to expect supplies from a jealous senate, who had never looked upon this diversion with approbation. That Hannibal should have been driven out of Italy is, then, no longer a matter of astonishment ; the wonder lies, in his not having been, sooner, compelled to make a precipitate retreat : we must not admire the Romans, who fought in their own country, and were, constantly, able to oppose four armies, to a single army : it is Hannibal, whom we must applaud ; Hannibal, who, destitute of all supplies, and weakened even by his own victories, perceived himself forced to keep up a defensive war, in the very heart of a country, belonging to the enemy ; how. particularly is that superiority of genius to be commended, which taught him to bring into subjection, an assemblage of barbarous nations,

K 2   and

and to acquire fuch a dominion, over their difpofition, as empowered him, in every peculiar cafe of neceffity, to infpire them with cool perfeverance, in the place of too daring a confidence; and with a devoted obedience, inftead of too prefumptuous an oppofition to his directions!

Amidft fuch a multitude of celebrated events, which arofe during the fecond Punic war, it is impoffible for me to forget one event, apparently, ftill more aftonifhing, than the enterprife of Hannibal, fince it is fomething like a relapfe into the error committed by this great general. I allude to the fuccours led on by Afdrubal, and defeated by the confuls, Livius, and Nero: and here, I cannot avoid inveighing againft thofe partial prepoffeffions, which would not fuffer, even this circumftance, to pafs by, without drawing from it an opportunity of beftowing a profufion of applaufe on the Romans; as if any thing, but the heighth of folly, could have adopted the defign of marching from. Spain, and of croffing the Alps, and the Apennines, with the view of affifting an army, blocked up, as it were, in Brutium, and with difficulty, fupporting themfelves in this

extremity

extremity of Italy; and as if the ftolen march of Nero was not, in fuch a cafe, the moft obvious operation imaginable, and even the firft rudiment, and earlieft leffon, in the military fcience. Could Hannibal, reafonably, have flattered himfelf with the hopes of leading his army, without interruption, acrofs Apulia, Daunia, Samnium, and Picenum, in order to join Afdrubal, amongft the Ombri ? are not two armies, thus put in motion, from oppofite quarters, conftantly exposed to the probability of a defeat, whilft they form only a detached part of the whole body ? undoubtedly, he, whom we have obferved, victorious, almoft at the fame inftant of time, in Saxony, in Silefia, and in Pomerania ; he, who, finding himfelf hemmed in, by three formidable armies, and on the point of feeing a fourth army rufh forward to attack him, knew how, by the combined force of military policy and fignal victories, to diffipate, in the fpace of fifteen days, thefe united ftorms ; this truly great man, who bears nothing about his character, that can eclipfe his glory, except the peculiarity of exifting in thefe modern times, would have felt himfelf exceedingly at eafe, had he been dictator

K 3   of

of Rome, when Hannibal made his entry
into Italy. He would have fmiled at the temerity of thefe barbarians ; and that conduct,
which in Livius was the effect of ignorance,
in him, had been the effect of policy; I
mean, that, inftead of blocking Afdrubal up
within the defiles of the Apennine mountains,
which might have been eafily accomplifhed,
by any one, the leaft verfed in the operations of a defenfive war, he would have permitted him to advance upon the plain, and
thus, have concerted the opportunity of deftroying him, by a fingle battle.

Such a multitude of errors, committed by
the Carthaginians, and the number of difafters,
which were the confequences of thofe errors,
might well accelerate the progrefs of the
Romans, in Spain and Sicily. Thus Scipio
propofed his celebrated diverfion, as an enterprize, the fuccefs of which, was to prove infallible. Even his departure bore rather the
air of a triumph than a dangerous expedition.
Hannibal flew to the relief of Carthage;
but what intelligent fpectator could, then,
have remained doubtful of the event? How
could it be fuppofed, that an army, harraffed
by a long and miferable war, would not be
intimidated

intimidated by that infufferable contraft, which they met with on the plains of Zama ? and, what was this army ? the Carthaginian Phalanx did not form a third part of it. The remainder confifted either of ill-difpofed auxiliaries, or difgufted mercenaries, who, deprived of the profpect of plunder, faw nothing before their eyes, but danger. Hannibal hath been blamed for placing thefe mercenaries, in the front ranks ; to have pitied him, had been more natural, fince he had reafon to miftruft them, to fo violent a degree, as to conceive no hopes of their making any efforts to conquer, unlefs fupported, or rather guarded by the national foldiers.

But under whatfoever difadvantages Hannibal may have laboured, yet, nothing can impair the glory of Scipio.(d) This hero,

K 4   even

_____

(d) The encomiums, which our ingenious author hath beftowed on Scipio, are, at once, warm and juft. That illuftrious Roman poffeffed the happy art of blending the accomplifhments of the gentleman, and the fcholar, with the conduct and intrepidity of the foldier. Learned, and admiring learning, he patronized and retained about him, the moft eminent in the liberal fciences. If he retired from his military employments, it was only to cultivate the fruits of

peace.

even in his firft enterprizes, blazed out with
a peculiar luftre : fomething divine predo-
minates over his character, and is vifible in
all the inftances of his fortune.   Happy
Rome ! thou native land of the Scipios, and
the Æmilii, why fhouldft thou be debafed by
frivolous and pedantic praife ? why fhould
thy encomiafts affect to honour thee, by opinions,

---

peace. Bufied either in ftudy, or in arms, his mind
was as much difciplined by fcience, as his body was
expofed to peril. Till this memorable period, the
Romans had but little knowledge of, and perhaps,
lefs paffion for the works of art. The introduction of
the fineft models of this kind was referved for Scipio,
Marcellus, Paulus Æmilius, and even Mummius, the
ignorant Mummius, fo ridiculous a contraft to thefe
celebrated chiefs, that he threatened the perfons, who
were intrufted with the carriage of fome pictures and
ftatues, taken at Corinth, that if they loft thofe, they
fhould give him new ones. The rage for poffeffing
thefe elegant collections became fo violent, that the de-
predations of Verres were not either without advocates,
or imitators. What the Romans could not buy, like
true virtuofi, they ftole: Livy, mentioning the introduction of the ftatues from Syracufe, makes this
obfervation. Cæterum inde primum initium mirandi
Græcarum artium opera, licentiæque huic facra, pro-
fanaque omnia vulgò fpoliandi, factum eft, quæ pof-
tremo in Roma, nos deos, templum id ipfum primum,
quod a Marcello eximie ornatum eft, vertit...... *See a
character of Scipio in the Connoiffeur.* K.

nions, fo different from thofe, which thou
draweft upon thyfelf? were I to offer thee,
the homage of my admiration, my fancy
would tranfport me to the public ftanding
places, where I might behold Marcellus,
difplaying to thy view, the wonders of Sicily ;
or rather, where I might fee Emilius, leading
at his chariot wheels, a train of kings, preceded by their riches : then, fhould I, with
tranfport, give thee thofe titles, which thou
hadft arrogated to thyfelf. I applaud thy
fortune, that fortune, of which thou waft,
in former ages, fo vain, and to which thou
haft gloried in attributing power, rather than
to thy barbarous infancy, thy unfettled laws,
thy tempeftuous government, and even thy
vertues, which were never more celebrated
than in thofe miferable times, when thou hadft
only preceptors, in the place of heroes. (e)

From

(e) Proinde ab hoc orfurus aliquis initio..... ipfos
in teftimonium vocaverit Romanos, ut qui plus fortunæ
quam virtuti refulerint. (Plut. de fort. Rom.)

This little treatife, by Plutarch, is worth reading. It
will, there, be feen that, exclufive of fome fuperftitious
ideas, his opinions concerning the Roman affairs are,
apparently, like thofe, which we have prefumed to
advance. Now, as Plutarch cannot be fufpected of
having

From the conqueſt of Carthage, Rome aroſe the miſtreſs of the whole world: from that period, what power could have oppoſed her? Could Philip, Antiochus, or Perſius, ſurrounded as they were by jealous neighbouring ſtates, and kings who were their enemies, have amuſed themſelves with the hopes of doing more than Carthage did? It is, at this period, in particular, that the fortune of the Romans becomes ſo conſpicuous. Rome, triumphant, or rather entering into the poſſeſſion of riches, might have ſunk into effeminacy; affluence might have introduced luxury; to luxury might have ſucceeded jealouſies amongſt the citizens, and theſe jealouſies would, in their turn, have brought on troubles, and civil diſcord: ſome few years of repoſe would have given birth to all theſe

---

having treated with injuſtice, the Romans, on whom he hath laviſhly beſtowed the moſt flattering encomiums, there is reaſon to believe that theſe ſentiments were not offenſive to them. It is well known that the Roman emperors were accuſtomed to place in their own chamber, a golden ſtatue, repreſenting fortune. Marcus Aurelius, perceiving himſelf at the point of death, ordered this ſtatue to be carried to his ſucceſſor; and this action was ſuppoſed to be the ſignal of his renunciation of the empire.

thefe evils: but the bad policy of Philip, and the prefumption of Antiochus, preferved the Romans from this danger. Inftead of temporifing, inftead of raifing, as it were, a bank to repel the torrent, thefe two princes were fo rafh as to turn their arms againft a people, inured to war, by a long feries of military operations, and elevated with the moft fignal fucceffes. This was a madnefs, fo ftrikingly marked, as almoft to render an enquiry into the motives of it difgufting: but as true philofophy doth not deem it a fufficient intelligence, if fhe difcover the mif-takes of human nature, nor reft till fhe hath feen from whence thofe miftakes fprang, we fhall rifque fome reflections, on the caufes of thefe fingular events.

It cannot be denied, that whatfcever ad-vantages Rome might, hitherto, have gained, fhe neverthelefs had not yet acquired any great eftimation amongft the Greeks. They faw all thefe exploits, in the light of wars be-tween Barbarians, and were more accuftomed to dwell on the expedition of Pyrrhus, than on the battle of Zama. One may even per-ceive that at the opening of the Macedonian war, the Romans had no allies, except the

Etolians;

Etolians; a people hated, and difcredited throughout all Greece; but who, notwith-ftanding, attributed to themfelves, all the fuccefs of the battle of Cynofcephalus, and boafted that they, alone, had triumphed over Philip. Pride, and a vain prefumption, were vices, peculiar to the Greeks, of thofe times. There is every reafon to imagine, that they did not begin to fear the power of the Romans, but in the moment, when they felt the fatal effects of it. As to Attalus, and Eumenes, his fon, who affifted the Ro-mans, during the Macedonian and Syrian wars, they can only be regarded as the kings of fortune. Wavering and ill-eftablifhed, but, above all, exceedingly jealous of the great, neighbouring monarchies, they perceived no danger in feconding a republic, from whom they conjectured that they had lefs to fear, than to hope.

In the midft of thefe rifing, or expiring monarchies; in the midft of the convulfions with which thofe new empires, the relics of the power of Alexander, were inceffantly agitated, the Grecian republics, too weak, too difunited, to exift merely by their own power, did not fail to add a confiderable

force

force to the party, which they embraced. They were weights, which ferved to adjuft the ballance, and which, perpetually, paffed from one fcale into the other fcale : and yet, lulled by the remembrance of liberty and independency, they extended their open arms to the firft ftate, which prefented to them a picture of thefe bleffings. Now, the Romans having made a proclamation, which was delivered by Quintus Flaminius, of their intention to reftore Greece to her freedom, and to deliver all the cities, from the burden of foreign garrifons, the Greeks were fuch dupes, as to fuppofe that the whole face of their country would be changed, and that Rome would affift them, in the total abolition of arbitrary power. It is, indeed, well deferving our notice, that, prior to the conquefts of Alexander, defpotifm was unknown in Europe, except in the neighbourhood of the Perfians. It, then, fallied forth, at once, from the midft of the Grecian army ; but unattended, either by the antiquity of empires, or the long anceftry of royal houfes, the ufual fupport of authority, its reign was conftantly precarious, nor had it, yet, acquired any ftability. The people, therefore,

returned

returned to their liberty, as to their natural condition. The fnare laid by the Romans, to entrap this moft enlightened quarter of the world was, indeed, terrible ; and this apparent beneficence had no other effect, than to break down all covenants, all bonds, and all political fyftems, amidft thefe unfortunate people, who, now, in exchange for the fweet fentiments of liberty, felt nothing but the conviction of their own weaknefs.

The Greeks had, undoubtedly acted more prudently, if, in order to prevent the Romans from rifing, at their fide, to fuch a pitch of grandeur, they had united themfelves, firmly, to each other, or even formed an alliance with Philip : but the members of fmall republics, in which the fpirit of party, ufurps the place of the fpirit of patriotifm, chufe rather to perifh with their enemies, than to yield to them the moft infignificant advantage. There was no tyrant whatfoever, whom a faction would not have preferred to the chief of an oppofite faction : and the confederacy of the Achaians, who were not apprehenfive of the confequences of calling Philip to their affiftance, when the intended war againft the Etolians was in agitation,

tation, deferted Perfius, when it became neceffary to oppofe the Romans. As to Antio-
,chus, his prefumption, his Afiatic pride,
the diftance at which he, ftill, viewed the forces
of the Romans, and above all, the feeds of
difcontent which he fowed amongft the Rho-
dians, were the caufes of his ruin. I fhall
fay nothing of Perfius, fince that prince af-
cended the throne, involved in fuch unhappy
circumftances, as to have felt no alternative
between war and bondage. Thus, whatfoever ill fuccefs, he had reafon to expect
from his enterprifes, they were, notwithftanding, become neceffary.

Such were the errors in policy, which
cleared the path, along which the Romans
were to pafs, ere they arrived at univerfal
monarchy. We have obferved this people,
giving laws to Europe, to Afia, and to Africa; but, like thofe emiffaries who, previous to the breaking out of war, are fent to
fathom the defigns of princes, to examine
into the ftate of their forces, and difcover
what fupplies may be expected from them,
we have traverfed the whole world, that we
might form a jufter idea of the enterprizes of
the Romans, and of the reafons of their fuccefs:

cefs : in this refpect, we have purfued a plan, far different from that plan adopted by thofe writers, who have limited all their refearches to the ftudy of the Roman laws, and who may be compared to thofe inactive citizens, whom Paulus Æmilius upbraided with idly difcuffing, in the forum, the pofture of affairs, and contenting themfelves, in the moment, when the conful was departing on fome important expedition, with merely attending him to the gates of Rome, and wifhing him a fortunate fuccefs.(f) From the refult of our reflections, we derive a conviction that the principles of the Roman power, exifted rather beyond, than within this celebrated republic. Let us, now, examine the effects of the Roman government, in its more immediate relation to its own particulars, and the influence which it poffeffed over the fortune of other nations.

CHAP.

(f) Examine the oration, which Plutarch makes Paulus Emilius deliver, on his departure for Macedon. It is a curious paffage, and capable of diminifhing the opinion, which may have been conceived of the Romans in thofe times.

CHAP. VI.

The influence of the Roman government over the happiness of the people: the condition of the Romans till the time of Cæfar.

THE title of this chapter fufficiently intimates, that the conquefts of the Romans, and even their heroic vertues, are, no longer to be the objects of our attention.   Were the people happy? was it fortunate to live at Rome? fuch are the queftions, which we muft now refolve, as if we were in the place of Lucumo(*g*) or Appius, when thefe two ftrangers came to eftablifh themfelves in this city.

Vol. I.   L   It

(*g*) " *Afterwards, Lucius Tarquinius Prifcus.*"

It is needlefs to declare, that we fhall not confider this queftion, relatively to the paffions and manners of our contemporaries. Were it even to be proved, that the condition of the Romans did not appear to merit the envy of the French, or the Englifh, it would not, therefore, follow, that this condition was, in itfelf, unhappy. In fact, whatfoever inclination we may have, to refer every thing to our own peculiar ideas, we have been long fince accuftomed to the admiffion of fome particular fuppofitions, by which, we are contented to regulate the feelings of our mind! thus, frequently, a philofophical and paffive fpectator bears a part in the frenzy of Seide, or the enthufiafm of Polieuctes: but there is fomething more than this; there are certain generalities, certain marks, by which, the condition of a nation is manifefted in the abftract. As groaning is a fign of pain; fo complaints, debates, and quarrels, are proofs of the difcontentment, and almoft univerfal mifery of the people: and without alluding to civil wars, famine, contagion, and the like calamities; is not the ferocity of individuals, a conftant fymptom of habitual fufferings ? nothing,

thing, therefore, prevents us from judging of the antients, as we fhould judge of each other ; neither are we precluded from the application of thefe great objects, to the moft known principles of morality and politics. But, amidft fo many revolutions, and fuch a multitude of alterations, made in the forms of the Roman government, how can we, poffibly, advance an opinion concerning it, with any degree of precifion, unlefs we divide its hiftory into feveral epochas ?

From the foundation of Rome, to the expulfion of the kings, may be included a period of about two hundred and forty years ; from the expulfion of the kings, to the entire conqueft of Italy, may be allowed the fame fpace of time ; from the firft Punic war, to the deftruction of Carthage, may be reckoned at about one hundred and twenty years ; and from that event, to the fubverfion of the republic, about fifty, or fixty years, at the moft,(b) thefe four different epochas muft

L 2   ferve

(b) If I miftake not, the banifhment of Tarquin, and the total deftruction of the regal power were effected in the two hundred and forty-fifth year of Rome ; Italy was entirely conquered in the year 489. Carthage

was

ferve us, as four different points of view, in which, we may behold the Roman people. We only intreat the reader to be fatisfied, although we fhould not call thefe epochas, the four ages of the republic. He will, doubtlefs, difpenfe with our diftinguifhing its infancy, its youth, its manhood, and its old age. All this infignificance of low rhe-toric, and bad policy, could tend to no ufeful purpofe, except a demonftration of the too general abufe of words, and the in-fluence, which language may poffefs over opinions. In fact, as foon as men became fo weak, as to efteem the frivolous flights of intellects, which are more fubtle, than pene-trating, they were, by degrees, accuftomed to affix to them fome meaning; and they no longer confidered republics, or, even governments, but as kinds of phyfical beings, whofe difeafes, habitudes, regimen, &c. it was neceffary to examine. The reafon of all

this,

_____

was overthrown in 621; and the republic was extin-guifhed in 706. It was not neceffary for the ingeni-ous and elegant author to write with the precifion of an arithmetician. It is rather the philofopher, and friend of human nature, than the formal chronologift, who, to communicate his refearches with the greater perfpicuity to the reader, divides this period into four æras. K.

this, is, that nothing exercifes and fatigues
the mind more than abftraction; and that
this act of withdrawing fome part of the idea
from the other parts of it, hath need of fupporting itfelf on fenfible circumftances.
Hence, it is, that the language of argument
is, conftantly, on the point of running out
into a figurative ftile; a ftile, equally vicious
and incorrect, of which, allegory is the worft
abufe. Thus, it may be obferved, that the
more ignorant and unpolifhed a nation is,
the more its language abounds with meta-
phors and comparifons. They are the art-
ful expedients of the mind, to elude that
exact definition, which fo frequently baffles
all her powers. Are the principles of a republic to be unfolded? it is compared to a
living being. Are the properties of a juft
man to be explained? He is likened to a republic. Thus, are we, inceffantly, turning
round, within a circle of errors, where every
thing meets with its refemblance, and where
nothing is decifive.(*i*) But it is not fufficient

L 3

to

(*i*) Plato, in writing his treatife on a republic, feems
to have had no object in view, except the teaching us
in what juftice confifted. He compares man to a republic,

to condemn, and avoid thefe abufes, introduced before our time, it may, perhaps, be
neceffary to open, for ourfelves, new roads ;
and fince we muft difcover fome means, of
afcertaining the fpirit of the different political
conftitutions, it might not, probably, be improper to confider, whether, inftead of fixing our whole attention on laws, and inftitutions, which are, frequently, the effect of
chance,

---

public, in which reafon is the monarch, and where the
paffions form the common people. To this fubtle idea,
we owe thofe ingenious extravagancies, which fome
modern authors are, ftill, now and then, reviving;
to the difgrace of philofophy ! as to the reft, Plato was
not always fo allegorical ; nor hath he, at times, been
above defcending into exact definitions. Diogenes La-
ertius obferves, that he made the excellence of government confift in three circumftances. Firft, in the
goodnefs of the laws ; fecondly, in the obedience,
which the people paid to thofe laws ; and thirdly, in
the exiftence of fuch cuftoms, and rules, as were able
to fupply any defect in the laws. In like manner, to
difcover the vices in a government, Plato propofed the
examination of three things, in particular ; firft, if the
laws were not ferviceable, either to the fubject-inhabi-
tants of the kingdom, or to foreigners ; fecondly, if
thefe laws may be tranfgreffed with impunity ; thirdly,
if there be no laws, and if tyranny, folely, predomi-
nate in the ftate. There may be lefs of ingenuity in
this, but it is much more intelligible.

chance, it were not better to employ ourfelves,
particularly, in the inveftigation of thofe circumftances, under which, a people may have
formed themfelves, and in an enquiry, concerning the character and interefts peculiar
to mankind, in the moment when they entered into a fociety, and had enacted their
laws. In fact, the people muft have exifted
prior to the eftablifhment of laws; and the
founders, either of republics, or of empires,
could, fcarcely, have been, all, in the fame
pofition, when they had fettled their forms of
government. Now, there is reafon to fuppofe
that, thefe firft moments threw a very confiderable influence over the future; fo
much, indeed, that one might propofe this
political problem : from the given circumftances, attending the eftablifhment of a
people, find out the appertaining fpirit and
character(k). Thus, for inftance, one might

L 4   be

***

(k) I cannot determine whether this obfervation
hath been neglected by political authors, or whether I
have never been ftricken with it, in any part of their
works : but I have a particular pleafure, in paying a
tribute of applaufe to the writer, to whom I am indebted
for it. I mean the author of l'hiftoire politique du
gouvernement Romain.

be convinced, that, whatever modifications were defigned to have been introduced, amongft the governments of Tyre, Sparta, and Athens, the ſpirit of commerce ought to have reigned in the firſt, the ſpirit of equality, in the ſecond, and the ſpirit of in-dependance, in the third. (*l*)

This

(*l*) I cannot diſpenſe with obſerving, in this place, that the above cited idea, differs, widely, from the maxim, advanced by Machiavel, in his diſcourſe on Livy. He, there, aſſerts, that, to enable a ſtate to exiſt, for any long period, it is neceſſary to call it, frequently, back to the firſt principles of its conſtitu-tion. It appears to me that almoſt every ſtate hath been eſtabliſhed in circumſtances, quite oppoſite to thoſe circumſtances, in which, in proceſs of time, it became involved ; and that, therefore, it would be uſeleſs, and even detrimental, to have recourſe to ſuch a remedy ; every alteration in a ſtate is not a certain ſign of the corruption of the people. The variations introduced by particular circumſtances, may, and, even, ought to have a great influence upon the government. A bar-barous and unpoliſhed nation may become commer-cial, and engaged in agriculture ; whilſt a commercial nation may grow warlike. It is, therefore, highly ne-ceſſary, amidſt theſe changes of government to diſtin-guiſh with preciſion, that which appertains to the na-ture of things, and that which relates to the corruption of mankind. Idleneſs, pride, and diſobedience are certain marks of corruption ; but the changes of fortune,

new

This method of confidering our fubjeft, feems to throw it into a new, and more per-fpicuous light. But, amidft the different applications, in which we might employ it, we fhall confine ourfelves to the Romans, and examine under what circumftances, their firft legiflation endeavoured to give fome form to the ftate.

Let

---

new pretenfions, and alterations in ranks, and dig-nities, flow not from the fame principle. At Rome, for inftance, a Plebeian might ftand for the confulfhip, and yet the republic would not have been corrupted : and in like manner, at London, a merchant might fit in the houfe of commons, without any difparagement to the nation. At Rome, the perpetuity of families, the honours conferred in time of war, vertues, and manners, foon raifed the confequence of the Plebeians. At London, the fpirit of commerce hath rendered the merchant, as important as the man of quality. The Plebeian, in the time of Canuleius, could not have been compared to the Plebeian in the time of Valerius ; neither is there any refemblance between the modern merchant of London, and the merchant in the reign of Edward the third : now, to have pretended, at a par-ticular crifis, to have brought back a ftate, to its firft principles, would, if at Rome, have reduced a power-ful and refpeftable peuple, to their original mifery, and debafement ; and, if in England, it would have eftablifhed a feodal government, in the place of a go-vernment, founded on property, and equal reprefenta-

tion;

ˉLet us recollect what hath been obſervéd, in the preceding chapter, and we ſhall perceive that, according to all appearance, Romulus was but an adventurer, of whom Numitor availed himſelf, to be revenged on Amulius, and who ſoon afterwards was, in his turn, ſo ſuſpected by Numitor, that this prince knew of no circumſtance, which he, ſo eagerly, deſired, as the immediate opportunity of getting rid of him, by furniſhing him with means, wherewith to eſtabliſh a colony. Romulus, therefore, aſſembled ſome young men, belonging to the city of Alba, with whom he joined thoſe adventurers, who choſe

---

tion; we muſt enquire, then, firſt, what hath been the character of a nation, at the time of its eſtabliſhment. Secondly, what influence this national character had upon the conſtitution of the ſtate. Thirdly, if the firſt cuſtoms, and primitive laws are ſo good, as ˉto merit the being preſerved, or if the alterations in circumſtances have drawn them into the legiſlation. It is in this laſt caſe, that the original, and, primitive character of a nation, may find itſelf acting in oppoſition to its intereſts ; and then great care muſt be taken, leſt it be led back to its firſt principles : it is even neceſſary to ſuffer them to be obliterated, as much as poſſible, for fear that the people, always willing to become, again, what they had been, might never prove what they ought to be.

chofe to offer themfelves. Amongſt theſe
laſt were fome individuals, whoſe birth, or
affluence entitled them to a fuperior diſtinc-
tion; they were feparated from the lower
claſs of the people, and united with the chief
of the Albans; they conſtituted the body of
Patricians. No fovereign, who doth not
eſtabliſh his power, either by force of arms,
or by fome particular revolution, can become
arbitrary. It was, therefore, the duty of
Romulus, to pay the greateſt attention to the
principal members of his colony. From
hence, aroſe that fpirit of ariſtocracy, and
that charaＣteriſtic of fiercenefs, which it
always preferved. A colony eſtabliſhed,
without any regard to commerce and induſtry, muſt of courfe be driven into aＣts
of plunder; from plunder ariſe reprifals;
and reprifals render a ſtate of war neceſſary,
and habitual. From hence, may be derived
the firſt interior arrangement of the city of
Rome: from hence, proceeded the plan of
throwing the Roman people into the form
of a legion; a form, the beſt adapted to their
fituation, at that period, when the women
were fo few in number, within this infant
colony,

colony, that it might be confidered as a little
army.

The firft want, of which a warlike colony
becomes fenfible, is the want of population.
As pillage is more attended to than the cultivation of the earth, and war more purfued
than commerce, foldiers are more neceffary
than flaves ; hence, arifes the principle of
putting no individual to the fword, and of reducing no enemy into captivity, who delivers
up his arms; a principle, which merits the
ftricteft attention, fince it may be confidered, as the fource of all the fuccefs, which
waited upon the Romans.

A colony, expofed to the dangers of war,
fhould always be prepared for battle; nor
can it difpenfe with keeping its members,
as nearly collected together, as poffible.
From hence, proceed a limitation of eftates,
and the neceffity of confining the heads of families to the cultivation of, only, a fmall
portion of land. This neceffity gives birth
to frugality; and frugality introduces aufterity of manners, &c.

A colony, in which, about the time of its
eftablifhment, the number of women was
extremely inconfiderable, and conquered, alfo,

by

by the power of the fword, would, of courfe,
reduce thefe women into a fubjeftion to the
moft rigorous laws ; nor would the children
be exempted from the fame fevere regulations.*(m)* From hence, mzy be derived, that
cruel

(m) It is certain that the wives were punifhed with
death, for the flighteft offences : for example, if they
had drunk wine. Fathers enjoyed the power of life
and death over their children, and this barbarous authority included a right to fell them, as flaves. Dionyfius Halicarnaffius hath obferved, that all legiflators
have thought it proper, to fix the length of time, during
which, the children were to remain fubjeft to paternal
authority ; that the entrance into the age of puberty
was the period appointed by fome legiflators, for their
enfranchifement; whilft others had determined that
they fhould receive it, on the inftant of their marriage:
but that the Romans, more wife than all the reft of the
world, had appointed no particular limits to this authority.

The inhuman cuftom, which Lycurgus eftablifhed at
Sparta, was adopted by Romulus, with only one foften-
ing reftriction. The latter, inftead of permitting the
Romans to expofe their weak and deformed children,
in the firft moments of their exiftence, gave orders, that
they fhould be preferved, during three years ; as in thac
interval, either receiving health and ftrength, their
limbs might knit themfelves into better proportion ; or,
their parents might acquire an affection for them, which
they were too unnatural to feel before. Although this
law was confirmed by the laws of the twelve tables, it
was

cruel authority, exercifed by hufbands over their wives, and, even, by fathers over their offspring. The power of fathers is, always, more fharp, and more abfolute than the power of mothers. A mother may be confidered as the chief moderatrix of paternal defpotifm.

Such are the obfervations, which the Roman people, in their infant ftate, naturally, fuggeft to us. However inconfiderable the number

---

was, yet, too frequently, tranfgreffed : it would be natural to imagine, that paternal authority, fo barbaroufly exerted, muft have extinguifhed all traces of filial piety ; but Rome abounded with ftriking inftances of the prevalence of this vertue ; and, as a proof, that the feverity of thofe laws, to which the wives were fubject, was kept inactive, by their exemplary behaviour, let it be remembered, that more than four ages had elapfed, when Carvilius Ruga, by repudiating his wife, occafioned the very firft divorce. K.

It had not the appearance of a modern feparation. The chaftity of the fair Roman was unfullied by fufpicion. Sterility, a misfortune, but not a crime, was all the hufband could alledge againft her; it was ufual for the citizens to fwear that they married, with the view of having children. Refpect for the oath which he had taken, alone, induced Carvilius to diffolve the union. The motive was, at leaft, plaufible; and yet all Rome beheld him, during the remainder of his life, with indignation. K.

number of thefe colonifts may be, they, notwithftanding, afford us an ample intimation,
that they were deftined to prove, conftantly,
ambitious in their projects, fierce in their
modes of government, and ferocious in their
manners. However, the admiffion of the
Sabines, into the city of Rome; however the
peaceable reign of a foreign legiflator,(n) who
attempted, with the affiftance of religion, and
the laws, to foften the manners of a barbarous people; and however, the more fplendid
reign of another foreigner,(o) who extricated
the Romans, from their groveling fituation,
by providing for their earlieft, and moft effential wants, may have, fomewhat, modified their original characteriftic, we are, ftill,
certain of tracing it, from the affaffination of
Camillus, down to the profcriptions of Sylla.

But, were it even true, that the vertues of
infant Rome had fo far prevailed over her
vices, that happinefs may be faid to have
refided within her firft cottages, what confequences can be drawn from hence, condu-
cive to the welfare of mankind? would it
follow

(n) Numa Pompilius.
(o) Tarquin, the elder.

follow that the people muſt, generally, enjoy'
the greateſt ſhare of felicity, in a newly-riſing
ſtate ? but the beginnings of empires are,
only as moments, in the ſeries of ages; and
the object of a good government ſhould be
to give permanence to public happineſs.
Rome, inceſſantly, engaged in battles, that
ſhe might procure ſome ſheaves of corns;
Rome, at once, a ſtranger to the tranquility
of ſocial life, and the activity of induſtry;
Rome, ſtill poor, ſtill deſtitute of power,
doth not preſent to our view a very flattering
proſpect ? and what, at the bottom, could
the common people be, who ſuffered themſelves to be governed, during the ſpace of
eight days, by a king,(p) already, in his
grave, a prey to worms; who, at length,
received from a female hand, a ſlave for their
monarch; and who, ſoon afterwards, became
victims to a deteſtable tyrant, from whoſe
yoke, they, perhaps, could never have been
freed, if the ſenſe of honour, had not been

more

(p) Tanaquilla, the wife of Tarquin the elder,
thought it proper to conceal the death of this prince,
until Servius Tullius ſhould have fixed his plan to ſuc-
ceed him. Servius Tullius was born a ſlave.

more violent, than the fenfe of liberty? and, let it not be imagined, that a certain eafe of life, a kind of fatisfaction which fprings from an equality of fortunes, could have indemnified the Romans for what they might have felt from other quarters, fince the mifery of the people, the tyranny of the rich, the rigour of impofitions, and the weight of ufury had, all, rifen to excefs, from the time of Servius Tullius.((*q*) It muft be confeffed, therefore, that this firft epocha of the government of kings doth no where afford us a picture of happinefs.

In the fucceeding times, we fhall, probably, perceive more grandeur than happinefs; more vertue than confolation. Their kings had, fcarcely, been expelled, when a cruel war was kindled to accomplifh their re-eftablifhment. Infpite of her victories, gained at the lake Regillus, Rome perceived her

VOL. I.　　　　M　　　　enemies

(*q*) See the oration, in which Dionyfius Halicarnaffius fuppofes this king to have declared to the Roman people, that, by ordering a general Cenfus, he only meant to diftribute lands amongft thofe, who had none, and to remedy the bad effects of ufury, which is a natural confequence of the difficulty attending the payment of taxes.

enemies encamped upon the Mons Janiculus; and nothing but the intrepidity of a single man effected the preservation of all.*(r)* The death of Tarquin, indeed, dissipated the alarms of the new republic ; but the people, in the room of one tyrant, whom they had lost, found a thousand tyrants, amidst the Patricians. Were I desirous of fixing an opinion, concerning the happiness of the Romans, during this epocha, I should not ask for any assistance, except the perusal of the marginal notes of Livy ; they would furnish us, solely, with instances, either of exterior wars, or of interior troubles ; these last

were

(r) It may easily be guessed, that I mean Horatius Cocles. As to the story of Mutius Scævola, I shall allude to it, in this note, for no other reason, than that I may remark, how greatly a taste for the marvellous still prevails among us. Dionysius Halicarnassius makes no mention of this singular action of Mutius, who burns his hand, in attestation of a falsehood ; but the fact is extraordinary, and we seem so much more pleased to follow Livy, than Dionysius, that we do not give ourselves the trouble, to observe the difference so remarkable between the narratives of the two authors. Mr. de Pouilli, in his learned work, entitled "Dissertation sur l'incertitude de l'histoire des quatre premiers siecles de Rome," proves that this account of Scævola was an imitation of the recital of a similar transaction, taken from a Greek historian.

were ſtill more terrible than their battles, becauſe war was eſteemed a remedy for, or, at
leaſt, an allevation of the public misfortunes.
How deplorable muſt that condition have
proved, in which this ſcourge became deſira-
ble ; in which, the tears of the people could
not have been dried up, until the ſtreams of
human blood began to flow !

Amidſt theſe habitual evils, what calamities poured in from foreign quarters ! the
city taken by enemies, hitherto, unknown !
a general ſcarcity of proviſions ! contagions !
miſeries of every kind ! . . . . . . (s)

M 2   But

(s) My readers will, probably, be ſurpriſed, whilſt
they obſerve me placing to the ſame account famine,
and, particularly, contagions. Their aſtoniſhment would
be juſt, were theſe calamities the effects of accident. It
is well known, that the cultivation of the earth prevents
famine, but it is no leſs certain, that it prevents diſ-
eaſes : firſt, becauſe famines are the general ſources of
epidemical diſorders : ſecondly, becauſe the air is the
moſt wholſome, when the earth is in the beſt ſtate of cultivation : thirdly, becauſe peace, and plenty, furniſh
the means of preſerving health, by uſeful eſtabliſhments,
ſuch as aqueducts, common ſewers, neatneſs in houſes,
and cloathing, a choice of aliment, ſalutary liquors,
gardening, &c. Mr. Corbyn Morris, (in his " collection of bills of mortality," quarto) hath remarked, that

ſince

But it will be faid ; " *what a terrible enu-meration have we, here, of thofe evils, which the Roman people fuffered. You will the more eafily reap an advantage from it, becaufe, mif-fortune being the common lot of humanity, the idea of that misfortune, is but too confpicuous to the view of all mankind. But love for ones country, an attachment to the laws, and the enthufiafm of glory are all factitious paffions, and, to be known, they muft have been experi-enced. Thus, whilft you give a loofe to thefe fpeculations, you become more fenfible of the mi-fery of the Romans, than of the happinefs, which they may have enjoyed ; and whilft your mind compares, your too partial imagination turns the fcale."* . . . Not to neglect this objec-tion, let us enter more particularly into the fubject.

The ftrongeft paffion which hath been at-tributed to the Romans, is the love of glory. Let us, for a moment, adopt this general opinion, and endeavour to apply it to the welfare

fince the Englifh have entered fo much into gardening, the frequent epidemical diforders, to which they gave the name of plagues, have been lefs common, and fatal, than they were before. . .

welfare of the people. We shall, doubtlefs, perceive a militia, trained up to war, continually, defiring that they might be led on to conqueft. The loweft citizens, as they walked along the forum,. would draw out the plan of operations, and fix the æra of victory. Even the moft tender wives, the moft timid mothers would catch the univerfal enthufiafm, and the people, intoxicated with fuccefs, would eafily forget their hardfhips.

How different is this. reprefentation from the reality! let us no longer judge of Rome, by what hiftorians tell us, but by what they teach us. Let us, in imagination, tranfport ourfelves into the heart of this city, and, there, perceive a forrowful, and unhappy populace trembling before the fenate. Let us hear them implore this fenate, at one moment, with fighs, and at another moment with threats, that they would deign to grant them fome acres of land, for their fubfiftance. Let us liften to the cries of thofe brave foldiers, who fhew, amidft their honourable fcars, the difgraceful marks of whips, and chains; unhappy wretches, thrown, without diftinction, amongft the meaneft flaves, be-

caufe

caufe they could not pay for the arms, with
which they had pierced their enemies, and
the bread, which they had eaten, on the day
of battle !..... The gates open ; the fenators
appear ; their favage looks declare their projects ; a barbarous joy exults in every feature.
What are they preparing to announce to the
people ? the alleviation of the public calamities, tranquility, plenty ?...... No ; but,
the enemy, tempted, either by the fecret intrigues of the fenate, or, by that confidence,
which long diffenfions could not have failed
to infpire, advances with hafty ftrides, and
will, foon, appear before the gates of the
city.   Already, the confuls, feated in their
Curule chairs, fummon the young men to
their tribunal. To-morrow, the enemy is to be
attacked.   The glory of repelling them may,
perhaps, be bought with the blood of three
thoufand citizens.   Perhaps, too, this enemy
may carry fire, and the fword, even into the
capital.   But what doth it fignify ? at this
time, the Agrarian law fhall not be proclaimed.

It is thus, that wars are kindled; it is thus,
that the love of glory intoxicates the Romans ;

mans; it is thus, that they march on towards the conqueſt of the world.*(t)*

But, what will be the iſſue of this war? ſome few equivocal ſucceſſes. The enemy will be repulſed, or, perhaps, retire of their own accord. However it be, 'the Romans will not think of profiting by the advantages which they may have gained over them: they will, purpoſely, avoid purſuing them into their own territories, and, ſoon, return to Rome, to demand bread from the ſenate.

M 4   Ano-

(t) "Di modo che volendo Roma levare le cagion" de' tumulti levava ancora la cagion dell' ampliare."

. Machiavelli de diſcorſi, liv. 2. pag. 20.

" Had Rome been willing to have removed the occaſion of the tumult, ſhe ſhould alſo have removed every occaſion capable of increaſing it. K.

Saint Auguſtin, (de civitate Dei, lib. 3. cap. 10.) after having deſcribed the continual wars, in which the Romans were engaged, makes a reflection ſomething ſimilar to that cf Machiavel. Perhaps (ſays he) theſe continual wars were neceſſary to the aggrandizement of the Romans, but what individual would wiſh to acquire a gigantic ſtature, at the expence of his health? idonea verò cauſa ut magnum eſſet imperium, cur eſſe deberet inquietum? nonne in corporibus hominum ſatius eſt modicam ſtaturam cum ſanitate habere, quam ad molem aliquam giganteam perpetuis afflictionibus pervenire?

Another objection. .... " The Romans, (it will be faid) were poor; true; but this poverty, far from being a misfortune, became a treafure to them. Frugality was to them, a fubftitute for affluence, and as they had no wants, they were ignorant of the value of opulence.".... They were ignorant of the value of opulence? whence came it, then, that the Patricians had gotten poffeffion of all the lands belonging to the people, by ufury, and of all the lands belonging to the republic, by fraud? why had thefe proud men fuch vaft eftates, replenifhed with thofe, who were, at firft, reduced to flavery, by the chance of war, and then, purchafed, at a low rate, from the needy foldiers? why did they, by a hundred times, prefer driving the republic on the brink of its deftruction, to the parting with a fingle inch of their lands? why did they rather chufe to offer the people a facrifice of rank magiftracy, and even religion, (*u*)

than

(*u*) None but the nobility enjoyed the privilege of taking the aufpices: for this reafon, the fpirit of ariftocracy, and the fpirit of fuperftition were infeparable. We fhall have occafion, in the courfe of this work, to prove

than relinquifh their riches? *(x)* It were needlefs to deny, that at Rome, the people were poor, and difcontented, and the great, rich, and avaritious. Thus, in the midft of troubles and revolutions, after the tyranny of the Decemvirs, the ravages of the Gauls, and the invafion of Pyrrhus; after one hundred and fifty years, all fpent in war, againft the Æqui, the Volfcians, and the Etrufcans; after forty years of perpetual engagements, with the Samnites, Rome, conftantly torn by divifions and always poor, arrived, as we have already fhewn, at the third epocha; that is, at the conqueft of Italy, and the beginning of the firft Punic war.

I muft confefs that this æra is not without its attractions. The fame gloom no longer feems to hang about the picture of the Roman

---

prove that, with ariftocracy, all the religion of the Romans became extirpated; an opening was made for the fects of Stoics, and Epicureans; and from hence, likewife, may we trace one of thofe concealed paths, which led to the eftablifhment of chriftianity.

(x) It was only to avoid the Agrarian law, that the Patricians permitted the Lex Sicinia, and the Lex Licinia to pafs: by thefe, marriages and divifions of magiftracies between the Plebeians, and the Patricians, were permitted, for the firft time.

man hiftory. Civil difcords are appeafed, the moft fignal victories become the rewards of military toils, and Rome is beholden with awe, by nations beyond the bounds of Italy. Were authors to be confulted, we fhould read that this moment was the moment in which the fucceffes of the republic had not, yet, altered the vertues of its members. Rome, if we are to abide by our references to thefe hiftorians, was already powerful, and hitherto uncorrupted. But, far from adopting fuch an opinion, we fhall, on the contrary, endeavour to form a more exact idea of the morals, and felicity of the Roman people.

The people, who can live upon a little, are not, therefore, happy; the Goths and Vandals lived upon a little, and yet, they marched, in fearch of plenty, into other climates. The people, who are inured to toil and fatigue, are not, therefore, happy; the Goths and Vandals were inured to toil, and fatigue, and yet, they paffed into other countries, in queft of luxury and repofe. The people, who are the moft powerful in battle, are not, therefore, happy; they engage in battle, only, to obtain peace, and the con-

veniences

veniencies of life. The people, enjoying eafe, and liberty ; attached to their property; and, above all, defiring no change of con-' dition, are happy. Now, one proof that the Romans never partook of fuch happinefs, is, that from the very firft moment of their having known what riches were, they coveted them, with a degree of fury, and to that luft, facrificed all their principles and manners.

In the four hundred, and thirteenth year, from her foundation Rome acquired the fovereignty of Capua. Scarcely had the army taken up their quarters, in this country, fo celebrated for its alluring productions, before the fpirit of revolt invaded it. The foldiers fpurned at the authority of their chiefs, and concerted a plan, whereby to eftablifh themfelves in Capua. What treafons poured in at once! defertions, breach of oaths, and contempt of military power! no confideration, no circumftance, however, could controul thefe men, fo greedy after riches. The army is feparated ; the precaution was ufelefs: the greater part of the army, perfifted in rebellion, and marched directly to Rome.

Shortly

Shortly afterwards, the city of Rhegium
demands fuccours from Rome. A legion is
granted to them. How are thefe vertuous
men employed? without any attention to the
faith of treaties, and without the leaft regard
to hofpitality, they maffacre all the citizens,
compel the widows to receive them, as their
hufbands, and thus, take the poffeffion of
this unhappy town: to fuch an excefs can
beings of a favage mind be driven, by the
irrefiftable allurements of a life, in which
every convenience might be enjoyed, with
indolence! thefe two pictures will, fufficiently, enable the reader to judge if the Romans
were happy at Rome, and if they preferred
their condition, to the condition of other
nations.

The firft Punic war plunged the republic
once more into new troubles. In fact, although during the courfe of this war, Rome
was more fuccefsful, than unfortunate, yet
the people did not receive from thefe advantages, a compenfation for the defeat of
Regulus, and the lofs of their three fleets,
which were either taken or funk. A victory,
frequently, reftores the poffeffion of a coun-

try,

try, which had been feized on, in confequence of a former defeat; but never can it reftore the hufband, to the widow, or the father, to the orphan. It is difficult to defcribe a more fhocking fituation, than the fituation, in which the republic found itfelf, after the firft fifteen years of the Punic war. Not to mention the perpetual humiliations, which it underwent, the Cenfus of its citizens, diminifhed almoft to within one half, is an ample proof of the fenfible loffes, under which it laboured.

When Carthage became humbled, then, arofe an uninterupted feries of good fortune, in which every fuccefs was more fplendid than the former; thus, the conclufion of our third period makes amends for the beginning. It was, then, that war appeared ufeful, becaufe the fpoils of all the nations were regularly brought to Rome.(y) But, who profited

---

(y) Metellus hath been reproached, for having difplayed, during his triumph, the ftatues, and other works of art, which he brought from Syracufe. No cenfure can be more frivolous. Why did the Romans fight? you will anfwer, to be the mafters of the world. And why, did they defire to be the mafters of the world,

fited by this plunder? firft, the public treafury, every thing having been carried either
thither, or to the temples; next, fome avaritious generals; and laftly, the order of
knights, who enjoyed no fhare of thefe riches,
until the duties had been fettled. Now, all
thefe conquefts might, indeed, have produced
to the Roman people, fome public fights,
fome feftivals, and fome games; but never
did they fcatter plenty amongft the neceffi-
tous. An inftance may be met with, in the
hiftory of the Gracchi. Tiberius, in his harangue from the tribunal, was not apprehenfive of exclaiming, thus: " the wild beafts
have caverns, and dens, whither they can retire, whilft the citizens of Rome can neither
find a roof, nor fhed, beneath the covering of
which, they might enjoy a fhelter, from the
inclemency of the weather; deprived of any
fettled refidence, and precluded from any
habitation, they wander, like unhappy outlaws, even within the bofom of their own
country.

but to enjoy riches, arts, and every thing which renders
life agreeable? To praife a people for their frugality,
during their infant ftate, is fomething like commending
a rich principal in office, for not having kept a coach,
when he was, only, a poor deputy.

country. You are called the lords and mafters of the univerfe. What lords! what
mafters! you! to whom they have not even
left an inch of land, to ferve you for a
grave." ...... However exaggerated this
picture may have been, the difturbance which
it occafioned amongft the people, is a proof
that it was not, abfolutely, a faint refemblance, nor inapplicable to fome of the citizens. Befides, it is well known, that riches,
acquired without toil, and divided amongft a
very fmall number of perfons, introduce luxury, and corruption; (z) or rather, every
thing is already corrupted, when luxury appears; for luxury is but an effect, erected
into a principle. It comes not, until all
order hath, already, been deftroyed, and
whether it arife from the inequality of circumftances, or whether it flow from the abufe
of

(z) In the year 572, which was long before the ruin
of Carthage, Caius Mænius, the prætor, was directed
by the fenate, to obtain a lift of all the poifoners, which
might be found either at Rome, or within ten miles of
the place: at the end of fome few days, this magiftrate
wrote word to the fenate, that he had already difcovered
three thoufand, and that the number feemed to increafe,
in proportion to his enquiries.

of affluence, it, conftantly, maintains a fuppofition that, there are eafy and rapid means
of acquiring money, and that paffions exift,
which are equally contrary to decency and
honefty.

The opinion of all mankind, and the fentiments of every age, exempt us from the
neceffity of levelling our cenfures againft
that epocha, which we had fixed upon, as the
fourth epocha.   No one can perufe, without
horror, the account of the revolutions, during
the times of the Gracchi, of Marius, and of
Sylla.   We will turn afide from the fight of
this fatal picture, and, at once, conclude with
obferving, that Rome hath not, in any of thofe
æras, into which we have directed our refearches, enjoyed a meafure of felicity, capable of making her condition envied, and
her forms of government admired.(a)

CHAP.

___

(a) The gloomy fadnefs, peculiar to the Romans,
until the reign of Auguftus, is another objection to their
pretended happinefs. When Cato accufed Murena, the
bitterest reproach, which he levelled at him, was his
having danced. His advocate, Cicero, exclaimed againft
the cruelty of this allegation, and afferted, that it was
impoffible to impute to a man the crime of dancing,
                                                    without

C H A P. VII.

The influence of the Roman government over the
happiness of all the different foreign states.
The situation of the world, at the æra of the
subversion of the republic.

IN proportion to the advances which we
make, in our obfervations on the hiftory of
human kind, we perceive ourfelves more and
more ftricken with aftonifhment; not that we
admire, with the multitude, that fucceffion

without fuppofing that he had, previous to the commiffion of the act, given a loofe to intoxication, and
every other kind of debauchery.

It may be, farther, obferved, that the religion of the
Romans was, conftantly, as ferocious as their manners.
After the battle of Cannæ, they thought it expedient
to bury alive, a male and female Gaul, and a Grecian

of events, and that variety of scenes, which
occupy the surface of our globe; but rather,
because, whilst we were employed in this attempt, it became impossible for us, to sacrifice to the study of facts, the sublime con-
templations of ancient nature, without being
surprised, and even humbled, by the difference, which exists between the history of the
world and the history of man. Here, we
see

---

cian man and woman, that the gods might be appeased.
This abominable barbarity was, amongst them, nothing
more than customary. Besides, religion was equally intolerant during the æra of ancient, and the æra of modern Rome. When the magistrate perceived, in the
second Punic war, that several new rites and some foreign modes of worship, had been introduced into the
city, it was decreed, that all these forms should be sur-
rendered up to the prætor; nor was the observation of
them, any more permitted. This intolerant spirit, not
confined to religion, infected even literature. In the
five hundred and ninety-first year, from the foundation
of Rome, all the Rhetoricians were driven from the
city. In the six hundred and sixtyeth year, some Latin
Rhetoricians, desirous of establishing schools, in con-
junction with the Greek Rhetoricians, were forbidden
to teach, whilst these last were confirmed in their exclusive privileges. There is, indeed, but little reason
to be astonished at such extravagancies, when we observe, in the " Testament politique," attributed to Cardinal de Richlieu, a minister gravely agitating this
question:

fee the waters preparing the earth, which we
are to cultivate, whether their flow retreat
forms the different beds, of which it is compofed, or whether their more rapid courfe
marks out the vallies, and the mountains.
Myriads of aquatic animals feem to have
crouded, as it were, upon each other, to have
exifted, and to have perifhed in heaps, only
to furnifh the materials, wherewith we raife

N 2   our

---

queftion: "fhould the care of public education, be
committed, exclufively, to the Jefuits, or to the Fran-
cifcans ?"

Such a queftion might, naturally, proceed from the
bigotted, and perfecuting Richlieu; but as he was not
the author of the above-mentioned work, this abfurdity
cannot, pofitively, be attributed to him. The " Teftament politique" was written by another, who, to fix
the reputation of his produ&ion, with the public, had
fheltered it under the name of the minifter. Controver-
fial and religious tra&s were the only papers, belonging to the cardinal, which were difcovered, after his
death. His niece the Dutchefs d'Aguillon ordered thefe
to be revifed, corre&ed, and publifhed. On politics,
a fubje&t which Richlieu always mentioned with great
referve, he wrote nothing. In France, the death of a
celebrated minifter hath been as regularly followed by
his political teftament, as by his funeral. Colbert,
Alberoni, and the Marfhal de Bellifle, were fcarcely in
their graves, when they aftonifhed us with fentences,
which, when living, they neither wrote, nor fpoke.
The teftament of Bellifle was made by Chevrier. K.

our edifices; whilft devouring fires, iffuing from the entrails of the earth, have thrown into the cavities of the rocks, the metals neceffary in the ftructure of thefe works. There, piles of ftones arife, like immenfe towers, whofe heighth feems to command the univerfe: in one place, the enormous mafs aftonifhes by its irregularity; and in another place, by its perfect fymmetry. Here, dreadful alluvions open a paffage for the ocean, and conduct it into the midft of the land. The black fea breaks over its bounds, and forms the Archipelago of Greece, whilft other inundations divide America into two diftricts, and bear away, from it, the Antilles. Marine monfters lie buried on the tops of mountains. The vaft fize of the bones of the terreftrial animals is a proof of the antiquity of their race, and points out the gradual degradation of the fpecies, whilft, at the fame time, vegetation fprings forward towards perfection, and feems to receive from man, a kind of new education.

Such are the magnificent objects, which the hiftory of the world prefents to our view. What fhall we difcover in the hiftory of mankind?

kind? facts imperfectly known, and yet, extremely recent. Thirty ages, at the moft, form the domain of hiftory: a fmall number of dynaftics, three, or four nations, celebrated by their conquefts, compofe, if I may be allowed the expreffion, the fole titles of nobility, in the political world. Let us, however, run over this brief genealogy, and only confider what, generally, concerns the fituation of mankind.

We fhall not pretend to examine, whether, as an ingenious author hath affected to prove, a defpotic form of government drew its beginning from a principle of fear, which fome revolutions, effected in different parts of the world, had infufed into the human mind; or whether this government, patriarchial in its origin, be more natural to an indigenous people: it appears exceedingly certain, that a power, vefted in a fingle man, fubfifted in Afia, from time immemorial; whereas the firft examples of a republican government, are to be met with amongft newly-rifing colonies. We perceive, then, that from the firft, the great monarchies appeared upon the theatre of the world, which was, then, con-

fined

fined to Afia, and to Ægypt. Several colonies fettled themfelves, afterwards, in Afia
Minor, and in Greece; and thefe colonies
having, in their turn, fent out other colonies,
the republican form of government, more
fuitable to men, living in a ftate of equality,
eafily propagated itfelf in thefe new eftablifhments. Here, alfo, it introduced that profperity, which fo ufually attends its progrefs.
Soon, this modern fociety of men, different
in their manners, and principles, contend
with the ancient fociety, and conquer: but
an ambitious youth, already corrupted by
his good fortune, prefers the manners of the
vanquifhed, to the manners of the victors.
Incapable of raifing himfelf to an equal rank
with gods, he debafes his fubjects, below the
condition of humanity, and thus, degrading
his exploits, proves that it was, only, the
defpot, and not defpotifm, whom he was
anxious to attack. The period, during which,
mankind groaned under the laws of this fenfe-
lefs mafter, was fhort: but, at his deceafe,
conquefts were fo recent, the martial genius
fo predominant, and the interefts of the conquerors, fo clofely connected with the fyftem
of

of oppreffion, that military defpotifm was eafily fubftituted in the place of hereditary defpotifm. Shortly afterwards, this government, which had been adopted by the Greeks, ran back from Afia into Europe, and fpread itfelf through Macedonia, Thrace, Illyrium, Epirus, &c. It was then, that liberty, driven towards the Weft, took refuge at Carthage, and at Rome: but Rome, having quickly triumphed over her rival, her infatiable ambition occafioned the defpotifm of kings to be fucceeded by the defpotifm of the people; and this tyranny was the moft fatal of all tyrannies. Thus, in few words, may be perufed the account of that fmall number of general facts, with which hiftory prefents us, and which lead us to fuch reflexions, as compofe the fubject of this chapter.

The maxim, "il mondo invecchia, e invecchiando intriftifce," (that as the world grows old it becomes the more wicked) was but too true, during the epoch under our examination; but I do not fuppofe it applicable to the prefent times. The conquefts of Alexander were, to mankind, a fignal of depravation; before this period, the known world

was divided into two parts, one of which
parts was filled with little flourishing republics, and the other part occupied by a vaft,
and ancient monarchy. On the one hand,
profperity was in the place of repofe; and
on the other hand, repofe was in the place of
profperity. In this fituation, the republics
received, in the enjoyment of their liberty,
amends for their perpetual diffenfions; and
the fubjects of the great king felt a fatiffaction in the midft of flavery, becaufe they
had been long accuftomed to tranquility.
Alexander, in the courfe of ten years, altered
the fituation of all thefe people. He died in
the arms of victory ; and yet, fcarcely were
his eyes clofed, when his generals waged,
againft each other, the moft bloody wars.
When nothing was left for the Macedonians
to deftroy, they mutually turned upon themfelves, and tore each other in pieces; like
thofe rats, the plagues of the North, which,
covering whole countries, perpetually ravage
the land, as they proceed, till, not finding
any more fubfiftance, they devour one another. The univerfe was, indeed, revenged,
but dear was the price of that revenge ; all
upon the furface of the globe was over-
thrown·

thrown. The republics preferved only the
vain appearance of liberty, which left them
the vices of the government, without preferving its advantages. Inquietude fupplied
the place of force. Factions became multiplied and irreconcileable. Yet all their difputes were confined to their choice of tyrants.
Shall the preference be given to the Seleucides,
the Lagides, or the kings of Macedonia ? to
whom fhall crowns be decreed, and whofe
ftatues fhall be thrown down ?(b) fuch is the
fubject of all their deliberations. And here,
I muft beg leave to obferve, that nothing can
be more deplorable, and at the fame time,
more contemptible than republics in their decline. Their ancient cuftoms feem to be new
fources of vice and ignominy. Their public councils become, henceforward, no better
than the vulgar bawlings of the market, or
the abufive clamors, which prevail amongft
the meetings of the mob. The love of glory
is extinguifhed, and in its place, appear an
empty

(b) The cuftom of erecting ftatues, through flattery,
and then, throwing them down, that, in purfuance of
the fame principles, they might raife others in their
places, became fo common, that, at length, they were
contented to faw off the head of a ftatue and fix on the
head of the new tyrant.

empty oftentation, and a mean prefumption; which render thefe vices, thus odious in themfelves, fo particularly ridiculous. They debate, they wrangle, and they threaten ; at length, this farce performed, even by fellow-citizens, is interrupted on the arrival of an officer, belonging to a neighbouring defpot, who comes to deliver the commands of his mafter. Then, their language undergoes a thorough alteration. They bend, they cringe, they promife every thing ; and this flave, this inftrument of the tyrant is conducted back, loaden with honours.

On the other hand, if any circumftance can adminifter confolation to the people, who live under on abfolute government, it muft arife from the confideration, that fuch a government is, at once, ancient and extenfive. In the firft inftance, mankind, always led by cuftom and opinion, are eafily induced to imagine that they who have governed them, during a long fpace of time, have, effectively, a right to govern them : in the fecond inftance, defpotifm being, conftantly and invariably, the work of force, the more the principle of this force is fituated at a diftance, the more is its activity impaired. Thus, fe-

veral

veral provinces of the Ottoman empire, fuch. as Dalmatia, Tranfilvania, Bofnia, ftill enjoy a kind of liberty.

Let us, then, call to our ideas, the fate of thefe vaft regions of Afia; when they found themfelves a prey to the firft powerful warrior, who defigned to invade them. I do not allude, merely, to Ptolemy, Caffander, Antigonus, and Eumenes, ftill fhining with that luftre which they had borrowed from Alexander; all the little ufurpers, who fucceeded thefe princes, the kings of Bithynia, of Pergamus, of Cappadocia, of Pontus, &c. &c. muft be included in the number. What motive, except fear, could have attached the people to fuch a form of government? and, what motive, except avarice, could have attached the prince to the people?

It was, in fimilar circumftances that Rome, the fovereign of Italy, and victorious in Africa, extended her ambitious views over the reft of the world. Surely the blood of two millions of men, fpilt in the fecond Punic war,(c) and the yet recent recollection of the

triumphs

_____

(c) I have been at the pains of calculating the number of men, which (as hiftorians inform us) pe-

rifhed

triumphs of Hannibal might have infpired
this nation with more pacific fentiments.
What a favourable moment! had they but
known how to have turned it to their advantage! had fome new Cyneas entered into
the fenate, and fpoken thus: " If, confcript
fathers! at the time, when Romulus founded
this city; or rather, when, after the expulfion of the kings, your generous anceftors
called,

---

rifhed in the different wars, waged by the Romans,
from the five hundred, and thirty-third year, after the
foundation of Rome, to the year 577; that is forty-
four years. This number amounts to 959,846. But
hiftorians have mentioned many of thefe battles, without fpecifying the loffes on either fide; fo that one
may add to this number, upwards of half as many
more, at the leaft, which will make, nearly, 1,400,000
men: to which add feveral fleets funk, and thofe who
perifhed, either through difeafe, or mifery, and the
number will amount to more than two millions of men,
all facrificed in war, during a fpace of time, fcarcely
exceeding the length of life, ufually allotted to every
human creature, and including only half of that portion of time which is called the age of man. It muft be
farther obferved, that this lofs was by fo much the
greater, as it referred only to the free-men, who formed
but a part of the general population. One may even
prefume that a greater number of flaves, attending the
fervice of the army, underwent the fame fate.

In

called you forth to the enjoyment of liberty,
fome divinely infpired man had arifen to
declare to you, that the gods were refolved to
render this bleffing perpetual, all your wifhes
would have been accomplifhed, and you
muft have fuppofed yourfelves the happieft
of mortals. But, with what rivulets of blood,
have you not been conftrained to purchafe
this ineftimable felicity! How much time
have you not fpent in fighting to defend it,
without ever prefuming that you could have
referved it for yourfelves, unlefs you tore it
from

In thefe modern times when, as the poet ingenioufly
obferves, we have " fitted murder to the rules of art,"
a military author afferts, that in a pitched battle every
eighth man is either killed or wounded. If the fables,
with which the hiftory of the fiege of Troy is interwoven, have not much weakened its credibility, we may
perceive what a multitude of the human fpecies were facrificed during the few years continuance of a contemptible quarrel. In the war, between the Greeks
and the Trojans, the former loft eight hundred and
eighty-fix thoufand men; and the number of the flain,
amongft the latter, amounted to fix hundred, and fixty-
fix thoufand men. All this for Helen; the wife, or
rather the proftitute of five, at leaft; who was enjoyed
by Thefeus, Menelaus, Paris, Deiphobus, and Achil-
les; and who, at length, was hanged, in the ifle of
Rhodes, by the maid fervants of Polixo. K.

from your rivals ? yet fuch is the depravity of mankind, and fuch, in particular, was the barbarifm of your neighbours, that, for a long period, to avoid oppreffion, it became neceffary that you fhould opprefs. I fay, for a long period; becaufe there is a point, at which ftates, ftrong within themfelves, ftand in no need of being aggrandized; then the fpirit of conqueft is no more than an abufe of the fpirit of prefervation. Thus, thofe inflaming liquors, which are defigned to reanimate our debilitated ftrength, when taken to excefs, infect us with illufory wants, and whilft they, always, feem to increafe our vigour, lead only to annihilation. Be fure, therefore, O citizens! that you are not arrived at this point of power, the paffing of which, is often dangerous and conftantly unjuft: you are obeyed by Italy; Africa is humbled; and Afia beholds you with refpect: but Italy is depopulated; Africa is plunged in barbarifm; and Afia groans beneath the yoke of flavery. Then, fertilize Italy, polifh Africa, and give freedom to Afia. This is, undoubtedly, your duty: nay, I will go farther; it is your intereft: and thus I prove it.

I perceive

I perceive but two objects to which your
desire of making conquests can extend:
either, you wish to enjoy, to a certainty, a
lasting repose, and, in the place of enemies,
to possess only subjects; or you are anxious
to become rich, and, in endeavouring to accomplish this point, you are ready to plunder
all other nations. If it be the duration of
peace which you are eager to obtain, why
do you not acquire, solely by policy, that
which you expect from force ? Can you believe 'that two or three legions are sufficient
to subdue the people of Taurus, and of Cau-
casus? do you suppose that your proconsuls
can preserve, for the republic, this empire,
which the generals of Alexander could not
preserve for themselves? how will you maintain discipline amongst your troops ? how will
you confine an army, accustomed to pillage,
within proper regulations? how will you fix
the obedience of a consul, instructed to go
beyond your orders? but you fear Antiochus;
but you fear Philip. Shall I, instantly, sup-
ply you with formidable armies, to keep these
princes in awe? restore to Greece her ancient forms: re-establish the republican government in all Asia Minor: Philip shall

tremble,

tremble, even in Macedon; and Antiochus fhall be driven towards the center of Afia. You fhall govern the world as you fit within the fenate; and, without throwing afide your robes, you fhall gain battles, in which, the earth fhall not be drenched with the blood of the Romans.

Let us, now, fuppofe what, however, is far diftant from my thoughts, that this fierce and warlike people, tired of the aufterities of life, fhould demand from the univerfe the reward of their long labours. You, O Romans! may demand it. Your frugality and difcipline may yet obtain for you that which will not fail to deftroy both. Well then! be rich! I agree to it. But tell me; who will have a right to thefe riches? will they belong to the army, who bore them off? then, none, except the foldiers, could be happy, or opulent. Will they become the property of all the Roman people? but, if each citizen be rich, who will enlift himfelf amongft the legions? who will carry burdens? who will undergo long marches, and the fatigues of encampments? I forefee your intentions: you will keep foreigners in pay, who may go to war, in your place. And, will you then be

rich

rich, whilſt others are becoming ſtrong?
ſhall you continue free, whilſt others remain
in arms? believe me, O Romans, if you are
weary of your ancient ſimplicity; if you, particularly, wiſh to be in poſſeſſion of the fine
arts, which ought to be the ſtudy of a great,
and happy people, do not import ſtatues, but
ſtatuaries; ſeize no more on pictures; but in-
ſtruct painters. It is the enjoyment of our
own workmanſhip, and not the enjoyment of
the workmanſhip, which we may have taken
from another, that proves ſo pleaſing. Let
me aſſure you, that the bread made of the
grain, which you may have ſown, will have
a ſweeter reliſh, than bread made of the corn
of Ægypt; and the marble, which may have
been hewn out under your own inſpection,
will be, in your imagination, a thouſand
times more precious, than the maſterpieces
of Phidias. Be then induſtrious, and politic
cultivators; but above all, be juſt; for the
order of the univerſe hath decreed, that the
welfare of a ſmall part of mankind cannot
long remain in oppoſition to the welfare of
the whole."

I know not if ſuch a ſpeech was ever made
in the ſenate; but the truths which it con-

tains, are fo ftriking, that the Romans, all intoxicated as they were with fuccefs, did not feem abfolure ftrangers to the leffons, which it inculcates. After the battle of Cynocephalus, Quintus Flaminius proclaimed, throughout the cities of Greece, a decree of the Roman people, directing that they fhould be reftored to their liberty. The exceffive joy, with which this news was received, muft naturally embitter our regret, when we obferve that this apparent beneficence was only granted for a moment, to caft an additional horror, over the miferies, with which Greece was fhortly afterwards loaden. In fact, it was not long, before the mafk fell from the ferocious character of the Romans; and this implacable republic was feen to exercife a tyranny, till then, unknown.(d)

We have remarked, in the courfe of the preceding chapters, that the frequency of civil diffenfions, amongft the governments of ancient Greece, became one of the greateft afflictions of humanity. We have obferved that, whilft thefe principal republics, namely, the

----

(d) Inter impotentes, et vallidos, falfò quiefcas. Ubi manû agitur, modeftia, ac probitas nomina fuperioris funt. Tacit. de. mor. Germ.

the republics of Athens, and of Sparta, in-
terpofed in the feveral difputes, and altered,
according to their pleafure, the form of the
government, fuch innovations were conftantly
fealed with the blood of a multitude of citizens. Thefe maffacres, however, bore the
appearance of acts of juftice, inflicted by the
prevailing faction, which, then, became the
legiflative authority; whilft the vanquifhed
party was treated like a rebellious confederacy. The Romans adopted a different principle. They concluded themfelves to have
been, apparently, born the mafters of the
world; and, in confequence of this fuppofition, they treated all other nations, not as
conquered enemies, but as revolted fubjects.
This fhocking principle, particularly, difplayed itfelf in its blackeft light, after the victory
gained by Paulus Emilius.

Rhodes, a republic, flourifhing with commerce, and with navigation; Rhodes, the
precious remains of ancient Greece, perceived herfelf, becaufe fhe had for a moment
ceafed from favouring the Romans, compelled to fubmit to an inquifition of their embaffadors, and threatened with a total deftruction. She had no method of avoiding

O 2   this

this calamity, but by putting to death every one of her citizens, who had voted againſt Rome. Shortly afterwards, Bæbius, the lieutenant of Paulus Emilius, hurried away by a particular hatred, which he had conceived againſt ſome of the Etolians, ordered five hundred and fifty of the chief perſons, amongſt this unhappy people, to be ſlaughtered. But theſe abominable tranſactions were only the prelude to a ſeries of cruelties, exerciſed by the Romans. The avarice and iniquity of individuals was ſoon blended with the barbarous maxims of the government. It is impoſſible to read the hiſtory of the war in Spain, without ſhuddering with horror. I do not, merely, allude to a Lucullus, who, introducing himſelf into a city, under the ſanction of articles of capitulation, violated the faith of treaties, and put twenty thouſand inhabitants to the ſword ; nor to a Galba, who, deceiving a whole nation, by a pretended peace, contrived to collect them together, like a herd of deer, within a proper incloſure, and maſſacre every one ; nor to an Aquileius, who, the more eaſily to deſtroy thoſe enemies, whom he durſt not encounter, was baſe enough to poiſon all the ſprings in the pro-

vince :

vince: a tear of more affecting forrow trickles
down my cheek, whilft I reflect on Scipio,
the wife, the illuftrious Scipio, who ordered
his executioners to cut off the hands of four
hundred young men, belonging to the little
city of Lutia, whofe only guilt was, the
having affifted the Numantians, their allies.(e) No; to deny it, were a vain attempt.
Such tranfgreffions can never be ftiled the
crimes, either of a general, or of fome few-
foldiers. A whole nation muft have proved
ferocious, to have been capable of producing

O 3   fuch

(e) The learned reader, whilft he recollects the melancholy ftory of the Numantians, muft pay a tribute of
admiration, to the intrepidity of a little band of heroes,
whom multitudes were unable to fubdue; and who had
the vertue to prefer death, within the arms of their expiring liberty, to a life of flavery, beneath the tyranny
of the Roman yoke. Although their number was confined to four thoufand men, yet they refifted, during
fourteen years, the attacks of forty thoufand foldiers.
At length, when the feverities of the famine, which
raged within, had cut off every poffibility of refifting
the army, which endeavoured to deftroy them, from
without, they, nobly, raifed a kind of funeral pile, with
their effects, and cafting themfelves upon it, perifhed
in the flames. The difappointment of Scipio, who faw
no monuments of the glory of his conquefts, except the
bare walls, and the afhes of the dead, may account,
but cannot apologize for his inhumanity. K.

such execrable villains, as the instruments of
their barbarity. And what heart, but must
be melted, at perceiving, almost in the same
instant, two splendid cities, two wonders of
the world, Carthage, and Corinth, reduced
to ashes? in vain, did the past ages, in vain,
did the whole world exert all their power, in
the embellishment of these magnificent monuments of ancient felicity: *the majesty of the
Roman people* required that they should be
crumbled into dust.*(f)*

Nevertheless, the proconsuls, and the greedy
prætors carry off those treasures, which the
fire and the sword had spared. To have
seen their warriors fall in battle; to have lost
their forms of government, and their freedom,
were but trifling afflictions to the people; the
weight of impositions was added to the
weight of slavery. A barbarous usury was
practised by the extortioners themselves: the
governors, and the collectors of the taxes
were like so many crows, disputing about the
carcases. But, if the oppressed universe cannot recover her ancient prosperity, at least,
let her derive some consolation, from the
hope

(f) Ecce quam feliciter Roma vincit, tam infeliciter
quidquid extra Romam vincitur. Paul. Oros. l. 5.

hope of vengeance... O Mithridates! O Viriatus! delay no longer your appearance!*(g)* Afia and Europe call upon you. Wait not, until thefe cruel conquerors fhall have done juftice on themfelves; for, foon, abject flaves, infamous gladiators, a Tryption, and a Spartacus, fhall be fubftituted to Carthage, and Numantia; and if, at length, they difappear, it will be only to give place to Marius, to

O 4   Sylla,

(g) The vertues, the abilities, and the fate of Mithridates are well known; but it is fingular, that Ammianus Marcellinus fhould have been the only hiftorian (Appian not excepted, the unwearied collector of almoft every circumftance, relating to this unhappy prince) who hath recorded the peculiar conduct of Menophilus. When Manlius Prifcus, in obedience to the orders, which he received from Pompey, commanded this eunuch to throw open the gates of the caftle, and, with himfelf, deliver up the daughter of Mithridates, he firft, ftabbed her, and then, plunged the dagger into his own bofom; determined that neither fhould furvive the fortunes of his mafter. . . . . Viriatus, in the earlier part of life, exchanged the peaceable employments of a fhepherd, for the more active toils of hunting? he, became, at length, a public robber, and by a natural gradation, rofe to the command of a formidable army. Ventidius, and Plancius fled before him; and Rome, beheld with terror, a chief, to whom all Portugal had fubmitted, when the fword of an affaffin, by depriving him of life, accomplifhed that which the legions of the miftrefs of the world had vainly ftriven to effect. K.

Sylla, to Octavius, ... But I stop short,
and feel myself conscious, that whilst the object of my pursuit, is an enquiry into the
condition of mankind, during this dreadful
æra, I cannot, with such circumstances before me, support the calmness, so requisite
in this discussion.(b) Must I, then, enter
coldly into the detail of so many atrocious
facts? and will it not be sufficient to excite
the indignation of every feeling reader, if he
be told to recollect, that, in a very short space
of time, Carthage, Corinth, Numantia, and
Athens were destroyed? that, without mentioning millions of men, who were slaughter-
ed in Spain, in Africa, and in Asia;(i) the
war of the slaves, in Italy, and Sicily only,
was attended with the loss of one million of
men; and that, in Italy; exclusively, three
hundred thousand men, perished, during the
war of the allies. Add to all this, proscrip-
tions,

(b) Cogit enim excedere propositi formam operis,
erumpens animo, ac pectore indignatio. Velleius Pa-
terculus. l. 2.

(i) It is well known, that Mithridates ordered a
hundred and fifty thousand Romans, found within his
state, to be destroyed on one day. This cruelty, all horrible as it appears, was yet no more than a reprisal for
those injuries, which he had received from the Romans.

tions and civil wars. Remember, alfo, that Cæfar boafted of having either taken, or reduced eight hundred cities ; fubdued three hundred nations; engaged with three millions of men, a million of whom remained upon the field of battle, ' whilft another million were throne into captivity. In fhort, recall to mind, the wars of Numidia;' the punifhment of Jugurtha; kings funk into the condition of mere vaffals; the people reduced to the moft abject ftate of flavery; and you will, in few words, form an idea of the influence of the Roman people, over the happinefs of mankind.(k)

CHAP.

(k) Raptores orbis, poftquam cuncta vaftantibus defuere terræ, et mare fcrutantur: fi locuples hoftis eft, avari, fi pauper, ambitiofi; quos non oriens, non occidens fatiaverit, foli omnium opes, atque inopiam pari affectu concupifcunt. Auferre, trucidare, rapere falfis nominibus imperium, atque ubi folitudinem faciunt, pacem appellant. Tacit. vit. Agric.

CHAP. VIII.

*Remarks cn the state of the Roman empire,
under the reigns of Augustus, and his successors.*

I Have, hitherto, only pointed out those
horrible tragedies, those times of murder,
and of carnage, when Rome, torn by civil
discords, avenged, herself, the cause of the
conquered nations, but oppressed them still
more.   This republic,   at once victorious,
and expiring, resembled a sick man, whose
entrails are devoured by a burning fever, but
whose arms, still robust, receive from the
crisis of his pain, a more energetic, and more
dangerous force.   Whilst Cinna, and Marius
were spilling the blood of the citizens, Sylla
extirminated the inhabitants of Pontus, and

of

of Cappadocia; and whilſt Octavius, and
Lepidus, under the ſanction of treaties, reciprocally ſacrificed their parents, and their
friends,(*l*) Anthony annoyed the Parthians,
and the Ægyptians, with his military forces.
During this diſaſtrous epoch, the univerſe,
every where, refounded with the clamours of
rage, and the ſighs of miſery. Could there
have been a picture, more afflicting to humanity, and, at the ſame time, more replete
with conſolations, for the preſent age? but
as our aim is not ſo much to ſtir up the paſſi-
ons, as to aſcertain their progreſs, and eſtimate their conſequences, we ſhall not dwell
upon facts, which the opinion of all mankind
hath devoted to the horror of poſterity. It
is not ſo neceſſary to turn the human mind
aſide from the love of civil war, as from that
vain enthuſiaſm of glory, that military, and
conquering ſpirit, which only ſerves to ſharpen
during

(*l*) Ne quid ulli ſanctum relinqueretur velut in dotem
invitamentumque ſceleris, Antonius L. Cæſarem avun-
culum, Lepidus Paulum fratrem proſcripſerant. Nec
Planco gratia defuit ad impetrandum, ut frater ejus
Plancus Plautius proſcriberetur. Atque inter jocos mi-
litares qui currum Lepidi, Plancique ſecuti erant, inter
execrationem civium uſurpabant hunc verſum: *de Ger-
manis, non de Gallis duo triumphant Conſules.* Vell. Paterc.

during fome time, thofe arms, with which
the citizens are deftined, one day, to murder
each other.   May we have accomplifhed this
objeā in the foregoing chapters. 'May we,
in the chapters which are to follow, adhere,
invariably, to that coolnefs of difcuffion, which
can, alone, convince, and thofe ingenuous
fentiments, which can, alone, perfuade!

A new queftion courts our examination.
We have perceived, that all legiflators, having
been employed rather in rendering mankind
powerful, than happy, the feveral people
were, in their turn, either flaves or ufurpers,
without ever attaining to a permanent felicity.
But, if the diverfity of laws, interefts, manners, and cuftoms, was an infurmountable
obftacle to a general peace, could there have
been a furer method of uniting men, than by
throwing them all into a ftate of fubjeētion?
could the repofe of the world have been more
firmly eftablifhed, than under an univerfal
monarchy? This queftion, in an age, when
geography hath fo enlarged the boundaries of
the world, that we know of a fingle kingdom,
more populous, and more extenfive than the
whole Roman empire, becomes abfurd; but
it is a queftion, which would have feemed
                                    plaufible,.

plaufible, in the times of Auguftus and Tiberius : nay, were it not to be taken in its full
extent, there would be reafon to fuppofe,
that fome ftrefs might have been laid upon
it, even in more modern times. It is certain
that Philip the fecond never felt the neceffity
of drawing within his ambitious grafp, the
empires of China, and of Ruffia. Fixed as
he was, upon the throne of England, by his
marriage with Mary, could he have rendered
France fubject to his dominion, the houfe of
Auftria muft have proved the miftrefs of the
whole chriftian world ; a fovereignty, likely,
in the end, to have included the fovereignty
of the univerfe. But Auguftus found himfelf naturally fituated in thofe circumftances,
to which Philip would, willingly, have attained. If we except fome barbarous nations,
whom the Romans judged unworthy of being
conquered, all the people, at that time known,
were their tributaries, and Rome, become
pacific, had banifhed war from the furface of
the earth. The good order of adminiftration
was re-eftablifhed ; juftice refumed her rights ;
and the polite arts, more attached to tranquility and plenty, than to vertue and liberty,
foon deferted the porticos of Greece, to dwell
within

within the court of a magnificent, and enlightened defpot. The reign of this prince
would, doubtlefs, have proved the happieft
æra for the Romans, could the beneficence of
Auguftus, have funk in oblivion, the cruelty
of Octavius. In fact, the hands, which fcattered favours, were ftill tinged with blood;
and the people, like foldiers, whom the fatigue of battle had overpowered with flumber,
could only lie down to reft upon an heap of
carcafes. But it muft alfo be obferved, that,
on the one hand, the citizens of Rome, alone,
felt their happinefs affected by this painful
recollection; and that, on the other hand,
the proftitution into which thefe very citizens
had fallen, at once, deprived them of all re-
fentment of injuries, and infected their minds
with the meaneft felf-intereft, and the moft
abject propenfity to flattery. The individuals amongft the Romans, who had reafon
to weep over the lofs of a father, or avenge
the fate of a brother, enjoyed an ample fatisfaction in the fmiles of their prince, or in
fome empty title annexed to magiftracy.
Thus, the provinces rejoiced at this revolution of affairs, whilft Rome no longer poffeffed
the merit of feeling it with concern.

Tiberius

Tiberius, equally inferior to, equally unworthy of his predeceffor, by his vices, and
even his vertues, was, for fome time, capable
of putting into practice the leffons which he
had received from Auguftus. The public
happinefs met with no difturbance, until the
adminiftration of Sejanus; and I am not furprifed that fo long a calm, before the breaking out of the political ftorms, fhould have
given rife to the fuppofition, that an univerfal
monarchy, or, at leaft, a monarchy, the extent, and preponderance of which, might be
very great, would prove a particular advantage to mankind. Some authors, too fond
of paradoxes, have even ventured to affert,
that fo conftant a peace, had, fufficiently, indemnified the Romans, for the barbarities of
Claudius, Caligula, and Nero; becaufe that,
in the times, when thefe monfters were glut-
ting themfelves with the blood of the fenators,
the people, at leaft, were happy and quiet.
It would be eafy to return them for anfwer,
that, unlefs, by the word people, they mean
what is commonly called the dregs of the
people, that is, an abject mob, without property, and without abilities, it is exceedingly
certain, that the Roman people underwent
great

great fufferings, during the reigns of thofe tyrants, who filled up the fpace, from Auguftus to Vefpafian. But, without dwelling on this particular queftion, which, furely, could never have been agitated in earneft, we will endeavour to eftimate, as clearly as poffible, that happinefs, which the Romans are imagined to have enjoyed, under their emperors.

To take in the full fcope of our defign, fome idea fhould be formed of the fituation of the Romans, when Auguftus, after the battle of Actium, remained the fole mafter of all. Rome was no longer, as formerly, the cradle of the kings of the world. The families which were become illuftrious, by the melancholy fate of nations, had already expiated their ancient, and guilty fplendor; and the inheritors of the moft celebrated names had yielded up their necks to the executioners. Freed-men, or Burgeffes, *(m)* iffuing

---

(m) All the people of Italy were become citizens of Rome. In the reign of Claudius, this privilege was, at firft, extended to the inhabitants of Tranfalpine Gaul, and, fhortly afterwards, to all the provinces of the empire. It is neceffary to read the fpeech, which Tacitus hath put into the mouth of Claudius, who, amongft

iſſuing from all the towns of Italy, had raiſed themſelves on the ruins of the ancient houſes; but theſe new citizens did not equal thoſe citizens whom they replaced, either in birth, or in affluence: public paraſites, deſtitute of all patriotic zeal, and having no concern in the management of affairs, came to Rome, that they might partake of the diſtributions of proviſions, and money, which were kinds of temporary alms, diſpenſed by the orders of the ſovereign; but particularly, that they might enjoy thoſe long and magnificent ſights, which, by amuſing, turned aſide their attention to their misfortunes. If ſome rich individuals ſtill exiſted, they were not thoſe great proprietaries, ſo reſpectable in all the ſtates; but Proconſuls, Pretors, and Queſtors, who, by pillaging the provinces, were become opulent; and more eſpecially, the Roman knights,(n) who having engroſſed to them-

Vol. I.　　　P　　　　　ſelves

amongſt ſeveral other plauſible reaſons, produces the examples of the Athenians and Lacedemonians, whoſe ruin, he attributed to that ridiculous jealouſy, which prevented them from admitting ſtrangers into the number of their fellow-citizens.

(n) Amongſt the Romans, as amongſt ourſelves, there were but two ſorts of nobility: the one ſort ſeemed acknowledged

felves all the bufinefs of the finances, foon
acquired immenfe fortunes in money ; a manifeft fymptom of a ftate in her decline. The
perplexity of Auguftus, when he undertook

. to

knowledged by the general opinion, and proceeded from
the antiquity and dignity of families, honourable employments, military crowns, the images of anceftors,
&c. (See Gravina de origine Juris). The other fort
belonged to the conftitution, and was that which conferred a real rank, by diftinguifhing the Patrician, and
the Senators, from the Knights, and the Plebeians.
Now, this laft order of nobility was founded only in
riches, in the Cenfus. Thus, the claffes, formerly inftituted with a different intention, by Servius Tullius,
were, by the lapfe of time, unavoidably drawn into a
contradiction, to the principles of the government,
fince they put men, who had, accidentally, made a
fortune, and fometimes, even gamblers, on a footing
with the citizen, fprung from the moft illuftrious parents,
and enjoying the advantages of the beft education. I
am furprifed that all authors, and, chiefly, Mr. de
Montefquieu, fhould have paid fo little attention to that
fimilarity which exifts in the condition of the nobility,
amongft the Romans, and the nobility, amongft ourfelves. He might have obferved how, in all governments, and in all ftates, confequence is attached to affluence ; and how impoffible it is for fortune to difpenfe
with confequence. In fpite of the numerous fatires,
which the juftice, the malignity, or the jealoufy of the
public, may have levelled againft the receivers of the

kings

to reform the fenate, is well known. The greateft part of the younger branches of the moft illuftrious families, wanted the poffeffi-ons neceffary to qualify them for that order, and this prince was obliged to fupply their

P 2   exi-

kings revenues, they are become amongft us, what the Roman knights were at Rome, a clafs apart, deriving a confequence from their affluence. And this con-fequence would, doubtlefs, have become more confi-derable, and more marked, if the marriages of the rich heireffes, had not diverted the money from its original channel, and caufed it to be fcattered abroad and diffipated. No fooner did thefe Financiers become de-firous of fhining with a borrowed luftre, than they di-minifhed the luftre which was peculiar to them. And yet, they not only form a clafs apart, as hath been al-ready obferved, but they recruit, as it were, the ancient nobility, which by degrees, become extinct, and make way for the modern nobility. Why the fortunes ac-quired by the adventurers in commerce, or the mer-chants, have not, like the fortunes acquired by the Fi-nanciers, eftablifhed a new order of citizens, would be no incurious queftion. But, here, it cannot be refolved. I fhall content myfelf with obferving, firft, that com-merce is generally the moft flourifhing in democratical ftates. Secondly, that the individuals, who engage in commerce, are of a rank, too diftant from the great, to endeavour to be affimilated with them. The com-mercial man avoids fplendor. The Financier loves it, and finifhes with the attainment of it.

exigencies with his bounty.*(o)* In fpite of the admiffion of the people of Italy, to the privileges of citizens ; in fpite of all thofe recruits fo little worthy of the metropolis; when Auguftus, in the beginning of his reign, gave orders for the Cenfus, the number of citizens did not exceed four millions, one hundred and fixty-three thoufand ; the majority of which muft have perifhed with famine, had they not partaken of the diftributions of the fovereign.*(p)* Such were the mafters of the world, or rather, fuch were the firft flaves of Auguftus; without means, without property, tranfported from Calabria into Tufcany, and from Tufcany into Lombardy, juft as it became neceffary either to recompence fome veteran foldiers, or to celebrate fome illuftrious names by eftablifhing a colony; thefe unhappy perfons, always confidered as ftrangers, even in Rome, ftrolled about under the porticos, and dwelled in cabbins.

Add

(o) Cæfar admitted fuch a number of ftrangers and new men into the fenate, that an humorous edict was fixed up, in which were the following words in great letters : *all perfons whatfoever are ftrictly commanded not to refufe fhewing a fenator the way to the fenate.*

(p) See Dion.

Add to thefe, fome Greek Rhetoricians, foreign adventurers, a multitude of flaves,*(q)*
and a great number of gladiators, wreftlers,
comedians, and proftitutes, and then, fome
idea may be formed of the fituation of Rome,
under her emperors.

P 3 ,

The

(q) The excefs to which the cuftom of keeping a
multitude of flaves, was, at that time, carried, might
eafily be afcertained; fome judgement in this matter
may be formed from the following circumftances. Pedanius Secundus was affaffinated by one of his flaves;
it was debated, whether, according to the laws, all
thofe flaves, who were in the houfe, during the perpetration of the crime, fhould be fentenced to death.
Caius Caffius voted for the queftion, and Tacitus,
amongft other reafons, hath made him affign the following reafon: quem numerus fervorum tuebitur, cum Pe-
danium Secundum quadringenti non protexerint? (fee
Annal. l. 14.) Pedanius had, at that time, four
hundred flaves. It is impoffible to read, without horror, that all thefe unfortunate wretches fuffered death
for the crime of a fingle man. Dion relates that Æg-
natius Rufus boafted, during his Edilefhip, that he had
extinguifhed a fire by the fingle affiftance of his own
flaves; Auguftus, who was difpleafed with this magiftrate, and who, befides, did not chufe that an individual fhould arrogate to himfelf the merit of having
provided for the public quiet and welfare, fet apart,
for this employment, only, fix hundred flaves, fallen
to him by the fucceffion of Agrippa. This immenfe
body of flaves was rather an alarming circumftance.

Tacitus

The provinces, long accuftomed to the tyranny of the proconfuls, the avarice of the queftors, and the ufury of the Roman knights, had every reafon to regard the eftablifhment of good order, throughout all the depart-ments of adminiftration, as an advantageous circumftance. But this was but a temporary bleffing,

Tacitus (l. 4.) in relating to us, that under the reign of Tiberius, it was, for a moment, apprehended that they might revolt, hath taken care to acquaint us, that this report had fpread terror through Rome: ob mul-titudinem familiarum quæ glifcebat immenfum minore in dies plebe ingenua. In the letter, which Tiberius wrote to the fenate, concerning the complaints which had been made againft luxury, we find thefe remark-able words: quid enim primum prohibere, et prifcum ad morem recipere adgrediar ? villarum infinita fpatia ? familiarum numerum, et nationes ? (Tac. ann. l. 3.) Treinfhemius explains the term, nationes, by obferving, that the Romans had fo great a number of flaves, that they diftinguifhed them by nations. Juftus Lipfius, alfo, cites on this fubject, a paffage from Pliny, who obferves that one Nicilius Ifidorus kept five thoufand flaves: he, likewife, produces another quotation from Athenæus, in which the number of flaves, belonging to fome of the Romans, is eftimated, even at thirty thoufand. (See Tacit. Varior. l. 3.) I fhall conclude this note with obferving, that in the fame letter alluded to above, Ti-berius declares that the prevalence of corruption, amongft the Romans, is not aftonifhing, fince they only formed a mixture of every kind of nations.

blefling, their condition became better, but
their ftate was not changed. We know that,
even during the reign of Auguftus, fome of
the pretors were guilty of a barbarous abufe
of that arbitrary power, which had been entrufted within their hands. Dion informs us
that one Licinius, in the courfe of the year,
impudently extorted from the Gauls, fourteen
inftead of twelve months tribute; but this
act, the violence of which was far from being
without examples, muft appear to us, in a
more fhocking light, when confidered as a
fpecies of rapine, exercifed by the government. In fact, Licinius, who had the prefence of mind to offer Auguftus, the money
which he had exacted, found no difficulty in
perfuading him, that a double ufe, might
arife from plundering the Gauls of their treafures, and throwing them into the coffers of
the emperor. As this fact hath reached pofterity, one may naturally fuppofe that many
other fimilar facts have perifhed in oblivion.
The complaints of the unhappy are not preferved fo long as the panegyrics of orators.
And what muft have been the condition of a
people, governed by two foreigners, who,
with the titles of proconful, and queftor,

were

were reciprocal fpies, or accomplices in the fame crimes; who could neither have played into each others hands, without ruining the province, nor have engaged in mutual oppofition, without fcattering through the fame province, trouble and confufion?(r)

But, however ftrict the integrity of thefe magiftrates might have been, the number, and even the mode of the taxes, were fufficient to reduce the people to the greateft diftrefs. The human mind, always fertile in inventions, had already concerted thofe numerous impofitions, which are the fcourges of our contemporaries; and the ingenious author,(s) who hath proved that almoft all the difcoveries, attributed to the moderns, are owing to the ancients, might have added to the examples, which he hath produced, in fupport of his affertion, the long-fince in-
vented

(r) Tacitus (Vit. Agric.) hath taken care to tranf-mit to us the complaints of the Britons, againft the Roman government. Singulos fibi olim reges fuiffe, nunc binos imponi; equibus legatus in fanguinem, procurator in bona faeviret: aeque difcordiam praepofitorum, aeque concordiam fubjectis exitiofam, &c.

(s) Mr. Du Tens.

vented art of working a province with taxes,
or rather of working a people with taxes.*(t)*

Whilft the frontiers we galled by the payment of tributes, and harraffed by the prefence of armies, they felt the additional mif-
fortune of being frequently expofed to the
incurfions of the enemy. In fact, although
Auguftus was not engaged in any very calamitous wars; and although the centre of the
empire was at peace, yet the Germans, the
Rhetians, the Pannonians, and the Cantabrians, were conftantly committing great
diforders, and exercifing much cruelty, not
only againft the Romans, but againft their
allies; for fuch were the extent and the fortune of this empire, that all who were neither
allied

(t) L'Abb: du Bos hath proved that the emperors
levied from their fubjects, but particularly, from the
Gauls, taxes of every kind, fuch as a tithe of fruits,
in the conquered lands, and farmed under the name,
Decuma: a fifth of all the productions not fown,
whether of wood, vines, meadows, &c. A general
land-tax, or if it be a more proper expreffion, an acre-
tax, called jugeratio; a capitation, or perfonal tax,
paid by every freeman; and in fhort, the duties of the
cuftoms, on exportation, and importation; the fortieth
penny on effects fold, &c. &c. (See l'hiftoire de l'eta-
bliffement de la Monarch. Franc. Chap. 11. 12. 13.
Tom. 1. Liv. 1.)

allied to, nor tributaries of the Romans, compofed a barbarous people, at once lawlefs and unpolifhed.

This induces us to extend our reflections ftill farther, and endeavour to form fome eftimation of the ftate of the known world, at that period. It is but too true that we perceive upon this vaft theatre, merely a debafed, indolent, and frivolous people ;(u) kingdoms converted into oppreffed and languifhing provinces ; and, at a greater diftance, barbarous nations, equally ignorant of commerce, and of agriculture, and exifting only in a ftate of war. Where is the philofopher who can, at any time, be led to envy thofe, whom fate had deftined to live, during this æra ? but, let us, inftead of loitering over thefe general views, follow the hiftory with a clofer ftep.

It

(u) The Romans had, from the beginning of the civil wars, fo entirely neglefted agriculture, that Auguftus was induced, in order to re-eftablifh it, to curtail the diftributions of corn, amongft the people, fince they exempted them from the neceffity of cultivating the earth. but Suetonius pretends that he was deterred, by the apprehenfion that, one day, the re-eftablifhment of this cuftom, might prove too great an opening to ambition, and too eafy a ftep to the attainment of popularity.

It is certain that Auguftus was a pacific prince ; and yet his legions were almoft conftantly engaged in war; his friends, his children were fcarcely to be found, but at the head of the armies ; and even he, in fpite of old age, in fpite of his averfion to a martial life, was frequently obliged to undertake long voyages, that he might be at hand, to direct the military operations. Did not the revolts of the Germans, the Cantabrians, and the other people above-mentioned, keep the Roman forces, always, in action? and was not the beginning of the reign of Tiberius difturbed with the din of battle? it is certain that all this never reached Rome; but what is Rome, when compared with the univerfe? befides, if even Auguftus, feated within the very bofom of fortune, lamented over the death of a fon, who perifhed miferably amidft foreign wars, is it poffible to believe that the inhabitants of Rome were happier, than he was? can we fuppofe that the defeat of Varus, and the bloody victories of Agrippa, of Drufus, and of Germanicus, had not often proved the caufe of mourning, in the moft illuftrious families? we muft not judge of the Auguftan age, by the works of

con-

contemporary poets; but had the fine verses
of Horace and of Virgil expreffed the fincere
meaning of the heart, no more could be gathered from this circumftance, than that the
artifts, and the men of letters enjoyed a ftate
of welfare; or rather, that the happinefs,
which they celebrated, like the rays of the
fun, after a ftorm, owed a great part of its
value to thofe horrible moments, which preceded it? and what dependance could have
been placed on this felicity, the only bafis,
the only fupport of which, were the days of
an old man? who, poffeffed of any feeling
but muft have trembled, when he reflected
that Tiberius, and Pofthumus Agrippa,
were the neareft heirs to the throne? After
the facrifices which had been made to Auguftus, what refource remained againft his
fucceffors? woe to the people, who have
been fubdued by enthufiafm! forgers of their
own chains, they have contrived to fit them
on in fuch a manner as to render it almoft
impoffible that they fhould be broken; as if
it were neceffary, in exchange for benefits,
to fupply a king with power; and whilft we
are rewarding a good prince, to make preparations for a tyrant. Monarchy, like nobility,

lity, which is the fupport of monarchy, to be refpectable, fhould be ancient. From a fortunate experience of authority, and from a fettled habit of obedience, may arife a kind of conftitution, which, in the end, becomes almoft unalterable : becaufe there is a point, beyond which the materials of a republic, exift no longer in a monarchy, whilft the materials of a monarchy, exift always in a republic.

There is but little room to doubt that the Romans gave way to fome reflections, fuch as thefe; and although the majority fuffered themfelves to be feduced, as much by the dignities which Auguftus lavifhed on them, as by that refemblance of a republic, which he ftill preferved, yet they could not avoid forefeeing what happened afterwards : but fuch was the artifice which prevailed in the conduct of this fortunate ufurper, that good and evil, hope and fear, the empty name and the reality were fo happily blended, and fo judicioufly counter-ballanced, that the Romans remained in that divided ftate, which leaves more room for doubts and fears, than for confidence and refolution. I infift the more particularly on this epoch of the reign

of

of Auguftus, becaufe the mere names of Tiberius, Caligula, Claudius, and Nero, are
fufficient to ftrike horror into every feeling
heart.   No one is fo barbarous, as not to de-
plore the fate of thofe unhappy wretches,
who lived under thefe execrable reigns ; and
yet they were reigns, which, of all others,
made the leaft fhew of war.(x)   If war was,
fometimes, kindled in Britain, or towards
Armenia, the center of the empire fcarcely
knew any thing about it ; but that kind of
bloody peace which prevailed muft frequently have become a motive for regretting the
horrors of battle.   The death of Nero brought
trouble and confufion back into the bofom
of Italy ; and the engagements between the
armies of Otho, and Vitellius, and of Vefpafian and Galba, again drenched in human
gore, thofe fields, which, fince the battle of
Mantua, had never refounded with the din of
arms.   Vefpafian eftablifhed peace in the empire : but his reign is precifely the reign which
prefents us with a picture of all the moft
                                     fhocking

_____

(x) Tacitus, on the fubject of the legions, which
Corbulo led into Armenia, faith : fatis conftitit fuiffe
in eo exercitu veteranos qui non ftationem, non vigilias
iniffent. Tac. ann. l. 13.

ſhocking circumſtances, which have, at any
time been produced by ambition, on the one,
and fanaticiſm, on the other hand. It may
eaſily be gueſſed, that I allude to the war of
the Jews, in which, during the ſpace of
two years, more than thirteen hundred thouſand ſouls periſhed; and which, rekindled
under Trajan, and under Adrian,(y) occaſioned the total deſtruction of fifty fortified
cities, and nine hundred and eighty-five
boroughs, or villages. This horrible ſcourge
of humanity too much outweighed the advantages, which aroſe in the reign of Veſpaſian. Titus can only be ſaid to have juſt
ſeated himſelf on the throne. It ſeems as if
that deſtiny, which had formed him a pattern
for ſucceeding kings, was contented with
barely ſhewing him as an eternal example to
every future age. I ſhall not mention Domitian, whom a ſeries of cruelties have rendered too notorious ; but I muſt obſerve that

Trajan,

(y) If Xiphilinus, the abridger of Dion, may be
credited, this revolt of the Jews was attended with the
loſs of two hundred thouſand men at Cyrene ; and two
hundred and fifty thouſand men in the Iſle of Cyprus.
The cruelties which this hiſtorian imputes to the Jews,
make the hair ſtand on end, and are ſcarcely credible.

Trajan, whofe vertues, and whofe goodnefs
fhould have proved the delights of the Roman people, difturbed, of his own accord,
by a paffion for war, the ferenity of thofe happier days, to which he had given birth. This
obfervation becomes more confiderably important, fince it enables us to eftimate the
morality of this age. I repeat it: I fhall frequently have occafion to repeat it: a love for
their country, popularity, and generofity,
were vertues common to the ancients; but
true philanthropy, a regard for public welfare, and general order, are fentiments, to
which the paft ages were abfolutely ftrangers.
And how, indeed, could fuch fentiments
have exifted amongft men, accuftomed from
their infancy, to behold thoufands of gladiators, mutually flaughtering one another,
and perifhing even amidft the acclamations of
the women? fuch exalted feelings as thefe
could never have animated a people, who fo
frequently faw prifoners of war, chiefs and
kings publicly conducted, in purfuance of a
decree, to execution, and completing, by their
deaths, the feftivity of a triumph. It muft
be confeffed that vertue hath been, in every
æra, what beauty ftill is, amongft different
nations;

nations; not that which nature hath produced
the moſt perfect, but the greateſt perfection
of features which ſhe may have given to each
nation, and in each climate. As in the an-
tique ſtatues, the countenances of a Venus,
or an Helen, preſerve a certain expreſſion
of auſterity, in our eyes, extremely inconſiſ-
tent with thoſe graces diffuſed through other
forms, ſo the vertues of the ancients were
continually tinged with the vices of their
age.(z)

VOL. I.　　　　Q　　　　If

(z) I have, hitherto, neglected to obſerve, that the
Romans were ſo rigorous, in all their criminal proſe-
cutions, as never to ſuppoſe that the number of the
guilty could ſuggeſt a reaſon why any ſhould be par-
doned. Seneca relates, that Voluſius Meſſala, having
ordered three hundred men, to be beheaded, on one
day, boaſted of his conduct, and thought the perpetration of this barbarity a truly royal action. When
Claudius exhibited that remarkable ſpectacle, on the
Lacus Fucinus, there were more than nineteen thouſand criminals all doomed to death; as may be ſeen
in a paſſage which Suetonius hath tranſmitted to us.
This author ſaith, that all theſe unfortunate wretches
cried out to the emperor, as they paſſed before him:
ave imperator, morituri te ſalutant; and that Claudius anſwering, from abſence of mind, avete vos, they
underſtood this expreſſion to mean a pardon, and would
not

If Trajan and Marcus Aurelius have been blamed for engaging too much in war, yet, it muſt be confeſſed, that many reaſons may be alledged in their favour. In faſt, if we examine the conſtitution of the empire of the Cæſars, and the ſlight baſis on which their authority reſted, we ſhall be convinced, that it was almoſt impoſſible to maintain peace at home, but by waging war abroad. War is, unfortunately, a great mean of government, it employs every mind, it reduces all forms into one plain ſyſtem, and keeps each diſ-

cuſſion

not engage, until they had been compelled to it, by threats and intreaties. Mr. Crevier (Hiſt. des Emp.) obſerves on this occaſion, that it was an aſtoniſhing circumſtance that nineteen thouſand criminals ſhould be found in the Roman empire, worthy of death, unleſs they had collected them, for ſome time before, from all the provinces of the empire.... But, we know that the Romans had but too many reſources, wherewith to ſupply their ſanguinary amuſements. Priſoners taken in war, foreigners condemned for different crimes, and more particularly the ſlaves, ſerved as food for their cruelty. The barbarous power which they exerciſed over theſe laſt, is well known, and we may recollect an horrible inſtance, from the unfeeling malignity of Vedius Pollio, who, becauſe a ſlave broke a glaſs, would have thrown him, even in the preſence

of

cuſſion at a diſtance. I am, alſo, exceedingly
inclined to believe, that thoſe kings, who
were always the moſt engaged in war, were
not the kings who ſtood in the greateſt need
of genius ; and that politic princes are as
much ſuperior to martial princes, as the art
of governing is more difficult, than the art of
commanding. The emperors, ſituated between the people, and the army, but more
embarraſſed by the laſt, ought to have deſired war, that they might have employed
the one, and amuſed the other. And yet a

Q 2   ſingle

---

of Auguſtus, to ſome ſea monſters, which he kept in a
pond. It may be, that theſe examples of inhumanity
were uncommon ; but it is at leaſt apparent that a generally eſtabliſhed cuſtom required that all fugitive
ſlaves ſhould be expoſed to wild beaſts.

Amidſt ſo many atrocious actions, of which the Romans were guilty, the greateſt reproach which they
have incurred, is, in my opinion, on account of their
having never treated man, in general, as a kind of fellow creature. The extreme rigour of their puniſhments
might, perhaps, have been excuſable, had it been
founded on a love of order, and had it been extended,
with equal ſeverity, againſt all. But who will not be
ſurpriſed, at perceiving that theſe ſanguinary judges
inflicted no other puniſhment, but the puniſhment of
ſending into exile, on a Roman citizen, even although
he might have committed a thouſand aſſaſſinations.

fingle obftacle defeated the effect of this policy. The Romans were too fuperior to
other ftates, the frontiers of the empire were
too diftant, and the neighbouring nations
were too intimidated; it, therefore, became
neceffary to go far off, in fearch of war, and,
then, the abfence of the mafter, of courfe,
diminifhed his power. Befides, fuch is the
misfortune entailed on a people, entirely military, that in the cafe, where war is fo diftant,
that the interior quarters do not feel its confequences, it will ceafe to be interefting, and
its fucceffes will become matters of indifference, whilft its loffes will be the more bit-
terly felt. Even the common foldier grows
fatigued, when toiling, without one object
in his view; he mutinies, and revolts. If
there be two armies, two parties are formed.
Frefh dangers may arife from the valour of
the officers, and the confidence of the forces.
They can no more remain attached to their
chief, without raifing him to the firft rank;
and the love of the foldiers foon induces the
generals to prove faithlefs? thus a misfortune
muft fpring out of one of thefe three circumftances. If war be difadvantageous, it brings
on the ruin of a nation: if it maintain only

an

an equal oppofition to the contending powers, it harraffes, and drains a nation ; and if it be advantageous, it introduces a diffolution of the armies, and of the government. I have not yet mentioned the danger which may accrue from particular bodies, fuch as the Pretorian guards, the Janiffaries, the Strelitzes, &c. becaufe all my readers well know that every defpot hath his fatellites, and that each of thefe fatellites are, in their turns, the tyrants of the defpot. Amongft three and twenty emperors, fixteen were flaughtered,(a)

Q 3 the

(a) It is remarkable that, out of forty-two emperors, who filled up the interval, between Julius Cæfar and Charlemagne, thirty, at leaft, died a violent death. Amongft thefe, four committed fuicide; and fix perifhed through the intrigues of their favourites, their brothers, their wives, and their children. It is not their dreadful difmiffion to eternity, but their fatal entrance into the world, at which the feeling reader will be apt to fhudder. The pen which writes the annals of the generality of kings, fhould, with propriety, be dipped in blood. A multitude of thofe monarchs, whom the fear, and adulation of their fubjects, have dignified with the titles of fathers of their country, were little better than the murderers of mankind. If their contemporaries durft have fpoken their fentiments with the fame freedom, which hath influenced the opinion of their.

the Roman empire was put up at auction, and fold to a contemptible individual; the revolutions of Ruſſia, of the empire of the Ottomans, and of that of the Mogul, are ample proofs that a government, founded in military deſpotiſm, is the worſt government of all, not only for princes, but for the people.

SECTION

their poſterity, the compoſitions of too many of our an- ceſtors, inſtead of being ſullied with panegyrics on royalty, would have glowed only with execrations againſt the flagrancy of arbitrary power. K.

SECTION II.

Confiderations on the lot of Humanity,
during the middle ages of hiftory.

CHAP. I.

On the inundation of the Barbarians.

WHILST we purfue our tafk of def-
cribing the misfortunes of mankind, we cannot obferve, without concern, the diverfity
prevailing through the feveral objects which
claim our attention. Evil is produced, and
generated under a thoufand different forms ;
and, without being hurried away by too
fplenetic an imagination, we may venture to

Q 4   affert

affert that, of all the prefents which were made to human nature, the box of Pandora was, indifputably, the moft complete, and the moft judicioufly afforted. The theatre of the world muft now undergo a confiderable alteration. In the place of either thofe rigid old men, who, feated on their curule chairs, decided, in three words, the deftruction of ftates; or of thofe young enthufiafts, who, for a crown of grafs, carried fire and the fword to the extremities of the earth, we fhall perceive a race of half-favages, a wandering multitude of Barbarians,(*b*) who, notwithftanding, more juft and more confiderate than the firft, felt only thofe paffions, to which their wants had given birth, and became the mafters of the world, folely, becaufe they were perifhing with hunger.

From

(*b*) (*Hordes.*) This expreffion is applicable to thofe large bodies of emigrants, thofe focieties of wandering Tartars, who, like the ancient Scythians, exift only in tents, in order the more conveniently to change their abode, whenfoever the provifions of the country become nearly confumed. Each troop of thefe emigrants formerly confifted of fifty, or fixty families, under the command of a captain, dependant on the general, or prince of the whole nation. K.

From whence came thefe people, known only by their invafions? how did it happen, that all unpolifhed, and divided as they were, they attained to the power of overthrowing that wonderful Coloffus, the Roman empire? (c) thefe are two important queftions. The invef-

---

(c) The rife and fall of Empires may be ranked amongft thofe events which, although common, do not ceafe to be remarkable. Infpiration only could have difcovered, that the primitive Romans, a vile, and abject people were deftined to clear the path, which conducted their future race to the fovereignty of the world. If, in the days of Julius Cæfar, a Roman Augur had pretended, that his *birds* informed him, that the diftant defcendants of the dictator, and his *invincible* countrymen, fhould be emafculated, and fing upon a ftage, before the pofterity of the conquered Britons, inftead of being reverenced as a prophet, he would have been ftoned, as a madman. Yet this, and ftranger things than this have happened. To what fate England, the envy, and admiration of every kingdom upon earth, may be referved, it is impoffible to determine: but an ingenious writer of effays, a Colman, or a Wharton, by purfuing this thought, might, at once, amufe and inftruct. A picture of England, funk into what Rome is at prefent, blended with the reprefentation of an American colony, fuperior in power and fplendour, to her unnatural mother, can, in this age, only be ideal; but the future reality is, to the full as probable, as was the deftruction of Rome, by the Barbarians, in the boafted reign of Auguftus. K.

inveſtigation of one queſtion is the province
of erudition; the inveſtigation of the other
queſtion is the province of the ſcience of politics. To diſcuſs them might ſeem a ſtriking
inſtance of temerity, on our part, if experience had not convinced us, that a little philoſophy can, ſometimes, throw a light over the
moſt intricate reſearches, and relieve us from
the toiis of learning. Let others diſplay a
vain, unneceſſary parade of knowledge: we
ſhall content ourſelves with confeſſing our ignorance of the hiſtory of that vaſt region of
the world, which contains Sweden, Ruſſia,
Poland, Tartary, China, and Indoſtan. Now
who can inform us, if the emigrations into
the Weſt did not originate from the North,
and the Eaſt? amongſt the people, who inhabited Germany, Bohemia, Hungary, and
Poland, there were but very few ſuppoſed to
be indigenous.(d) The majority of them came
from a greater diſtance, but they were not
known until after their laſt eſtabliſhment.
                                        Were

(d) There are very ſtrong proofs, that all theſe
people came from Scythia. The celebrated Odin had
conquered all the northern countries. See *Introduction
a l' hiſt. du Dannemark.*

Were thefe people repulfed, towards the Weft, by the Tartarian and Chinefe nations? or, did they not extend themfelves into the vicinity of the Roman empire, by reafon of too numerous a population? or, may we not rather fuppofe, that the world, becoming peopled, only by fucceffion, the countries neareft to the fea, were, at the firft, inhabited by a larger proportion of individuals, than the inland countries; from whence it muft have followed, that an equilibration could never have been eftablifhed amongft them, the progrefs of one part of thefe individuals, exactly correfponding with the decline of the other part.

The multiplication of queftions, is the multiplication of doubts. Firft, fuppofing that the barbarous nations had been repulfed towards the Weft, in confequence of thofe unfortunate wars, which raged within the Eaftern quarters, it muft be very aftonifhing, that there fhould have been no tradition preferved, relative to thefe events. Secondly, although it be generally allowed, that the women in Germany are more prolific than elfewhere, we do not perceive that this circumftance

cumftance extends farther to the North ; or
that Sweden and Ruffia have any reafon to
boaft of the fame fecundity. Thirdly, there
is no abfurdity in admitting, that the population of the world was, as yet, progreffive,
in thofe early times ; and that the effect of a
long feries of ages was univerfally manifefted,
almoft at the fame inftant. But, is it neceffary to fuppofe, that the population amongft
the Barbarians, and, particularly, amongft
the inhabitants of the North, was fo numerous ? let us fee what dependance can be
drawn from the calculations of hiftorians.
Shall we attempt to fide with them ? whenfoever I read in their works, that this emperor
attacked the Barbarians, and deftroyed one
hundred thoufand men; that another emperor defeated two hundred thoufand Goths ;
and that a third emperor vanquifhed three
hundred thoufand Sarmatians, I always tran-
flate thefe paffages, thus: fuch an emperor
attacked the Barbarians, and deftroyed a great
multitude. What ! if, in our times, when
the military ftate of each nation, is printed
and publifhed, we can never exactly afcertain
the number of the forces of our enemies, or
even

the number of the forces of our allies, fhall we pretend to reckon up the forces of the Barbarians, who had no mufter-rolls, no divifions of troops, nor any other method of marching, but in multitudes? it is, indeed, impoffible to avoid wondering at the confidence with which hiftorians tranfmit their details to pofterity. Had they not been obliged to furnifh out the greater part of their annals with materials, taken from the compofitions of the orators and panegyrifts, how could they have expected, that the Romans themfelves fhould have known the number of the forces of their enemies? is it not evident that either fear or vanity magnified every object; that, in order to fcatter terror through the ranks of the enemy, it was cuftomary to fpeak of the ftrength of their own army, as greater than it was; and that, when they had been defeated, it was equally ufual, to reprefent the ftrength of the oppofing army, as lefs than it was, that the difgrace of having been conquered, might admit of fome extenuation? befides, no province, whether in Germany, in France, or in Spain, is fo poor, as to prove incapable of

exciting

exciting the fears of neigbouring provinces, were all its inhabitants to take up arms, at once: and thefe apprehenfions muſt have been ſtill more violent, at a time when there were no military fortreſſes, to ſerve as barriers, of which the aſſailants could not have poſſeſſed themſelves, but by dint of ſkill, toil, and perſeverance.

The cuſtom which thefe barbarous nations had adopted, of tranſporting themſelves, to a man, from one climate, into another climate, feems, at the firſt glance, a more aſtoniſhing circumſtance, than any of the former circumſtances. And yet, if we do but reflect, we ſhall be no longer ſurprized at reading, in the pages of hiſtory, a relation of fimilar events, which happened at a period, much leſs remote from our own times. It is not a great while, fince we became acquainted with the interiour parts of America ; and we know that the nations which inhabit them have undergone the like revolutions. It is, ſtill, extremely common, to obſerve the ſavages, fettling themſelves in places, five, or fix hundred leagues diſtant from their original abode. Such, at this period, is the

fate

fate of the Tartars; and fuch will always be the deftiny of thofe people, who remain abfolute ftrangers, to the arts of agriculture. This, then, is the important fpeculation, on which we are to fix: if we defire to know what, in general, is the condition of the inhabitants of the world, we need only inform ourfelves, whether the number of cultivated lands be augmented, or diminifhed.

However fimple this method of invefti-gating our fubject may appear, we dare venture to affert, that it is not without its novelty; a novelty, arifing from the contempt, with which fuch difcuffions have been treated by all thofe political enthufiafts, who were only led afide by a vain glory, or a falfe vertue; forms, at once, gigantic and frivolous, incapable of exifting, but by mutually fupporting each other, and making humanity a conftant victim to their connexion.

We have, already, obferved how the arts, commerce and agriculture became, as it were, a conftituent part of Ægypt, of Phenicia, and at length of Greece, fpreading themfelves, as they conftantly kept near to the

the fea-fhore, through Italy, Sicily, the coafts of Africa, Spain, and even amongft the Gauls. This confideration may ferve to explain the reafon, why the nations, bordering on the ocean, always enjoyed more diftinguifhed advantages, than the nations inhabiting the inland countries. In fact, whilft Lycurgus, Solon, Romulus, and the reft, were putting their invention to the torture, that they might difcover the art of effectually vanquifhing their neighbours, nature, by flow degrees, conducted her rebellious children to that point, whereto fhe inceffantly tends, by a progrefs, at once, fecret and undifturbed. Whilft agriculture increafed the productions of the earth, commerce was taught to negotiate their exchange; and as a river, when iffuing from its bed, firft overflows its banks, and then, divides its waters into different channels, bending its courfe through every convenient winding; fo thefe ufeful difcoveries extended themfelves from the fea-coafts into the places more immediately within the reach of commerce, and from thence, into the inland countries. Thus, it may be faid that riches and induftry made the firft advances, and went in queft of the Barbarians,

before

before this people began to covet them. What, then, muft have happened, if the perverfenefs of mankind, but, more particularly, the perverfenefs of heroes, and legiflators, had not intruded itfelf to interrupt the order of nature? the induftrious nations would, by little and little, have mixed themfelves amongft other nations, either by commerce, or by alliance; nay, even by war, fince, if, of two contending powers, the one power be more civilized than the other power, only the moft ftupid pride and the moft mifguided policy, can hinder the conquerors from either adopting the manners of the conquered, or imparting to them their own manners. Unfortunately the philofophers had fo much underftanding, the chiefs fo much heroifm, and the people fo much vertue, that all, over the furface of the globe, was in a flame, whilft the perfection of human nature was thrown back to an extreme diftance. An ignorant people, entirely deftitute of laws, and ftrangers to cultivation, foon triumphed over the compatriots of Homer, of Plato, and of Lycurgus. They undertook to draw out their empire to a greater extent, than that extent which the empire of manners and legiflation had been able to reach : but quickly corrupted, divided and enfeebled, they preferved no traces of their ancient fplendor, except thofe atrocious principles which they had derived from it; and at a time when they were no longer capable of quelling a revolt, their conduct invited it to break out. The barbarous nations found themfelves, during that period, in a fingular fituation. Within the vicinity of opulence, and repulfed by a power who left them no fhare of it, they eagerly wifhed for all the foftnefs of luxury, whilft they dreaded left they fhould fall victims to oppreffion. There was no hope of thofe federal alliances, thofe intermarriages of fovereign houfes, which tended to affimilate and unite the neighbouring nations. In the place of the ancient apothegm, introduced by Cato; *delenda eft Carthago*, there was reafon to fubftitute ; *delenda eft Roma :* and, in fact, Rome was, already, deftroyed; the fenate was filled with foreigners; the Barbarians commanded an army almoft entirely compofed of Barbarians. The Pretorians, invincible tyrants in the capital, but pufillanimous citizens in the camp, after having created

ed and affaffinated emperors, were compelled to give the precedency to the Germans
and to the other foreigners, whom the Cæfars
had appointed to form their guards. Thefe
Barbarians, admitted into the firft rank, eftablifhed with their own nations a corref-
pondence which became pernicious to the
Romans; they fixed their eyes on this de-
graded ftate, in proportion to its becoming
forgetful of itfelf: the ambition of particular
individuals preceded the ambition of the
people; the chief employments were invaded,
and even the throne was ufurped in fuch a
manner, that the Barbarians may be faid to
have conquered the empire before they attacked it.

From hence, it follows that we muft feek
for the fources of the invafions of the Barbarians, hitherto fo difficult to be afcertained,
in the atrocity of the ancient principles of the
republic; in the vices peculiar to the modes
of government, adopted by the emperors;
and, efpecially, in the vaft extent of their
dominions. But, whatfoever may have been
the caufe of thefe invafions, it will always remain an incontrovertible point, that they
ought to be regarded, as fome of the moft

bitter

bitter calamities, which ever afflicted human
nature. The numerous and bloody battles,
which they have occasioned, may be referred
to thofe firft principles of war, defcribed at
the beginning of this work; the defire of
quitting a rigorous climate, for a more whole-
fome climate; a barren land, for a more
fertile land, &c. Now, wars of this kind
are the moft cruel and difaftrous; not being
fo much the contention of rival warriors, as
the obftinate oppofition of one nation againft
another nation. On the one hand, the im-
poffibility of drawing off, and on the other
hand, the neceffity of preferving the means
of fubfiftance, render the deftruction of the
enemy a neceffary confequence of victory.
What can be more melancholy and difquiet-
ing, than the picture of humanity, during
the times, which preceded the feparation of
the Roman empire? nations deftroyed through
principles of policy: other nations over-
whelming and laying wafte whole countries;
and a third affemblage of nations, more dangerous than the former, exifting, folely, by
acts of theft and piracy; the emperors tranfplanting whole colonies from Germany, into
Britain;

Britain ; from Afia, into Africa ; and from
Africa, into Europe. The univerfe refem-
bled one vaft field of battle, where the bodies of forces, not employed in fight, are
engaged in continual evolutions, and, inceffantly, change their ground. *(e)*

R 3   C H A P.

(e) Thefe frequent emigrations, thefe perpetual
changes in the eftablifhment of nations, were, after the
war, amongft the greateft misfortunes, entailed on human nature. Let the reader judge from the following
circumftances. Probus, unable to keep the Barbarians, in a ftate of peace, refolved to tranfplant feveral
nations, into the lands belonging to the empire. Only
one colony fucceeded. It was compofed of a hundred
thoufand of the Baftarnæ, a people of Scythia, who
had fettled in Thrace. The Gedinians, the Vandals,
and the Franks could not be prevailed on to fix themfelves, but committed their ufual acts of plunder, in
the places, where it had been attempted to eftablifh
them. It became neceffary to deftroy them, by force
of arms. Dioclefian tranfported, into Pannonia, the
Carpian nations, inhabiting the vicinities of the Pontus
Euxinus ; and Conftantius Chlorus made the Bata-
vians pafs into the moft depopulated provinces of Gaul.
The manner in which they waged war againft thefe
Barbarians may be difcovered, in a paffage, from Vopifcus, who informs us, that the emperor Probus, not
contented with having flaughtered, in one battle, four
hundred thoufand Barbarians, confifting of Burgun-
dians, Franks, and Germans, fet a price upon the
heads

C H A P. II.

The firſt appearance of Chriſtianity.　The poli-
tical, and moral ſtate of Paganiſm, at the æra
of the eſtabliſhment of the Chriſtian religion.

THE dreadful convulſions, which ſhook
the political ſyſtem of the world, were not
ſufficient to fill up the meaſure of calamity.
A revolution, a thouſand times more aſtoniſhing, prepared itſelf to overthrow the empire of opinion; as if the time had been arrived

---

heads of all who remained, promiſing to each of the
ſoldiers a piece of gold, for every head which they
might bring. It is with ſingular ſatisfaction, that I
draw the contraſt to theſe cruel orders, whilſt I mention
what I recollect to have ſeen practiſed, during the laſt
war. Some commanders of light troops, anxious to
prevent

rived, at which, every thing on the furface
of the earth was to be altered, from the
power which commands, to the perfuafion,
which governs. A tumultuous war arofe in
the mind; nor did the individual, who had
retired to folitude, and contemplation, enjoy
more tranquility in his retreat, than the un-
ruly foldier, or the timid cultivator of the
ground. What an epoch was this, in which
hiftory, at once, prefents to us the deftruction of the Roman empire, and the fall of
paganifm ! new people, and a new mode of
worfhip are introduced upon the theatre of
the world ; it may even be faid, that a new
religion is introduced ; for, idly would men
alledge, that chriftianity, teaching, as its
firft dogma, the unity of God, and immediately deriving itfelf, from the faith of the If-
raelites, fhould trace its origin up to deifm
and judaifm : the myftery of the redemption,

R 4 its

---

prevent the fpilling of too much blood, concerted a
ftruggle, in the minds of the foldiers, between avarice
and cruelty, and inftituted a reward, for every one,
who might bring in a prifoner, fafe and found. Such
is the progrefs of manners and philofophy, that the
moderns, at this period, are not fo cruel, in the time
of war, as the ancients were, in times of peace,

its tenets relating to a future ſtate, its forms
of worſhip, its precepts, all anounce, all
declare a new order in ſpiritual matters.; all
charaċteriſe a revolution in the ſyſtem of religion.

But, howſoever this ſubjeċt ought to be
conſidered, there is only one method of enquiry, with which we can indulge ourſelves ;
and this method neceſſarily enters into the
plan of our work.   Thus, far from following
the example of ſome philoſophers, of the
preſent age, whoſe abilities we reſpeċt, but
whoſe fondneſs for diſcuſſion hath, perhaps,
led them into errors, we ſhall leave to Theologians, that which belongs inconteſtably to
their province, and enter ſolely into an examination of the influence of the Chriſtian religion over the happineſs of mankind, in its
excluſive relation to this life.   It is in conſequence of this principle, that, being obliged,
through the ſeries of our reflećtions, to unfold the origin and progreſs of chriſtianity,
we ſhall only mention thoſe human means, of
which providence hath made uſe; to theſe
means the fathers of the church have given
their aſſent ; and in this inveſtigation no
other means can be admitted, ſince it is im-
                                    poſſible

poffible for man, to trace the ways of God
through fupernatural events; and equally
as difficult, for our weak intellects, to affign
a motive, why he fometimes changes the
order of nature; as to explain the reafon,
why he doth not change it, either oftner, or
in a manner more adapted to the attainment
of thofe ends, to which, we imagine, that he
directs his purpofes. If, in the courfe of
this work, we have never affumed that ftile
of confidence, which pretends to teach; but
rather the language of criticifm, at once,
doubting and difcuffing, how much more
neceffary is it, that we fhould adhere to this
precaution, in a matter, where we cannot
boaft of having availed ourfelves of any affiftance, except that affiftance which arofe
from the light of hiftory, fupported by reflection.

Whilft mankind meditated upon this great
revolution in the moral world, they appear
to have been particularly ftricken with two
circumftances, the deftruction of an ancient
religion, and the eftablifhment of a new religion; or rather thefe two objects being confounded with each other, the human mind,
which conftantly endeavours to relieve herfelf
by

by abſtraction, from the fatigue of entering
into long details, ſaw only a war on foot, between two powerful rivals, and did not he-
ſitate to deſcribe chriſtianity, as engaged
againſt paganiſm. But was paganiſm a religion? far from it; the term Pagan was not
adopted until ſome ages after the appearance
of Jeſus Chriſt.*(f)* The Phenicians, the
Ægyptians, the Greeks, the Italians, and the
Celtæ, had all different ideas, not only of
the nature and origin of the gods, but of that
kind of adoration, which they imagined it
neceſſary to pay them. There were no relative ideas, no connection even between the
names.

(f) Pagan, from Pagus, a village, becauſe the
chriſtian emperors having baniſhed the idolaters from
all the cities, they were obliged to retire to the villages;
or rather becauſe Conſtantine drove out, from amongſt
his troops, and expelled into the villages, all thoſe who
were not chriſtians. Neither of theſe explanations is
ſatisfactory. The firſt mention which hiſtory makes of
the Gentiles, under the name of Pagans, is in the reign
of Valentinian, and in the three hundred and ſixty-fifth
year of Chriſt. See " Gothofredus de ſtatu Paganorum
ſub imperatoribus Chriſtianis." Echard imagines that
the inhabitants of the country, remaining longer attached to the worſhip of idols, than the inhabitants of
cities, the idolaters were therefore called Pagans. Pa-
gani. b. 7. c. 1.

names of their gods; nor did they barely admit of a tranflation from one language into another language. Examine all the ancient nations, and endeavour to form from their notions, with regard to *Taut, Brimba,* or *Brama, Tiphon, Ofiris, Zeus, Jupiter, Odin,* &c. a fyftem which conciliates every opinion, and forms a point of re-union againft a new religion. It may be faid that fuch a fyftem is vifible in *Polytheifm.* But this affertion is far from carrying conviction along with it; for we, in our turns, muft afk what is underftood by religion? doth it mean the opinion prevailing amongft the people? and yet, with ignorant men, all opinion degenerates into fuperftition, and all worfhip into idolatry. In this refpect, it will appear that even the chriftians poffeffed but very few advantages over the Pagans : for were we to enquire into the religious ftate of all the fouthern part of America, and of fome nations fituated to the North and South of Europe,*(g)* we fhould find that their notions on the Trinity, the Virgin, the Saints, the Angels, and the Devils, were

---

(g) The Ruffians ftill preferve their little idols, and render them the fame worfhip, which the Pagans rendered to their Penates.

were little fhort of idolatry. If, on the contrary, it be imagined that through every age,
and amidft every religion, the ideas of the
vulgar are to be rejected, we fhall, then, perceive that amongft the ancients, the priefts
referred all their doctrine to deifm, and all
their morality to politics. It is certain that
the dogma of one God alone was the firft
truth revealed in the Eleufinian myfteries.
Lactantius afferts, that Alexander learned this
truth from the mouth of the Hierophant;
and a very flight knowledge of antiquity may
convince us that this belief was the bafis of
all initiation, and the hidden principle of
every doctrine. The freedom with which
even the minifters of religion fpoke of their
divinities, is evident from the writings of
Cicero; and Diodorus Siculus accounts for
the origin of the popular opinions, relative
to the *Styx, Acheron, Minos, Rhadamanthus,*
&c. &c. It were a ftill more ufelefs tafk,
fhould we attempt to fearch for Polytheifm
amongft the philofophers. In whatfoever obfcurities their ideas, concerning the nature of
things and firft caufes, were involved, we
may affert, that no fect exifted, the principles
of

of which, had any thing in common with the religion of the people.

We ſhall not, in this place, trefpaſs upon the readers time, by endeavouring to ſhew what little ſolidity could have belonged to an edifice, without ſymmetry in any of its parts, and without the leaſt correſpondence to a general plan. The Pagan religion, defpiſed by its own miniſters, inveighed againſt by the philofophers, and neglected, the moſt frequently, by the people, was equally incapable of ſtriking a deep root, and of forming a a code of doctrines, difficult to be overthrown. The credit which it maintained during a length of time is, notwithſtanding, unqueſtionable. To account, therefore, for all this, we muſt have recourſe to ſome more diſtant cauſe ; for it is not ſufficient to demonſtrate with Mr. Hume, that Polytheiſm is the firſt religion which muſt have offered itſelf to an untutored ſet of men; it is not even ſufficient to have difcovered that this religion was mild, and that its modes of worſhip were agreeable and ingenious : on the one hand, it may be anſwered, that it exiſted during the moſt poliſhed ages ; and on the other hand, that the pain and cruelty, attending its practices,

have

have been already proved. We muft, therefore, lead our obfervations ftill farther, and
we fhall, then, difcover in the fyftem of politics, the true reafon of the long duration of
Polytheifm.

Would we, in general, comprehend fome
circumftance from antiquity, we muft not
lofe fight of two important facts, namely,
that Afia hath been, as it were, the cradle of
the fciences, and Greece, the cradle of poetry.
From this fingle confideration, a thoufand
confequences will naturally flow. The poets,
that is to fay, the *makers,*(*h*) the firft amongft
the Greeks who enjoyed the knowledge of
any thing, have arranged, as well as they
poffibly could, all the materials which they
were able to collect, from the fentiments of
the Phenicians and Ægyptians, relative to the
origin of the world, and the generation of
gods; but thefe *makers*, faithful to their
name, and their profeffion, forged many new
                                    fables,

_____

(*h*) Poet, Ποιητης, from Ποιεω, to make, to fabricate,
to compofe, &c. We do not, here, pretend to deny
that poetry is of an earlier date, and that the Greeks
received it from the Phenicians ; but we allude to a regular poem which, whilft it became the language of
the priefts and the legiflators, was the chief amufement of the people.

fables, which they mixed with the ancient fables, and, particularly, laboured at attempts to circulate delufive accounts, concerning the origin of the Greeks; an origin for which they blufhed to have been indebted to merchants, or a people of flaves. Amidft thefe *makers*, Homer quickly obtained the firft rank. He compofed fo many tales, and fpoke of fuch a multitude of things, that his books, in this refpect, like the Koran, were of themfelves fufficient to found a religion. And yet, the oracle of Delphos, another *maker*, who *worked* with hexameter verfes, Lycurgus, who made *metrical* laws, pretending, indeed, that they were dictated by Apollo, but which he had ftolen from the Cretans,(*i*) Hefiod, and many others, began to form, from a very fmall number of acquired intelligences, and from a very great number of ingenious conjectures, a monftrous and gigantic fcaffolding of materials. From all thefe poems, and all thefe oracles, arofe a particular language, ftiled μύϑος, in oppofition to λογός, which

(*i*) Rhetra, or oracle, an appellation given to the laws of Lycurgus, who pretended to have received them from the mouth of Apollo, whofe ufual manner of fpeaking to him was in numbers.

which was the language of reafon, and which
did not prevail until fome time afterwards.
But the μῦθος maintained its ground during
whole ages ; and as the poets had continually
treated of the moſt intereſting ſubjects, ſuch
as the origin of republics, the principles of
legiſlation, the rights of magiſtrates, the limits of ſtates, &c. poetry, or fable, or, if it
be a more proper expreſſion, religion became,
as it were, the general repoſitory of archives,
and the titles of the nobility of republics.
From thence ſprang the obligation which
united polity with religion, and the neceſſity
which preſerved tenets and ceremonies. The
oracles had frequently decided on the privileges of ſtates ; and theſe points had been
determined even by the authority of the
poets.(k)   Who could have queſtioned the
infallibility of the oracles ? who could have
treated Homer with diſreſpect ? !

Saint Auguſtin(l) quotes a beautiful definition from Varro, in which that author divides theology into three kinds: the fabulous
kind,

(k) Two verſes of Homer decided a conteſt between
two republics, which diſputed their metropolitical right
over a colony.

(l) De civitate Dei. l. 6. c. 6.

kind, μυθικον, the phyfical or natural kind,
and the civil or legal kind. The firft kind
contains fables, the metamorphofis, &c. the
fecond kind, which treats of the nature of
the gods, and of things, is taught only in the
fchools ; and the third kind, which is but the
ritual of feafts, or of facrifices, is entrufted
to the priefthood. Varro faith that, from
thefe three kinds of theology, we can only
felect the firft, and the laft kind, as proper to
be given up to the people. " Prima, inquit,
theologia maximè accomodata eft ad theatrum,
fecunda ad mundum, tertia ad urbem." But
this fabulous theology, which Varro particularly annexes to the theatre, was intimately connected with civil theology; and each
of thefe did not fail to unite themfelves
againft natural theology, which was their
greateft enemy. Natural theology unfortunately neglected, during a length of time,
the only arms which fhe might have employed with fuccefs ; obfervation and experience.
She was even weak enough to borrow frequently from the firft, her language, and
from the laft, her impoftures and her myf_
teries. Thefe three fyftems were fo ftrongly
re-acted upon, by one another, that religion

became allegorical, and philofophy fuperftitious.: but whilft the commerce of nations,
whilft voyages and conquefts multiplied the
objects of adoration, by the adoption of foreign rites, curiofity, emulation, and fubtilty
increafed the fects and the fchools. What
could have arifen from thence, except the
difcredit into which philofophy and religion
fell together? the extravagant cuftom of
adoring all forts of divinities, from the great
God Jupiter, down to the God Crepitus;
and of maintaining all kinds of opinions;
from the moft magifterial dogmatifm, to the
moft obftinate Pyrrhonifm, foon placed the
priefts and the fophifts in the fame rank, and
at length gave birth to that fentiment, which
they dread the moft amongft the Great, the
fentiment of indifference.

Amidft thefe difafters, religion ftill enjoyed two great fupports, in the vanity of the
people, and the polity adopted by the magiftrates. Greece was the receptacle of the
gods; in Greece every place feem filled with
their prefence. The *Olympic* and *Ifthmian*
games; the *Panathenæa*; all thofe magnificent
feftivals peculiar to each city; the great multitude of oracles, each in high reputation,
and

and each promifing to Greece an eternal
fplendor; what objects were thefe for a con-
fident and frivolous people! unfortunately,
whilft the Greeks were bufied in the contemplation of their actual glory, a man of Macedon, (to borrow an expreffion from Demofthenes) came to throw all their ideas into
confufion, by infulting over a legiflation, for
which, indeed, they felt but little anxiety,
and by difturbing their religious feafts, to the
celebration of which, they were attached with
the moft bigotted idolatry. To this man of
Macedon fucceeded another man from the
fame country, who, at once deftroyed and
eftablifhed tyranny; who overthrew an ancient monarchy, and gave birth to new dy-
nafties, all warlike and ferocious, whofe op-
preffive power overwhelmed the gods, the
priefts, the philofophers, and the people.

But this, as yet, was nothing, and there
had conftantly remained fome particulars belonging to thefe two fyftems of civil and dra-
matic theology, accomodatæ ad urbem, ad
theatrum. At length, a people confifting of
exceedingly bad theologians, but of excellent
warriors, arrive to overthrow the fucceffors
of the man of Macedon, and treat as vile

S 2   flaves,

flaves, the defcendants of gods, heroes, and
poets. Then every expectation was difappoint-
ed, and every prophecy was belied. Religion,
then, loft all her credit; if the leaft mark of
her footfteps was to be feen, it was confined
to the theatre, and owed its prefervation to
that happy alliance, which fhe had, for a
long time, contracted with the mufes and
the polite arts.

At the firft glance, the Romans feem to
have been fo powerful, that they might have
given law, even in matters of opinion, to the
whole univerfe; but, if I may be allowed the
paradox, they were neither fufficiently intelligent, nor fufficiently ignorant, to found a
religion. Their own dogmas did not belong
to them; they were incapable of forming a
code of doctrines; their firft notions of this
kind were derived from the Etrufcans, a
people much addicted to divination: thus,
the earlieft traces of religion, vifible amongft
them, may be difcovered in the cuftom of
confulting the aufpices, eftablifhed by Romulus.(m) Numa, originally a Sabine, and
better

_____

(m) Romulus confulted the flight of birds before he
began to build Rome.

better inftructed than the Romans, imagined that it was neceffary to deceive, before he could reduce a ferocious race of men, who had affaffinated a warlike prince, and the founder of the empire. He, therefore, introduced fuperftition to affift authority; but he was more engaged in the eftablifhment of ceremonies, than in the circulation of tenets. He was, in general, the mildeft of all the impofters, and merited the applaufe of pofterity. By little, and little, the feveral relations extended themfelves : on the one hand, the commerce carried on with the Grecian colonies, and on the other hand, the eftablifhment of the Tarquins, could not fail to fix a reputation upon fome new opinions. An attempt was made to reconcile thefe vulgar notions, with the more refined ideas of the people of Greece; but the names, and the rites, which underwent no alteration, were evident proofs of the effential difference, which exifted between thefe opinions, and the primitive dogmas. *(n)* Cicero derives the

S 3   word

(n) What relation is there between Cronos, Zeus, Ares, Hermes, Pofeidon, and Saturn, Jupiter, Mars, Mercury, Neptune?

word *Jupiter*, from *juvare*, to help,(*o*) to
affift; and indeed, the infcriptions, *Jovi
Statori, Jovi Feretrio*, frequently to be met
with on altars, feem to mean no more than
*to the affifting power, who ftopped the courfe of
the enemy ; to the affifting power, who ftruck
the enemy.* It is alfo very certain that the
whole hiftory of the Roman Mars, hath no
connection with the hiftory of the Grecian
Ares. Even Flora is abfolutely a Roman divinity. Lactantius(*p*) pretends that fhe was
indebted for her origin, to a courtezan, who,
having acquired a large fortune, left a confiderable fum, by will, to keep up the an-
nual celebration of public games, in honour
of her memory. This author adds, that
after a certain period, the fenate, humiliated
by the idea of having paid fuch homage to a
proftitute, thought it proper to turn her into
the goddefs of flowers. It is, in this place,
unneceffary to relate, how the Romans, not
much contented with their own gods, had
frequent

(*o*) Some have derived the word Jupiter, from *J A H*,
Jehova Pater; but I cannot think that this alliance of
the Greek word Pater, with the Hebrew word Jehovah,
appears very natural.

(*p*) Inftit. l. 4. c. 20.

frequent recourse to the gods of the Greeks; how they confulted their oracles, whenfoever they imagined that they might enjoy the power of drawing up the anfwers; and how they went in fearch of the god of Epidaurus, but had the addrefs to permit his efcape, left the dreadful ferpent, which reprefented Efculapius, might not be acknowledged. One very important obfervation is, that religion, whatfoever might be her nature, remained conftantly within the hands of the Great; and ferved them as a kind of *Ægis*, againft the tumultuous infurrections of the people, whom they opprefled.

We have already obferved, in the former part of this work, that the privilege of taking the aufpices, was a diftinguifhing mark of the effential difference exifting between the nobility, and the people. We have declared, that by this privilege alone, the condition of the citizens was enabled to ftand good in law; becaufe no other privilege could have ftampéd an authenticity on their marriages. The whole Roman hiftory teftifies, how neceffary it was, for all thofe, who were deftined to fill the firft offices of the magiftracy; and I could produce feveral inftances of confuls,

S 4 quitting

quitting the armies, becaufe fome formali⸭
ties had been wanting, during their inaugu-
ration. Every one can recollect the fine difcourfes, related by Livy, and Dionyfius Halicarnaffius, wherein thofe authors have fo
ably unfolded the principles on which the
Patricians grounded their claims, in fupport
of the exclufion of the Plebeians, from the
confulfhip. What! exclaimed the Appii,
and their adherents, fhall we, then fee at the
head of our armies, confuls who never took
the aufpices; inaufpicati confules! in fhort,
nothing hath been more clearly proved, than
that intimate union fubfifting, amongft the
Romans, between their government, and
their religion, but more particularly, between
religion and ariftocracy. Thus, we need
not hefitate to affert, that the efforts of the
people, ftruck equally againft the government and againft the religion: and as James
the firft was wont to obferve, *no bifhops, no
king*, fo, at Rome, it might have been faid,
the more nobles, the more religion.

Democracy, fhaken for a moment, by
Sylla, was continually acquiring frefh vigour
until, having degenerated into anarchy, the
licentioufnefs of all occafioned the defpotifm

tifm of a fingle one. But we muft not lofe
fight of a very important truth ; namely, that
the people never erect an individual into a
defpot, except from a principle of hatred
againft the great, who tyrannife over them.
We can produce a very recent inftance of
this, from Denmark ;(q) there, the people
erected an individual into a defpot, with an
enthufiafm equal to that enthufiafm which
animated the Romans, at the time of the expulfion of their kings. A very flight acquaintance with the Roman hiftory, is fufficient to convince us, that the moft difa-
proved emperors, fuch as Caligula, Nero,
and Commodus, had maintained fome degree
of favour, with the people, merely, becaufe
they defpifed the fenate, and perfecuted the
nobility. And yet, it was not neceffary to
have been a Caligula, or a Nero, but only a
politic prince, in order to have perceived,
that the people, becoming, from day to
day, more and more abject, might eafily
have been gained over, by diftributions and
fpectacles ; whereas the laft traces of the government fubfifted ftill amidft the fenate,
and

---

and the fmall number of nobles, who were
the relicts of thofe illuftrious families, the
ancient objects of public veneration. Now,
we have already explained the intimate union,
which fubfifted, for a long time, between
ariftocracy, and religion. Befides, every
thing which is ancient, every thing which acquires a particular and independant importance, wears, in the eyes of defpots, a kind of
pedantic characteriftic, which troubles them.
It was, therefore, as much through inclination, as policy, that the emperors fuffered all
religious opinions to fall into difgrace: *(r)*
and unfortunately for thefe opinions amidft
the fmall number of good princes, who fucceeded Auguftus, there were found only
philofophers, too vertuous to be expofed to
fear and repentance, the ufual food of fuperftition, and too enlightened to cherifh a
medley of abfurdities, with the fplendour,
which was reflected from the throne. It became ftill worfe, when foreigners fupplied
                                          the

(r) Tiberius, whofe policy aimed the moft dreadful
blows at the authority of the fenate, feems to have
been particularly free from all thofe fuperftitions of
his country, which he found acting in oppofition, to
his arbitrary views.

the place of princes, who were fcarcely Roman citizens, and of courfe, gave themfelves no concern about the nobility; when the principal employments, whether civil, or military, were entrufted to Barbarians, who had never read Homer, nor heard either of Mercury, or Apollo. Thefe ferocious men, accuftomed to worfhip their god, under the form of a wolf, and to revere only the fpirit of the mountain, or the genius of the tempefts, found themfelves exactly in the fame fituation, with thofe favages of America, whom the moft ignorant of our miffionaries converted, by thoufands. Full of contempt for the Romans, they rejected their gods, of whofe hiftory they were ignorant, and whofe power they defied.

This was the period at which the chriftian religion began to extend herfelf. Her members, more difperfed abroad, and more zealous, continually animated by the fpirit of making profelytes, frequently irritated by perfecution, and, moreover, inculcating a doctrine, very oppofite to that contempt which the Romans and the Greeks expreffed againft the Barbarians, muft, confequently,

have

have prefented themfelves to thefe laft in a
more favourable point of view; and the fimplicity of their dogmas, (for we fhall obferve
farther on, that nothing could have been
more fimple, than the tenets introduced by
the apoftles and their fucceffors) was much
better fuited to the comprehenfion of thefe
plain and properly-tempered minds, which
had not yet been either infected by fuperftitions, or fubtilifed by idle dialectics.

To fum up the whole, then, we may conclude that Greece was the land of paganifm;
that all the religious ideas, eftablifhed in this
country, and united to polity, were overthrown by the conquefts of the Romans; that
the Roman government becoming, at firft,
ariftocratical, then democratical, and at length
monarchial, religion which was the fupport
of ariftocracy muft neceffarily have fallen with
it; and, in fhort, that the invafions of the
Barbarians gave the finifhing ftroke to the deftruction of the laft remains of the ancient
opinions.

C H A P.

CHAP. III.

On the eſtabliſhment of Chriſtianity.

WE cannot too often repeat what hath
been already mentioned, namely, that we
have reſolved, whilſt we trace the progreſs of
chriſtianity, to enquire only into the human or
natural means; means, the importance of
which the theologians themſelves do not affect
to deny: but indeed, if providence had choſen
to eſtabliſh a ſyſtem of worſhip upon miracles,*(s)* it would have been ſufficient to
have

(s) Origen, in his defence againſt Celſus, agrees with
the Pagan philoſophy, in ſuppoſing that ſeveral miracles
might have been wrought by magic; and the only rule
which he preſcribes for diſtinguiſhing the miracles,
which proceeded from Heaven, is founded on the morality,

have wrought at Rome a fmall part of thofe
miracles, of which the Jews only were the
witneffes; or even to have fixed on thefe,
fuch a character of authenticity, as to have
rendered it impoffible that they fhould ever
have been called in queftion, or paffed over
in filence, which two of the moft learned
men of Judæa, have, notwithftanding,
done. *(t)* On the contrary, we perceive that
the firft advances of chriftianity were flow
and laborious, and particularly, whilft we
examine it under its political relations, and
by its influence over the ftate of fociety; this
fpecies of inveftigation being our chief object.

We muft, here, guard againft the indolence
of the human mind, againft that particular
kind

rality, the doctrine, and the manners of thofe who
worked thofe miracles. No one is ignorant of the prodigies brought forth by the magicians of Pharaoh; and
it is alfo well known, that when the heathens placed
the miracles of Apollonius Tyanus, in oppofition to the
miracles of Jefus Chrift, the chriftians, in anfwer to
this objection, were fatisfied with fcrutinizing the life
and character of this philofopher; as, in their opinion,
it was very immaterial, what miracle he might have performed, if it were certain that his doctrince and his
conduct deferved neither refpect nor confidence.

(t) Jofephus and Philo.

kind of curiofity, which flies from application, dreads the falling into doubt more than it likes inftruction, and is the oftneft fatisfied with fome principal points whereon it may reft its wavering opinion. We refemble thofe travellers, who cafting their eyes from the fummit of fome mountain upon an extenfive plain below, obferve here and there a tower and a fteeple, and then return, perfuaded that they are acquainted with the country. We know that Jefus Chrift hath given his name to that religion, which all, who are ftiled chriftians, at this time profefs; and we believe that immediately after Jefus Chrift, there was a chriftian religion. The extreme averfion, alfo, which prevails amongft the chriftians of our days, and the Jews, inclines us to fuppofe, that there muft have been, from the beginning, a very diftinguifhable fciffion, an openly-declared war between the two religions. All thefe opinions are not conformable to the facts. Several hiftorical monuments prove that the Romans for a long time confounded the Jews with the Chriftians. I fhall only produce one inftance, by a quotation from Suetonius, wherein that author, enumerating the laudable actions of Claudius,

at

at the beginning of his reign, faith, that he
drove from Rome the Jews, who continually
revolted, and were *fpurred on by Chriftus.(u)*
Now, Suetonius wrote under Trajan ; that is,
more than one hundred years after Jefus
Chrift. It is certain, that Tacitus, who lived
at the fame period, ufes the word Chriftian,
when he informs us, that Nero was defirous
of making that fufpicion generally circulated
concerning his having fet fire to Rome, alight
upon the chriftians ; but he fpeaks of them
as only a fociety of fectaries iffuing from Judæa ; " repreffaque in præfens exitiabilis fuperftitio rurfus erumpebat, non modo per
Judæam originem ejus mali, &c." The
chriftians themfelves did not immediately affume this refpectable name ;*(x)* fome ftiled
themfelves *Jeffeans*, from *Jeffe*, the father of
David ;

(u) Judæos impulfore Chrefto affiduè tumultuantes
Roma expulit. Dion mentions one Acilius Glabrio,
who, under the reign of Domitian, was accufed of
atheifm, becaufe he became a Jew ; Bingham fays that
we muft, here, underftand Chriftian. . . . See Antiquities of the church, b. 1. ch. 2.

(x) According to the acts of the apoftles, the faithful, that is, the new converts, took the name of
Chriftians at Antioch, from the time of the apoftles :
but it appears that this appellation did not grow common until a long while afterwards.

David; or rather from Jefus, their Mafter. Others were called *Therapeutæ*; others, the *faithful believers*, the *eleƈt*,*(y)* *contemplators*, &c. Some amongft them bore the appellation of *Pifciculi*, *little fifhes*, either becaufe they were engendered, or regenerated by the waters of baptifm; or on account of the initial letters of thefe words; Iησᵾς χριϛος Θεᵾ υιος Σωⁿηρ, *Jefus Chriftus*, *Dei filius*, *Servator*, which form the Greek word IXΘΥΣ, a fifh. Others even confented to pafs for a feƈt of philofophers, as may be colleƈted from thefe words of Melito, in his treatife *de Pafcha*: "hæc enim philofophiæ feƈta quam profitemur apud barbaros viguit."*(z)* Befides, as they had no temples, and as they celebrated no public worfhip, it became natural to confider them, rather as fimple feƈtaries, than as the apoftles of a new religion. Mr. Crevier obferves with juftice, that before the perfecution

VOL. I.   T   of

(y) Πιϛοι, εκλεκτοι, γνωϛοκοι. See Bingham's antiquities of the church.

(z) This feƈt of philofophers, to which we allude, began to acquire fome reputation amongft the Barbarians. See Eufeb. hift. eccles. l. 4.

of Maximin, that is to fay,(a) two hundred and forty years after Jefus Chrift, hiftory doth not, any where, affert that the chriftians had churches.(b) Arnobius, an author of the third age, pofitively faith, "we erect no altars, we offer no incenfe:"(c) and, alfo obferves, "that they believe not in the gods, who believe that their refidence is in the temples, and that they fhould offer up incenfe to them, and honour their images." Let me add, that if an emperor, fo well inftructed, fo well employed in the performance of his duty, as Trajan was, had no particular knowledge of the chriftian opinions; and if the hiftorians have fcarcely made any mention of them, till the reign of Conftantine, it is reafonable to conclude, that they were either very little expanded, at their firft opening, or that they were not feen in that important light, wherein their merit fhould have placed them.

If,

(a) Monfieur Crevier hath committed a fmall error in chronology. It was only in the 238th year of Chrift, that Maximin, after an ufurpation of almoft three years, was affaffinated. K.

(b) Hift. des Emp. tom. 5. p. 111.

(c) Non altaria fabricemus, non cæforum fanguinem ænimantium demus, non thura, &c. l. 6. adverfus gentes.

If, on the other hand, we examine with attention the works of the fathers of the church, or of thofe authors, whom fhe hath confecrated, fuch as Origen, Eufebius, Arnobius, Tertullian, Minucius Felix, &c. we fhall perceive that the feparation of the Chriftians and the Jews was not fo quickly brought about, as fome perfons have imagined. It appears, indeed, from the *acts of the apoftles*, that the preaching of Saint Paul, and the converfion of the Gentiles, gave birth to a fyftem of chriftianity, more pure, and more difengaged from judaical obfervances; and yet Saint Peter remained, for a long while, attached to thefe laft; and the church of Jerufalem adhered fo obftinately to them, that Eufebius pofitively afferts, that there was, in this city, a fucceffion of fifteen circumcifed bifhops.(d) The church, or the congregation(e) of Jerufalem had not, therefore, renounced the law of Mofes, although the preaching of Jefus Chrift was admitted. There is even every appearance, that the

Jews,

(d) See Hift. Eccl. l. 4. c. 5.

(e) The church, in Greek, Εκκλησια, fignifies an affembly, a congregation.

Jews, having been, for a long time, settled
at Rome, maintained a great influence over
the newly-rising state of christianity. This
may be seen from the letter ascribed to Saint
Clement, the Pope, and supposed to have been
written before the conquest of Jerusalem.
This letter doth not, in any manner, treat
of the tenets introduced by Jesus Christ, except that tenet, relative to the resurrection,
which was known to the Jews before ; and
this too is supported by the example of the
Phenix, a subject much more properly belonging to fable than to the gospel. The
principal point, into which Saint Clement
enters, is the ecclesiastical discipline which
had been disturbed at Corinth, by a sedition
amongst the faithful. He, very forcibly, and
with great latitude, inculcates an hierarchical
subordination ; but he draws all his arguments
from that subordination established at Jerusalem. He saith: " the high priest, the
sacrificing priests, and the Levites have all
their several functions. The Laity are obliged to follow the necessary precepts, &c."
A perpetual sacrifice is not offered in all
places ;

places ; nor is the facrifice of prayer, and for fin offered, except at Jerufalem. *(f)*

Thefe paffages clearly prove the union of the primitive Chriftians, with the metropolis of judaifm, and the temple of Jerufalem. In more than an age afterwards, Saint Juftin declares, that a man may be faved, if he obferve the fabbath ; but he adds that, the deftruction of the temple of Jerufalem hath rendered facrifices impoffible. *(g)* Origen, in his defence againft Celfus, violently repels the reproach of defertion, with which they were loaden, who forfook the law of Mofes; *h)* he anfwers, that they, who embraced the faith of Jefus Chrift, never quitted the ancient law ; that they called themfelves only Ebionites, that is, beggars, receivers of alms; *(i)* that Saint Peter was always attached

T 3   to

(f) See Hift. Eccl. de M. Fleury, tom. 1. 4to, p. 248.

(g) See his dialogue with Tripho.

(h) See l. 2. adverfus Celfum.

(i) The fpirit of charity and alms-giving which manifefted itfelf, from the firft appearance of chriftianity, hath contributed, not a little, to facilitate its progrefs. Under a defpotic government, like the government over which the emperors prefided, there muft neceffarily.

have

to the ancient law; that he even refused to confer with the Gentiles, left he might have alarmed the Jews; and that Saint Paul faith himself, that he became a Jew for the advantage

---

have been many indigent perfons and beggars; under a government, ftill preferving the traces of ariftocracy, foreigners, and newly-introduced individuals, could not avoid the being involved in many humiliating circumftances. The firft found a refource in the enjoyment of a fhare from the offerings. The laft received fome confolation from thofe ideas of equality and brotherhood which reigned amongft the Chriftians.

It feems as if the heathens were but little affected with this chriftian charity, which, indifcriminately, received with open arms, all conditions, all ages, and particularly the two fexes. On the contrary, they took, from hence, an advantage, to reproach the Chriftians with having difperfed their dogmas, only, either amongft children and filly women, *mulierculis*, or amongft the loweft artifans, fuch as coblers, dyers, &c. It may be feen, with what confidence, Origen (l. 3.) refutes this objection, by fhewing that, although thefe affemblies might have appeared contemptible, from the manner in which they were compofed, yet their object was facred and fublime; and that, after all, it was no great misfortune, if thofe children, whom they faw running to them, did efcape from their frivolous tutors, who were only capable of teaching them fables, &c. Such as wifh to fee a fuller account of the fituation of the primitive Chriftians, muft confult the learned differtation, by Mr. Lami, *de eruditione Apoftolorum.*

vantage of the Jews.(k) In fhort, it feems,
as if this wife man thought that the law fhould
fubfift, until the eyes of mankind might be
fufficiently opened, to difcern the myftical
meaning of the fcripture, and to underftand
all thofe figures concealed under vulgar expreffions. It is in this fenfe, that he cites a
paffage from the gofpel, in which Jefus
Chrift faith to his difciples: "adhuc multa
habeo vobis dicere, fed non poteftis portare
modo. Cum autem venerit fpiritus veritatis,
docebit vos omnem veritatem." "I have as
yet many things to fay unto you, but ye cannot bear them now; howbeit, when He, the
fpirit of truth is come, He will guide you into
all truth." (St. John, c. 16. v. 12. 13.) Ori-

T 4   .   gen

---

forum, in which he proyes, that the apoftles and difciples
were not only fimple and unpolifhed men, but that even
fome criminals were found amongft them. He, alfo,
difcovers beyond a contradiction, that the gofpels are
filled with errors in language, &c. Some learned men
have obferved that if the Vulgate Bible was written in
fuch bad Latin, it was, chiefly, becaufe the tranflation
was intended for thofe who did not underftand a more
elegant Latin.

(k) "Unto the Jews, I became as a Jew, that I
might gain the Jews." 1 Cor. c. 9. v. 20. Two paffages in the Acts confirm this circumftance. C. 16. v.
3. C. 21. v. 21, &c. K.

gen doth not fcruple to affert, that all the
chriftian doctrine is not comprifed in the Gofpel, Jefus Chrift having found his difciples
too·ignorant to receive the explanation of
the figurative and myftical fenfe of the
fcripture. (*l*)

Neverthelefs, the period was already arrived, at which the chriftians were to feparate
them-

(*l*) It were to be wifhed, that a paffion for the in-
terpretation.of figures and prophecies had not carried
the moft celebrated authors too far. I could indeed
furnifh a multitude of examples of the abufes which
have refulted from.this paffion, but I fhall content myfelf with producing only fome few inftances, and, folely
with the intention of proving how neceffary it is that a
writer fhould have recourfe to his reafon, even in the
very moment, when he has the ftrongeft grounds for
fuppofing himfelf infpired. St. Juftin introduces in his
firft apology, this paffage from Genefis, " non deficiet
princeps ex Juda, nec dux a femore ejus, donec veniat,
qui repofitus eft," or rather, "qui ftatutus eft," or
any expreffion, (for Le Clerc, in his " bibliotheque
choifie," hath proved that this paffage was fufpected to
have been interpolated,) " et ipfe erit expectatio gen-
tium, ligans ad vitem pullum fuum, et lavans in fanguine uvæ ftolam fuam." " A prince of the race of
Judah fhall not be wanting, nor a chief, iffuing from
his thigh, (or from his thighs) until he fhall come, who
is appointed to come; and he fhall be the expectation
of nations, binding his foal unto the vine, and wafhing
his

themfelves, entirely, from the Jews. After
the deftruction of the temple of Jerufalem,
there no longer remained a point of re-union
for thofe who continued attached to the ancient law. The centre of the Judaical Ca-
tholicity (if I may be allowed the expreffion)
could

---

his robe in the blood of the grape."* Now, according
to St. Juftin, thefe words, " binding his foal unto the
vine," mean Jefus Chrift, who, before he made his
entry into Jerufalem, unloofed an afs, which was tied
to the foot of the vine; "lavans in fanguine uvæ," the
blood of the grape fignifies the blood of Jefus Chrift,
who, not being made up of human blood, is better cha-
racterifed by the blood of the grape; " et ftolam ejus"
his tunic, his robe, allude to the faithful, who compofe, as it were, the cloathing of Jefus Chrift. Saint
Juftin doth not ftop even at this fingular commentary.
He faith, that the demons, in order to deceive mankind, have imitated all thefe figures in a fable of their
own

* *In our Englifh tranflation of the Bible, (Gen. c. 49. v.
10. 11) the paffage rvns thus: " the fceptre fhall not depart
from Judab, nor a lawgiver from between his feet, until
Shiloh come, and unto him fhall the gathering of the people be.
Binding his foal unto the vine, and his affes colt unto the choice
vine, he wafhed his garments in wine, and his clothes in the
blood of grapes." If the reader be defirous of perufing a very
learned explanation, he need only be informed, that the celebrated bifhop of Gloucefter hath written the Divine Legation.
The third and fourth fections of the fifth book, and the firft
parts of the fourth volume, abound with ftrokes of erudition,
peculiar to this right reverend author. It may, alfo, be proper to refer to the " letters on the Septuagint" by Mr.
Spearman. K.*

could no more recover itfelf: it was become
impoffible to facrifice at Jerufalem: the means,
therefore, of obferving the ancient law, were
all exterminated. It is this argument, which
St. Juftin employs againft Tripho; and it is
this argument, of which Tertullian hath alfo
availed

own produćtion. Thus, they have mentioned Bacchus,
as alluded to, in the paffage, "ligans ad vitem pullum
fuum, et lavans in fanguine uvæ," "binding unto the
vine, &c." "In faćt, (he adds) as they knew not
whether pullum figniñed a foal, or the colt of an afs,
they have introduced an afs into the myfteries of Bacchus; (probably the afs of Silenius:, and not to be de-
tećted in an error, in cafe that pullum fignified a foal,
they have alfo introduced the horfe Pegafus. With the
fame view, they have compofed the hiftory of Hercules,
to correfpond with that paffage relative to David,
"fortis ut Gigas." It is true (he proceeds) that they
have not mentioned the crofs; but to fupply this defećt
in prophecies and fables, God hath chofen that this
fign of redemption fhould be reprefented every where;
as in fhips, the mafts and yards of which form the fhape
of a crofs; amongft the implements of agriculture,
fuch as the rake; and even in the fhape of the human
frame, which is deftined to be upright like a pillar,
whilft the nofe, with the reft of the body, reprefents a
kind of crofs." The fame author, conftantly employed in difcovering the fymbol of the crofs, obferves, in
another place, that the Pafchal lamb fhould be eaten
roafted, becaufe a lamb on the gridiron, or the fpit,
refembles the figure of a crucified man.

Laĉtantius

availed himfelf, after him. Chriftianity muft
then have drawn a double advantage from
this event; for whilft it gave a mortal wound
to the Jews, by deftroying their political and
religious

Lactantius, that elegant and learned writer, falls into
the fame abfurdity, when he faith, that carnal circumcifion is no more than the figure of the fpiritual circumcifion, which difcovers the heart; for, according
to his opinion, there exifts a certain exterior likenefs
between the part which circumcifion lays open, and
the figure of a heart. " Quoniam pars illa que cir-
cumciditur, habet quandam fimilitudinem cordis."
(Inft. l. 4.)

Of all the ecclefiaftical authors, Origen is the moft
attached to the figurative fenfe. He feems to have involved this fyftem, even in cabaliftical ideas; for, in
refuting Celfus, who maintains that it is not ridiculous
to invoke the divinity by every kind of name, fuch as
Adonaï, Jupiter, Jehovah, &c. he afferts, that all the
names of the Patriarchs are myftical, or cabaliftical;
and that an invocation of demons could never fucceed,
if, inftead of making ufe of the names of Abraham,
Ifaac, and Jacob, they were to go through with it, in
the name of *Father of men, Wreftler, Chofen Being,* &c.

Even Saint Cyprian is not free from this reproach,
when, infifting upon the neceffity of confecrating the
wine, he faith, that Melchifedeck had confecrated
wine, and that Jefus Chrift, who is a facrificer of an
order, fuperior to Melchifedeck, cannot, properly,
confecrate with water: that as wine diffipates uneafinefs, fo the blood of our Lord drives away the old man;
that water reprefents the people; and the mixture of
the

religious empire, it prepared, at the-fame
time, new arms, wherewith to encounter Polytheifm, by fending out, into all the provinces of the empire, a great number of
men,

---

the two liquors, the union of Jefus Chrift, with the
church. (See hift. eccl. de Fleury, tom. 2. p. 190.)
But, Saint Barnabas, or the compofer of the letters
which pafs under his name, hath, if poffible, gone beyond all thefe abfurdities. He perceives within the
number of three hundred and eighteen perfons, whom
Abraham caufed to be circumcifed, the name of Jefus,
expreffed in a cypher, and his crofs reprefented by the
letter *Tau*, which enters into the cypher. In the three
conftitutions of Mofes, or rather in his prohibitions
againft the eating of unclean animals, he difcovers a
concealed precept, which he explains thus : " non le-
porem manducabis" " thou fhalt not eat of the hare,"
fignifies, thou fhalt not defile boys ; becaufe the hare,
or probably, the rabbit, every year makes a new hole.
" Belluam non manducabis," " thou fhalt not eat of
any wild beaft" fignifies, thou fhalt not be an adulterer,
lafcivious, becaufe the wild beafts (he undoubtedly
meant the hyæna) partake of the two fexes, and alter-
nately enjoy each. "Muftellam non manducabis,"
" thou fhalt not eat of the weafel," fignifies, thou fhalt
not proftitute thy mouth to the moft infamous of pol-
lutions, (the text is much plainer) "for the muftella, or
weafel, brings forth at the mouth." Here phyfic and
natural hiftory are as much at a fault as logic. It is
needlefs to extend this note any farther, as it, already,
fufficiently marks out the fpirit, in which the authors of
the firft ages of the church have drawn up their writings.

men, whofe religion was founded on Deifm, and whofe opinions approached much nearer to the doctrine of the Chriftians, than to the fables of Paganifm.

Many authors, aftonifhed at the filence of all the hiftorians, with regard to the Jewifh nation, have concluded themfelves juftified in fuppofing them to have been a poor, defpifed, and wandering multitude; but they muft acknowledge, that if their origin was obfcure, yet ample amends were made for this difadvantage, by their fubfequent condition. If we may credit Jofephus, the population of Judæa, confidering the fmall extent of this province, was very great; but feveral writers, lefs fufpected of partiality, than Jofephus, affert that, under the firft emperors, the Jews had fpread themfelves through Paleftine, Syria, Cilicia, a great part of the Archipelago, and almoft all Afia Minor. They had formed eftablifhments in moft of the great cities, but particularly at Cæfarea, at Alexandria, and even at Rome. But, after the bloody wars of Titus, and of Vefpafian, a ftill greater number came pouring in, amongft the provinces of the empire. The majority of thefe Jews, whether difperfed, and fugitives, or
whether

whether fettled, during a long period, in the
commercial cities, fo far from having been
concerned in the death of Jefus Chrift, were
even ignorant of his name. And as till then,
they had been attached to their religion, folely by thofe relations, which they preferved
with their Jerufalem, and by the cuftom of
either, fometimes going, or fending proxies
to offer facrifices in the temple, it became
eafy for them to accomodate themfelves to
the new law, which proved the inutility of
thefe facrifices, and which feemed fo fully
juftified by the event. But, whether they
confented to embrace the chriftian faith, or
whether they perfifted in the obfervation of
their ceremonies, and their dogmas, their
contempt for the Gods of the heathens, and
their averfion, from the mode in which thefe
Gods were worfhipped, fupplied the two religions with fufficient matter for reciprocal
and fatirical abufe. Hence, it hath happened, that the profane writers frequently confounded the Jews, and the Chriftians together, in thofe charges of atheifm, which
they have, on feveral occafions, levelled
againft them; but thefe odious imputations,
defigned, at all times, to irritate the people,
and

and fpur on the magiftrates, brought over feveral new converts to chriftianity.*(m)*

Many philofophers, who beheld with indignation, thofe fables with which the common people were amufed, and were weary of the vain difputes of the fchools, felt a growing partiality towards a religion, the bafis of which was the eftablifhed notion of the exiftence of ONE ALMIGHTY AND ONLY GOD. They foon endeavoured to unite themfelves with the Chriftians ; and they were not

lefs

(m) Much may be faid, concerning the manner in which the Chriftian religion was affected, by the deftruction of the temple of Jerufalem. A modern writer hath very ingenioufly obferved, that the clergy drew from this circumftance, an advantageous opportunity of increafing their own confequence. For the bifhops, or infpectors, *Epifcopoi*, the elders, or honourable perfons, *Prefbuteroi*, and the overfeers, or attending priefts, *Diaconoi*, who were but the minifters of a fociety, confidering equality as their firft principle, did not hefitate to liken themfelves to the Jewifh hierarchy ; the firft comparing themfelves to the great Pontiffs, the fecond to the priefts, *Sacerdotes*, and the laft to the Levites. "Cum poft urbem Hierofolymam denuò everfam, fpes omnis Judæis adempta effet rempublicam fuam inftaurandi, Epifcopi fimiles tum videri volebant Pontificis maximi Judæorum, Prefbites eodem quo facerdotes loco verfari dicebantur, Diaconi cum Levitis comparabantur. (Mofhemii inftit. Hift. Eccl. fect. 2. p. 2.)

lefs ftricken with the fimplicity of their doctrine, than with the mildnefs of their moral
fyftem. No fuperftition, no facrifices, no
exterior worfhip were found amongft them ;
the faithful were, then, fatisfied, if they affembled, from time to time, in fome great
hall, and moft frequently, at the houfes of
their particular friends : there, the Elder
(*Preſbus*) inftructed them in the moft familiar
manner ; this cuftom was either preceded, or
followed by fome lecture, taken out of the
Gofpel, or the Bible ; and the whole was
concluded with a fimple repaft, made up of
fuch offerings, as the faithful, each according to his abilities, had brought, whilft the
poor and the rich fat down, promifcuoufly,
to the fame meal. The bread, and the wine
were always bleffed by the Elder, and this
entertainment was either followed, or accompanied by fome canticles, in praife of God.(*n*)

Equality

(*n*) The form of the Chriftian affemblies, afterwards,
underwent fome alteration. The perfecutions to which
the faithful were expofed, frequently obliged them to
affemble before the break of day, in order to avoid the
being difcovered. They were, then, contented with
making their oblations, and bleffing the bread and
wine. The repaft was either neglected, or put off till
night,

Equality amongft mankind, charity, beneficence, and the diftributing of alms, were,
at once, recommended, and practifed, in
thefe pious affemblies: where could humanity,
where could true philofophy have feen a more
refpectable object ?

But chriftianity began to break loofe from
her once exclufive connexion, with fimple
and obfcure individuals. The fpirit of difcuffion, fo oppofite to the fpirit of charity,

VOL. I,   U   had

---

night, and a convenient place of meeting was fixed on,
againft that time. Two reafons rendered this arrangement neceffary ; firft, becaufe to have eaten early on
the morning muft have been an extraordinary circumftance, and efpecially, when this was done in com-
memoration of the laft fupper of Jefus Chrift; fecondly, becaufe the Chriftians were fearful, left it fhould
be perceived, that they had drunk wine before the hour
of dinner, the which circumftance, not being ufual,
might have detected them. When they afterwards began to enjoy more tranquility, they continued to affemble on the morning, and to diftribute the bread and
wine, as foon as their oblations and prayers were concluded. The divine fervice was then divided into two
parts: the *Catachumenes,* the Strangers, *Audientes,* the
Penitents, *Lugentes,* or *Hyemantes,* were admitted during
the lectures, and fome of the prayers, which were, for
the moft part, in the form of our litanies: they were,
then, fent away; and this was called " Miffa Cathecu-
menorum,"

had found means to introduce itſelf amongſt
the faithful, who, either compelled by perſecutions, to examine more narrowly into
their dogmas, or encouraged, and tempted
by their firſt ſucceſs, to engage in controverſy,
were ſoon obſerved to make their appearance
in public, and to grow familiar with the
ſchools. Platoniſm was, at that time, the
moſt faſhionable doctrine, amongſt the philoſophical dogmatiſts. It was, indeed, becoming corrupt, and ſo mingled with ideas
of

---

menorum," the diſmiſſion of the Catachumens. Then,
began the prayers, which were followed by a long
thanſgiving, or the *Euchariſt*, ευχαριϛιᾳ επι το πολλυ, and
the communion; after which the faithful were diſ-
miſſed; and this was called " Miſſa fidelium."

We muſt, however, confeſs that ſome abuſes crept
into theſe aſſemblies of the firſt Chriſtians, all ſacred
and reſpectable as they may appear to us. The biſhops
frequently reproached the rich, with having brought to
the repaſt and to the communion, nice meats, which
they reſerved, ſolely, for themſelves; whilſt the poor
had ſcarcely enough to ſatisfy their hunger. The contrary, ſometimes, happened, and the poor partook ſo
plentifully of the offerings, as to become intoxicated,
and that ſo violently, that it was neceſſary to carry them
away.

Conſult, on the foregoing ſubject of all this note,
the apology of Saint Juſtin, the letters of Pliny, and
Bingham's antiquities of the church, b. 15. &c.

of the force of Theurgy, or Magic, as to
have degenerated into a kind of fuperftitious
fyftem ; but yet the firft principle of this
philofophy was, conftantly, the eftablifhed
notion of ONE ETERNAL AND ONLY
GOD, who had acted upon matter, and given
a form to the chaos. Plato imagined that
God, who comprehended within Himfelf,
an univerfal idea of all poffible things, could
not have manifefted himfelf, but by means
of a Thought, an *Active Reafon*, which He
called the Son of God, His Firft-Born, His
Word, (λογος.) It was by the Word, that
God had placed in the World a vivifying
Spirit, an active foul. It was by the Word,
that Man had been created, and that a Soul
had fallen to his lot. It was by the Word,
alfo, that the univerfe had been peopled with
Genii, and Demons, (Δαιμονοι) who occupied the fpace between God, inhabiting
the upper regions, and man, dwelling on the
furface of the earth. Thefe ideas, borrowed, in a great meafure, from the Gymnofo-
phifts,(o) tallied much more eafily with
Chriftianity, than with the Materialifm of
U 2 Ariftotle,

***

(o) See Hyde, Holwell, &c.

Ariſtotle, and the atoms of Epicurus. Hence, aroſe that eagerneſs, with which the majority of the Fathers of the Church, ſo haſtily, availed themſelves of theſe ideas: hence aroſe that reſpect, and even that enthuſiaſm, with which they mentioned the divine Plato;(p) ſome aſſerting that God had revealed to him His Myſteries; others declaring that he had been in Judæa, and there received the know-ledge of His doctrine: but, to the laſt opi-nion, even Saint Auguſtin, in ſpite of his great veneration for this philoſopher, could not, poſſibly, ſubſcribe; nay, this author hath taken the pains to collect authorities, from which he proves, that Plato died long before the tranſlation of the Septuagint had enabled the Greeks to underſtand the books of Moſes.(q)

As

(p) See " de civitate Dei. l. 8. c. 2."

(q) All the works of the firſt fathers of the church, breathe the ſpirit of Platoniſm. Saint Juſtin expreſsly ſaith, that if he quitted the ſchools, in which the doc-trine of Plato was taught, it was not on account of its being contrary to the doctrine of the Chriſtians, but becauſe it was not entirely the ſame. " Non equidem quod alienæ ſunt a Chriſto Platonis doctrinæ, ſed quod non ſunt ex omni parte ſimiles." (Apolog. 1.) This philoſophy, involved in ſuch a ſimilitude to chriſtianity,

main-

As enthufiafm and fubtlety continually leap over all bounds, fome difadvantages, of courfe, refulted from this union between philofophy, and religion. In fact, if a fmall number of fimple and upright fouls were entrufted with the prefervation of the faith, yet the world was full of *Platonic Chriftians*, and

U 3   *Chriftian*

---

maintained an influence even over opinions, refpecting worfhip, or, to fpeak more properly, over the notions of the relation between the creature, and the Creator; to this philofophy, Quietifm feems indebted for its origin, as Saint Auguftin exprefsly afferts, that, according to the Platonic fyftem, the Philofopher ought to be in love with God; and that he who fhall have thus loved God, will be entitled to enjoy him. "Ipfum autem verum, ac fummum bonum Plato dicit Deum, unde vult effe philofophum amatorem Dei, ut quoniam philofophia ad beatam viam tendit, fruens Deo fit beatus qui Deum amaverit." (de civ. Dei. l. 8. c. 8.)

Origen; whofe character is that of having violated every principle, hath perverted the Platonic philofophy, more than any of the ecclefiaftical writers. I fhall only produce one example, from amongft a thoufand; it is taken from his Apology, (book 6.) where, quoting thefe very obfcure words of Plato; " in rebus omnibus quas ad fcientiam adhibere neceffe eft, tria funt, quartum autem ipfamet fcientia: horum primum eft nomen, alterum fermo, tertium idolum, quartum fcientia:" three things are neceffary to facilitate the attainment of knowledge, which is but the fourth thing; firft the

name,

Chriftian Platonifts. A paffion for Metaphyfics foon became connected with a paffion for Magic, and then, every thing was involved in controverfies, and in prodigies. Hence fprang thofe fchifins, and herefies, which, even in the moft profperous times, threw the church into divifions, and armed her children againft

---

name, fecondly, the difcourfe, or the word, thirdly, the image, or the figure, and fourthly, knowledge, or fcience. Origen obferves, that the Chriftians adopted the fame principle, and that Saint John, the Baptift, is the name, the voice, "vox clamantis in deferto;" Jefus Chrift, the difcourfe, or the word; that the fenfible form, ("forma quæ in anima impreffa manet poftquam in illa Chriftus fuum verbum, fua vulnera impreffit") anfwers to the image, or the figure, and in fhort, that the fame is, alfo, fcience or knowledge. It is this Platonic delirium, which makes Origen conftantly believe that the Angels, enjoyed within themfelves, a portion of the Divinity. He faith, "the reafon why I do not adore them, is, becaufe I have thought that, as men are frequently deceived, either by their own ideas, or by the miftakes of others, fo amongft the fouls, which have quitted the bodies, in which they refided, amongft even the Angels, and the Demons, fome may be found, who, feduced by certain probabilities, or led aftray by fome fophiftry, might become capable of pretending to be Gods. Now, as it is difficult for men to unravel all this myftery, the plaineft, and beft method is, to offer no adoration, to any beings of this order.

against each other. The sincerity of plain
dealing was soon sunk amidst the implacable
violence which infected the theological dis-
putes. Perplexed in their endeavours to support a set of frivolous and obscure opinions,
they were obliged to have recourse to artifice:
and as the simplicity of the true Christian
doctrine, disdained to mingle with all these
cavillings, they counterfeited books, and
forged the oracles of the Sibyls. Unfortunately, these illusions were not only elevated into credit, by a false and extravagant
zeal; but it too frequently happened, that
authors, reputable in every other respect,
fell into the snare, and thus, brought into
question the truths, which they were anxious
to inculcate. It is a matter of concern, to
observe such a writer, as Lactantius,(r) confidently, quoting passages from the works of
Mercurius Trismegistus, and the books of
the Erythræan Sibyl; productions acknowledged to have been counterfeited, and in
which the forgery betrays itself, by the bad
policy of their authors, who were so absurd
as to express their meaning, more clearly,

U 4   than

(r) See Instit. l. 4.

than all the ancient Prophets have expreſſed theirs.

The misfortune, entailed upon the majority of the Ecclefiaſtical writers, of the three firſt ages, of having fallen into ſome herefy, may be confidered as a puniſhment, inflicted upon them, becauſe they abandoned the ſimplicities of the Gofpel, for the ſubtleties of the ſchools. Indeed, not to mention the opinion of the Millenarians, which was, almoſt generally received amongſt them, it is evident, that, at one time, they maintained the Metempfycofis, or the tranfmigration of ſouls, into the bodies of animals; (a doctrine embraced by Saint Juſtin) *(s)* at another time, they aſſerted, (witneſs Tertullian) that the ſoul, and even God were material; *(t)* and,

---

(s) " Qui autem videndi (Deum) facultate indigni judicati funt, quidnam inquit (Triphon) patiuntur? in aliquo ferarum corpore velut in carcere vinciuntur, atque id ſupplicium eorum eſt." He faith, alfo, that ſouls, being created, as the world was created, are, like the world, periſhable. " Quâ de cauſâ, et moriuntur, et puniuntur." (Dialog.)

(t) " Nos autem animam corporalem, et hic profitemur, et in fuo volumine probamus habentem proprium genus ſubſtantiæ, et ſoliditatis, per quam quid, et fentire, et pati poſſit." And, in another place, " quis negabit Deum eſſe corpus? &c."

and, at another time, they denied, with Arnobius, the creation of man; and invalidated
the teftimonies from Genefis, relative to the
creation of the world.*(u)* With refpect to
all this, it may be remarked, that fuch hath
conftantly been the fate of thofe writers, who
were free, to follow the bent of their under-
ftandings; and that, if the fathers of the
church, in thefe later ages, have not met
with the fame misfortune, they were, in a
great

(*u*) See l. 2. adverfus gentes, where he obferves that,
perhaps, an infinity of ages hath paffed away, fince the
world was created; that it is impoffible to know the
defigns of God; and facrilege to believe, that he created men, fince experience proves, that they are very
wicked, and much inclined to evil.* It is fingular
that Arnobius, a well inftructed author, and who wrote
at the conclufion of the third age, fhould have been
ignorant of the doctrine of original fin.

* *If I am not miftaken, the learned author, in this place,*
alludes to the following paffage in Arnobius: " *fed procul ba-*
abeat fcelerata opinionis immanitas, ut Deus credatur om-
nipotens, magnarum, et invifibilium rerum Sator, et Con-
ditor, Procreator, tam mobiles animas genuiffe gravitatis, ac
ponderis, conftantiæque nullius: in vitia labiles, in pecca-
torum genera univerfa declives, &c." . . . . . . *I have taken*
the liberty to infert the Greek quotations in this laft note, ac-
cording to the original text. It is more than probable that the
paffages were written in the manufcript copy of this elegant
performance, exactly as they are, here, reftored, and that the
errors and omiffions have arifen, folely, from the negligence
of the printer. K.

great meafure, indebted for an exemption
from it, to the advantage of having known
the decifions of the Œcumenical church, and
to the happy neceffity, under which they
were laid, of fubmitting their reafon to the
canonical decrees.(*x*)

But,

(*x*) Before the patronage of the emperors permitted
the bifhops to affemble, and form œcumenical councils,
there was nothing, which could have ferved, as an eftablifhed rule, in the matter of doctrine. The church,
had, as yet, no vifible chief, whofe authority was acknowledged, or confirmed; for, fetting afide the privileges, which the bifhops of Rome might have claimed,
as the fucceffors of St. Peter, it is certain, that they
were, in fact, indebted, for their credit, to their pofition, that is, to the advantage which they enjoyed by
keeping their fee, at the capital. But, before the emperors had embraced the faith, and, particularly,
whilft they perfecuted it, this pre-eminence could not
have been very diftinguifhed. We may, indeed, perceive that, at the beginning of the fourth age, and at
the time of the celebrated quarrel between Donatus,
bifhop of Cafæ Nigræ, and Cæcilian, bifhop of Carthage,
Melchiades, the bifhop, or pope of Rome, (the two
words were fynonimous) having affembled a council at
Rome, the decrees of this council were not obferved;
fo that Conftantine was obliged to appoint another
council, to meet at Arles, at which council, pope Syl-
vefter did not affift, either in perfon, or by proxy; nor
did he even obtain any intelligence of its decrees, but
by common letter of advice, in which neither his affent,
nor

But, although thefe contradictions fomewhat expofed the reputation of the Chriftian
fchools, it muft be allowed, that they rendered them, from another quarter, very effential fervices; fince the new doctrine amply
regained, in a negative fenfe, the advantages
which it loft, in a pofitive fenfe. Saint Juftin,
Tatian,

---

nor his approbation were demanded. Eufebius, who
enters into a long detail of the hiftory of the Nicene
council, doth not appear to pay any attention to the
bifhop of Rome, and is fatisfied with merely obferving,
that "Της βασιλιυεσης πολιως ο μιν προισως υσιερι δια γηρας;
πρισβυτιροι δ' αυτε παροντις την αυτε ταξιν ιπληρουι. The bifhop of the royal city abfented himfelf on account of
his great age; fome of the elders, however, were prefent, who fupplied his place." (V. Eufeb. a Reading,
fol. v. 1. p. 580.) " Sozomenes hath written nearly
to the fame effect; Ιελιος δι οχ δια γηρας απιλιμπανι το,
but Julius, on account of his great age, was abfent."
(Sozomeni hift. fæc. 4. p. 34. c. 17. Reading, v. 2.)
If it fometimes happened that the metropolitan churches
were referred to, that they might fettle particular points
of doctrine, this was an advantage, which Rome only
enjoyed in common with the reft. Amidft a multitude
of authorities, which clearly prove it, I fhall cite one,
from Tertullian (de præfcriptione). This author, in-
forming us in what manner herefies are to be diftinguifhed, from the orthodox doctrine, faith, that recourfe muft be had to the traditions of the church;
" if in Achaia, confult Corinth; if in Macedonia,
confult Philippi, and Theffalonica; if in Afia, confult
Ephefus; and if in Italy, confult Rome."

Tatian, Minutius Felix, Origen, and Lactantius had examined, with the moſt ſcrupulous attention, all the dogmas of Paganiſm;
they had dared to pluck aſide the veil, which
covered this falſe religion; and as it frequently happens, that ideas, ſecretly ſpread-
ing themſelves through enlightened and judicious minds, wait but for the moment of
liberty, or the daring efforts of ſome author,
before they blaze out, at every point, and
avenge the rights of injured reaſon; ſo each
intelligent individual, who exiſted at that
period, read with avidity theſe intereſting
controverſies. It is even probable, that whilſt
ſuch controverſies beſtowed obligations, by
deſtroying prejudices at once ſo ridiculous,
and deeply rooted, they, at the ſame time,
ſtamped ſome degree of favour on the opinions, which were attempted to be eſtabliſhed
in their place.   In cheriſhing the Chriſtians,
men cheriſhed the enemies of the prieſts;
nor were they inſenſible of the kindneſs,
which they had received from them, by the
overthrow of ſo ancient an impoſture.   How
unfortunate a circumſtance muſt it have
proved, if a ſevere policy had, then, deprived us of thoſe learned productions, to
                                which,

which, amidſt many other valuable acquiſitions, we ſtand particularly indebted for the
precious illuſtrations of antiquity, and the
enlightened memorials of the long empire of
ſuperſtition! happily, the proſcription againſt
books, did not begin till towards the end of
the third age; for, although the philoſophical emperors, ſuch as Trajan, Antoninus,
and Marcus Aurelius, too rigorouſly, called
to an account, a ſect, whom they ought to
have tolerated, yet they never levelled their
perſecutions againſt the works, which the
leaders of this ſect had compoſed. They
judged it more becoming, to treat with reſpect, thoſe mute and peaceable depoſitaries
of the ſentiments of mankind ; and they regarded them, as ſacred aſylums, open to
every ſyſtem, whether founded in error, or
conceived in the ſpirit of truth. The Chriſtians exclaimed violently againſt the new tyranny, to which their books were expoſed:
they reſiſted the ſearch of the inquiſitors,
with the moſt unſhaken reſolution, com-
priſing within their anathemas all the *Tra-
ditcres*, that is, thoſe who were ſo puſilla-
nimous as to ſacrifice their books or bibles
to the magiſtrates.

As

As to the reſt, Perſecution ſerved only to caſt an additional luſtre over the reputation of the Chriſtians. Under a deſpotic government, every act of ſeverity is, at once, deemed unjuſt. And who, indeed, could have beheld without concern, the fate of theſe unhappy wretches, daily dragged to the tribunal of ſome freed-man, ſome creature lifted into place, who, inveſted with the title either of Pretor, or of Proconſul, concluded that he had a right to give laws to opinion, and paſs his judgement on the conſcience of another? Thus, all, except thoſe fanatics who had been infected by the ſuggeſtions of the prieſts, pitied and encouraged the Chriſtians, whoſe writings, every where, recommended that toleration which Jeſus Chriſt had taught them, and which, from the peculiarity of their lot, it was their intereſt to preach of. They were particularly careful to flee from the preſence of tyrannical magiſtrates; and they travelled into the remoteſt provinces of the empire, in order to reveal their dogmas to plain and untutored minds. They deſcribed a God of peace, a God, who conſidered all mankind as his children; and who admitted not of any difference

ʾerence between them, whether they were nobles, or plebeians, Romans, or Barbarians, free, or in flavery. Thus, was Chriſtianity extended throughout the provinces, but principally in Spain and Gaul, where it was fo generally propagated, that although Conſtantius, Chlorus, and Conſtantine, his ſucceſſor, did not totally embrace it, yet they thought it good policy to countenance it, with their favour, and to avail themſelves of it, in oppoſition to the preponderating influence of Dioclefian and Galerius.

As we have, now, carried our reflections, down to that important æra, in which, Conſtantine, having united in a ſubmiſſion to his laws, the largeſt empire that ever exiſted, employed his whole power, to render Chriſtianity the ruling religion, we ſhall, for a moment, fix our attention on the reign of this prince. Here, then, we conclude our remarks on Chriſtianity, the progreſs of which ceaſes to be extraordinary, when directed by the operations of the moſt powerful, and the moſt abſolute of all the emperors.

CHAP.

C H A P. IV.

On Conftantine.

THE fourth age of the church opened
under the moft unfortunate aufpices. An
empire divided amongft the chiefs of the
Barbarians, defolated by continual wars, and
ravaged by a foreign army; a religion, at
one moment, perfecuted by the prince, and
at another moment, tearing in pieces her own
entrails; now timid, now furious; then
weak, then fanatic; either condemned to
filence, or loft in herefies, conformably to
the caprice of fovereigns, and the revolutions
of the ftate; the deftruction of all public
morals; licentioufnefs, or defpotifm ufurp-
ing the place of a regular form of government;

ment; and avarice, and depredation feated on the tribunals, compofe the objects which fill up the picture, prefented to us, by the Roman empire, or rather, by the whole world. During this dreadful chaos, during this total overthrow of power and opinion, mankind waited in expectation of a mafter; one of thofe ferocious warriors, who, whilft he remained too formidable to dread an oppofition from the people, might prove equally invincible againft the attacks of rival nations, was all they afked for. Although no longer defirous of liberty, yet they were anxious to enjoy peace; the vigour of their minds was already bent; their intrepidity was·exhaufted; and whatfoever might have been the will of a defpot, an univerfal principle of adulation was prepared to adopt it. Dioclefian alike wearied with battles and with glory; at once loathing the occupations of a general, and the employments of a fovereign; but particularly difpleafed with the Romans, whofe bafenefs, and ingratitude he had experienced, defpifed the luftre, and apprehended the dangers, which furrounded the throne of the world, and this too, at a time when he was, of all others, the moft

Vol. I.   X   worthy

worthy of filling it. Unfortunately, he fore-
faw not, until it was too late, the part
which he was obliged to take ; but like a
commander, who difmantles the conquered
place before it be abandoned, he rendered
the poft, which he quitted, impoffible to be
maintained. The empire was divided into
four *diocefes,* or governments. An illufory
ballance of power had been eftablifhed,
amongft the chiefs, who under the titles of
either Cæfar, or Auguftus, prefided over the
feveral departments. The colleagues, united
only by illegal marriages, or forced adop-
tions, unavoidably, became mutual rivals;
and he who, firft, triumphed over his competitor, was fure of invefting himfelf, fhortly
afterwards, with the rank, and authority of
an univerfal monarch. It was under thefe
circumftances, that Conftantine, in the flower
of his age, and adorned with all the gifts of
nature, inherited a power, which Conftantius, his father, had made a favourite and de-
firable object. To reign, was, in fact, to
wage war. His firft exploits were directed
againft the Franks. A conqueror beyond the
Rhine, a peaceable fovereign amongft the
Gauls, he, quickly, fixed his views on Italy.
There

There, the fway of Maxentius was grown
deteftable. At once, cruel, and fuperftitious,
whilft he confulted the oracles, his hands
were imbrued in human blood. This period
was the empire of magic. Every place was
filled with the accounts of evocations, of facrifices, and of predictions. Whether, as
Eufebius faith, Conftantine, intimidated by
the inchantments of Maxentius, fought after
other arms, wherewith to oppofe him; or
whether his acquaintance with the difpofition
of a people, irritated by perfecutions, and inclined towards chriftianity, infpired him with
the idea of placing his fupport, upon a new
religion, it is certain that he was eager in tef-
tifying his averfion from thofe falfe deities,
and his attachment to the mode of worfhip,
peculiar to the Chriftians.

Nothing can be more obfcure, than the
hiftory of the *Labarum*, or crofs, which appeared to Conftantine, whilft he marched at
the head of his army. What hath been
written, either to confirm, or to confute this
circumftance, may be feen in a work publifhed by *Mr. Le Beau.(y)* I prefume it to

X 2   be

(y) Hift. du bas Emp. tom. 1.

be exceedingly clear, that the period, and the place, at which this event happened, are equally uncertain. Not only Origen, but all the profane hiftorians are filent, on the fub-ject.(z)   Even *Eufebius* doth not relate it, as a fact generally known, but as an incident mentioned to him by Conftantine ;(a) neither was there any vifible trace of the prodigious effect, which fuch a miracle ought to have produced, fince the army of this prince, ftill remained devoted to Paganifm, and fince he himfelf

---

(z) The author might have excepted the learned writers of the Univerfal Hiftory, whofe credulity, and complaifance have implicitly adopted from Eufebius, an account which that father only believed in part. K.

(a) Quod fi quidem ab alio quopiam diceretur, haud facile auditores fidem effent habituri. (*De vita Con-ftantini*, *lib.* 1. *cap.* 38. It is certain, that if Eufebius imagined that he was relating a fact, as fufficiently known, and as generally confeffed as this ought to have been, he would not either have written with fo much precaution, or have begun with agreeing, that if any other, except Conftantine, had mentioned this circum-ftance, his audience would not have given him much credit.   Thus the whole authenticity of this narrative, is confined to the teftimony of two perfons; the one, probably inftigated either by enthufiafm, or policy; and the other engaged by fituation, and 'intereft, to re-ceive the ftory, as a truth.

himfelf did not declare that he was become a
Chriftian, until fome time afterwards. It is
not, therefore, without reafon, that this hiftory hath been often called in queftion, and
confidered as a *picus fraud,*(b) which is the
worft of all falfities, becaufe by poifoning
even the very fource of truth, it expofes the
moft facred authorities, to all thofe doubts
which profane writers are fo ready to caft
upon them. But, whatever may have happened, it is a pofitive truth, that Conftantine
granted to the Chriftians, a protection fo
ftrikingly marked, that the firft ufe, which
he made of his victory over Maxentius, was
to engage Licinius to proclaim an act of toleration in their favour.

It is at this period, that we may fix the
beginning of the epoch, which we fhould
ftile the fine age of the church, if the difputes, the cabals, the fchifms, and the cruel
and extravagant errors, with which he was
agitated, had not tarnifhed the luftre of thefe
profperous days. Here, bifhops accufed bifhops of having ftolen the facred veffels, whilft
a woman gave away the chief fee in Africa.

X 3   There

(b) See Echard's Roman hiftory.

There, Chriftians, fcarcely efcaped from one
perfecution, carried on a fecond, ftill more
cruel than the firft; againft themfelves, by
turns reproaching one another, either with
defertion, or with treafon.(c)   And here, a
fet of zealots, lefs ambitious indeed, but
more fanatic, had fubftituted barbarity in the
place of outrage : it is impoffible to reflect
without horror, on thofe heretics, called
Circumcelliones, a kind of Maniacs, who, mif-
taking the words, *praife be to God*, for a fignal
to rally together, and not daring to tranfgrefs the precept of the gofpel, which for-
bade them to draw the fword, knocked down
with clubs, all thofe who refufed to embrace
their tenets ; and were fometimes fo tranfported with madnefs, as to precipitate themfelves into the fea ; as if there had been contagions, peculiar to the mind, as well as the
body ; and as if cruelty towards others, and
towards themfelves, had been as much a difeafe attending on the ignorant and fuperftitious man, as the leprofy is a diforder, which
naturally vifits the poor and the uncleanly
man.   No church enjoyed tranquility, no
afylum

(c) See Hift. eccl. de Fleury tom. 2.

afylum remained, in which peace, and charity could have refided; for, although the
controverfies which difturbed Afia, were not
attended with fuch cruel effects, as thofe controverfies by which the Eaft, Europe, and
Africa were torn, yet they were much more
vain and frivolous. I am pleafed with that
ingenuous manner, in which Eufebius writes,
when he relates thofe quarrels, which arofe,
at the time, when the paffover was to be celebrated. "Every one (faith he) differed in
opinion, from another; no two perfons could
agree about the ceremonies of religion, nor
was an individual found, who knew what remedy to apply; for amidft fuch a multitude
of different counfels, there was not the leaft
reafon advanced, why the fcale fhould be inclined more to the one, than to the other
fide."(d)

X 4   And

(d) "Itaque cum omnes ubique populi jam dudum
inter fe diffiderent, et facri religionis noftræ ritus con-
turbarentur, mortalium quidem nemo erat qui huic
malo remedium poffet adhibere, cum utrinque inter fe
diffentientes velut æquatâ lancê controverfia penderet."
I cannot refift the opportunity of introducing, on this
occafion, a paffage from Arnobius, which feems to be
.exceedingly

And yet, thefe internal diforders did not prevent Chriftianity from acquiring frefh vigour. In fpite of a reciprocal hatred, in fpite of a diverfity of opinions, the favour of the fovereign, and the extinction of Paganifm, was, as it were, the rallying point, to which every fect equally tended. The ecclefiaftical authority hath never been refufed to thofe princes, who countenanced the ecclefiaftics. Conftantine, fcarcely a Catechumen, and as yet half a Barbarian, ftained in his reputation, by feveral parricides, and furrounded with concubines, and an illegitimate offspring, was foon confidered as an oracle, in all matters

---

exceedingly judicious. *" Where (faith he, b. 2.) is the opinion, fo rational, and fo plaufible, that the fpirit of controverfy cannot fhake it ? can any pofition be fo abfurd, as to render fpecious arguments, incapable of fupporting it ? when a perfon is once convinced, either of the truth, ur of the falfity of any thing, he,

* *Quid eſt enim quod humana ingenia labefactare ſtudio contradiⳡionis non audeant ? quamvis illud quod infirmare moliuntur, fit purum, et liquidum, et veritatis obſignatione munitum ? aut quid rurſus aſſerere veriſimilibus argumentis non queunt, quamvis fit apertiſſimè falſum, quamvis evidens, manifeſtumque mendacium? cum enim fibi perſuaſerit quis eſſe aliquid, aut non eſſe, amat quod opinatur aſſerere, et acumine alios anteire, maximè ſi agatur res ſummota, et abdita, et caligine involuta naturæ. Arnob. l. 2.*

ters relating to doctrine. His mediation was invoked, during each controverfy, and his prefence was defired at every council. Nay, to fuch a length were thefe things carried, that he was requefted to deliver out fermons and paftoral inftructions. The reward of fo much adulation was the prefcription pronounced foon afterwards againft the Gods, their temples, and their minifters. Chriftianity oppreffed, preached in favour of toleration; but Chriftianity, when rendered the ruling religion, became intolerant in her turn; and the bifhops, at once forgetting the precepts

---

he, immediately, from a paffion for difputation, becomes attached to his own idea, and foon feeks, folely, to acquire a fuperiority over his adverfary, by dint of the powers of the imagination, and by fubtlety; efpecially when fome obfcure queftion, involved by its nature, in darknefs, is the point in debate." Such remarks frequently fall from the pen of this excellent author. It were to be wifhed that thofe, who, like him, have written in favour of religion, had been guided by the fame fpirit of difcernment and toleration. Bold, and earneft, whilft he refutes paganifm, and the ancient philofophy; modeft, and cautious, whenfoever new doctrines are to be eftablifhed, reducing all to the belief of ONE ONLY GOD, and to the practice of the natural law, he hath proved himfelf as much a friend to inquifitive doubt, as an enemy to fuperftition.

cepts of the gofpel, and their own true interefts, in order to fubdue their enemies, furnifhed the civil power with thofe arms, againft
the ufe of which, they had fo long inveighed.
They went ftill farther; and even thefe men,
who believed alfo in Jefus Chrift, who followed the fame difcipline, and obferved the
fame ceremonies, but who differed concerning
fome abftrufe, and fpeculative opinion, could
not make a proper ufe of that toleration,
which had been granted to the heathens, but
fome years before. The fame emperor, who
in his firft edict, in favour of the Chriftians,
had faid, in exprefs terms : "it is our will,
that fuch as follow the errors of the Gentiles,
fhould enjoy the fame tranquility, and the
fame repofe which the faithful enjoy ; and we
efteem this reciprocal toleration, to be the
beft mean of propagating the truth. Let no
one, therefore, prefume to moleft his fellow
creature; let every perfon live as he pleafeth;
and let thofe, who chufe to adhere to a falfe
religion, not only enjoy their forms of worfhip, but their temples." The fame Conftantine, when fome time had elapfed, iffued
an edict againft the heretics, in which he for-
bids them to have any oratories, and even
                    acquaints

acquaints them, that they muft not dare to affemble on any pretext whatfoever.*(e)* He fent foldiers into all the provinces of the empire, to pull down the temples, to break their idols in pieces, to imprifon their priefts, and to difperfe their worfhippers; and whilft he thus eftablifhed his tenets, by fire and the fword, he was himfelf inceffantly changing; perpetually paffing over from one party, to the other party; and preaching, and inculcating contradictory doctrines, until, at length, forgetting, through the excefs of zeal, to be baptized, he died an heretic.

To draw afide the mafk, beneath which feeble humanity hath frequently remained hidden, is conftantly a painful employment; but howfoever odious it may be in fociety, in all hiftorical refearches, it is at once noble and ufeful. In fact, if the ordinary courfe of juftice requires that a flow and impartial examination fhould rife up, after a long feries of years, to redrefs her errors, how much more is hiftory, placed at firft between the fycophant, and the carping fophifter, and then delivered over to the blind compiler, entitled

(e) See Eufeb. de vita Conft. l. 2. c. 46. and l. 3. c. 66.

entitled to enter her proteft, againft the fentence of the paft ages? Conftantine, by
throwing down the idols, had often applaud-
ed himfelf, for having convinced the people,
that thefe fplendid images, far from proving
afylums to the divinities, contained only
defpicable afhes, or the tainted bones of dead
bodies; but little did he perceive that thus
he infulted over his own deftiny. The tafk
of daring to penetrate into his foul, was referved for this enlightened age. The idol
being overthrown, and its rich covering deftroyed, what then remains? felf-intereft,
paffions, hypocrify, and the whole fkeleton of
humanity. Conftantine is, of all princes,
he who hath the moft influenced the ages
which fucceeded that age wherein he exifted.
The obje
cts to which he confecrated his reign
were the deftruction of the worfhip of falfe
deities, in order to fubftitute in its place, the
worfhip of Jefus Chrift; and the tranfportation
of the capital of the world, from the ancient
theatre of her glory, to a barbarous and un-
cultivated fhore. The laft ftep hath not met
with any apologifts; but the firft ftep, by
endearing his memory to the Chriftian world,
hath probably caft upon the author, too much
of

of the merit of the work. As for us, equally
removed from the bitternefs of Zofimus, and
the enthufiafm of Eufebius, we fhall not borrow opinions from thefe authors, but only
facts. We fhall even reft fatisfied, with
having placed the reader, in a fituation, to
judge for himfelf; and to follow a furer road,
in our obfervations, we fhall examine Conftantine, under three different points of view;
as a man, as a prince, and as a Chriftian.

Were it neceffary for the religion of Chrift,
to borrow fome luftre from her followers, we
fhould not have confeffed, but with uneafinefs,
how much we are conftrained to acknowledge
an extreme difference, between the great and
fublime minds of *Trajan*, and the *Antonini*,
and the yet barbarous character of *Conftantine*:
but the faith inculcated by the minifters of
the gofpel, hath nothing in common with the
perfonal vices of this prince; vices at once fo
ftriking, and fo odious, that we can neither
juftify, nor diffemble them. Perhaps, indeed,
he ought, in fome meafure, to be pitied, for
having been hurried away by the manners of
his times, whilft he treated with fo much
cruelty, the people of Germany, whom he
had conquered: but what pardon can be
granted

granted to thofe writers, who, notwithftanding that they were commendable in every
other refpeft, inftead of lamenting over thefe
horrid perpetrations, have ftriven to palliate,
and, as it were, to filch away the atrocity
that ftained them? I cannot, in this place,
avoid quoting a paffage from Mr. Crevier;
it may ferve as an inftance of the manner,
after which, hiftory is written in our times.
" Conftantine (faith he) paffed the Rhine,
and entered into the country of the *Brueteri*,
whom he gave up *to the fire, and the fword.*
Nothing was fpared. The villages were
burnt; the cattle were taken, or flaughtered;
the men and women were maffacred; and
they, who efcaped death, and whom he
made prifoners, underwent a fate ftill more
cruel. As he judged them incapable of ever
performing the leaft ufeful fervice to the
caufe, on account of their ungovernable
fiercenefs, and their perfidy, they were thrown
to the wild beafts, whofe ferocity they
imitated."(*f*)

What an artifice! what an effort to foften
fuch abominable crimes! and all this, becaufe
Con-

(*f*) Eufebius relates this faft with the fame indulgence.
See de vitâ Conft. l. 1. c. 25.

Conſtantine was the firſt Chriſtian emperor.
A partiality ſo peculiar to hiſtorians, ſometimes becomes amuſing, when it is not exerted on ſubjects which ſeem to riſe againſt
it. Amidſt ſo much guilt, a ſimple homicide,
though indeed exceedingly uſeleſs, and un-
merited, may be conſidered as a trifle; but I
cannot help taking under my protection, an
unfortunate eunuch, for whom *Mr. Le Beau,*
and *Mr. Crevier* have ſhewn no compaſſion.
Conſtantine had ſtrong reaſons to ſuſpect his
father-in-law *Maximian*; but he had determined to delay executing his revenge on him,
until he ſhould have taken him in an attempt
to commit the fact. Having, therefore,
been one day informed by his wife *Fauſta,*
that *Maximian* was to fulfil his intentions, on
the following night, and ſtab him in his bed,
he placed in it an eunuch, without doubt, a
contemptible creature, yet, at the ſame time,
very innocent; and one who had nothing to
do there. *Maximian* is deceived, and whilſt
he only kills the eunuch, ſuppoſes that he
ſlays a ſon-in-law. *Conſtantine* then ſteps forward, overwhelmed with joy at the diſcovery,
and orders his father-in-law to be immediately
put to death, to the great ſatisfaction of his
wife,

wife, and all the affiftants. Is it poffible, that
no hiftorian fhould have been induced to remark, that it would have been better not to
have taken away the life of a blamelefs individual; and to have faved his father from
the commiffion of an additional crime, and
himfelf from the guilt of parricide? but I am
in the wrong to expect that a poor eunuch,
fhould be mentioned with any pity, whilft
the fame hiftorians have expreffed none for
Cæfar Valens, and *Cæfar Martinianus*, whofe
only crime was, the having been raifed to the
firft rank by *Licinius*; and whilft, alfo, they
have fhewn as little commiferation, even for
Licinius, who, during a long time, coequal
with *Conftantine*, and, at length, fallen within his power, though under the fanction of a
treaty, was fhortly afterwards condemned to
death, upon the moft frivolous pretexts.
The execution of an *Auguftus*, and of the
two *Cæfars*; the violation of the public faith;
and treaties, either forgotten, or broken, are
all as nothing, for an emperor, who protected
bifhops, and compofed homilies.

What crimes could have been added to
thefe, unlefs they amounted to the having
put to death a wife, and a fon? and under
what

what circumftances were fuch cruelties committed? *Conftantine* returned in triumph from
the *Nicean* council; he was congratulating
himfelf on having given a dinner to more
than three hundred bifhops, and kiffed the
wounds of martyrs; when, on a fudden,
hurried away by mere fufpicions, and from
the fingle imputation of a crime, the hardeft
to be believed, he put to death his fon
Crifpus,(g) a youth of the moft promifing
hopes. Shortly afterwards, turning his fury
from the accufed, to the accufer, he ordered
that the emprefs Faufta fhould be fuffocated.
The ties of friendfhip were, in his eftimation,
no furer fafeguards than the ties of blood.
This ferocious, and irregular prince, all occupied as he was in accelerating the progrefs
of Chriftianity, had invited to his court,
Zopater, a Platonic philofopher, of the fchool
of *Jamblicus*. He foon permitted him to
enjoy fo great a fhare of his confidence, and
intimacy, that the unfortunate fage, deluded

VOL. I.   Y   away

(g) It is remarkable, that *Eufebius*, fearful of throwing too dark a fhade over his beautiful picture of Conftantine, hath not taken the leaft notice of the death,
or rather murder of *Crifpus*, who was compelled to
fwallow poifon. K.

away from his own country, could not efcape
the jealoufy of the Chriftians. Accufations
of forcery and magic had been whifpered
abroad, and a popular commotion had already
rifen, when the fleet, which was to import the
corn from Ægypt, became detained by contrary winds. The people, conftantly furious,
and driven almoft to madnefs, whenfoever
factious and interefted men alarm their minds
with apprehenfions of a famine,(b) did not
fail to direct their fury againft *Zopater*; whilft
Conftantine, at once a weak prince, and a
perfidious friend, delivered up to execution
this innocent philofopher. To a character
fo cruel, and inconftant, may be added an
unbridled paffion for oftentatious pomp, and
an immoderate thirft after every kind of glory:
from fuch marks, it is but too eafy to difcover, in the perfon of *Conftantine*, an odious
and contemptible individual, whofe vices, the
luftre of the purple, the laurels of victory,
and the adulation of ages, have long ftriven
to conceal. Let us now examine whether
the prince hath a better title to our efteem.

In

(b) Tacitus, fomewhere faith, " Plebs cui una ex
republica annonæ cura."

In this cafe, facts feem to fpeak for themfelves. *Conftantine*, born in the very midft of
dangers; expofed from his infancy, in the
character of an hoftage, to all the hatred of
his enemies; and at length, efcaping from
their hands, at the hazard of his life, no
fooner perceives himfelf placed at the head
of an army, than, being the abfolute mafter
of an extenfive part of the empire, he attempts to conquer the other part, and to feat
himfelf on the throne of the world.   What
fuccefs could have been more brilliant? what
a fubject for panegyric! but the philofopher,
who is never dazzled by the mere fplendor of
actions, foon withdraws his admiration, when
directing his refearches up to the origin of
victories, he beholds only a feries of battles
gained.   He is convinced, that from the moment, at which men began to repofe their
whole truft and intereft in their armies, it
muft neceffarily have happened, that the
event of battles, decided either in favour of
the one, or of the other; that the advantages
acquired by war, may be of high relative
value, but of very little pofitive value; and
that fignal fuccefles do not always form great
generals.   A player at chefs may take another

lefs

lefs ftrong than himfelf, and yet be very weak. In India, for inftance, we know that entire empires have been overthrown, by armies, who might have been forced to flee, before fix battalions of *Europæan* troops. It is not becaufe he defeated the duke de *Bcurnonville*; but becaufe he harraffed *Condé*, and *Montecuculli*, that *Turenne* is efteemed a great general. *(i)* So alfo, in politics, the citizen, who by dint of firmnefs and intrepidity, attains to the power of adding fome advantage to public liberty, is more refpectable than the prince, who, at the head of fifty fatellites, makes a people of flaves exchange one mafter for another mafter.

For

(i) The Chevalier Folard mentions this campaign, fatal to Turenne, with that enthufiafm, to which the merits of the French general, and his almoft-equally illuftrious competitor had fo ftrong a claim. " Celle ci fût le chef d'oeuvre du Vicomte de Turenne, et du Comte de Montecuculli; il n'y en a point de fi belle dans l'antiquité; il n'y a que les experts dans le métier qui puiffent en bien juger." Montecuculli, who, after the death of Turenne, quitted the profeffion of a foldier, gave this remarkable reafon for his retirement. " The man who has had the honour to engage with Turenne, muft not venture his reputation againft thofe who are but beginning to command armies." K. ·

For *Conftantine* to have vanquifhed *Licinius*, and to have triumphed over fome barbarous nations, is, without doubt, no inconfiderable circumftance ; and yet the little glory which he receives from it, can only laft, whilft we continue ignorant of the choice of his means, and the fagacity of his views. But this emperor, by placing his conduct in a more interefting light, hath given us a ftandard, whereby we may judge of him. He acted as a legiflator ; nor will the reader find it difficult to determine, whether our feverity be mifplaced, fhould he recollect that it is this prince, to whom we owe that vicious mixture of the *civil power*, and the *ecclefiaftical power*, which hath fcattered fo much diforder, during fifteen centuries, throughout the Chriftian world.

The firft traces of the intervention of the ecclefiaftical power, in civil matters, may be found in a law, enacted by Conftantine, and relative to the enfranchifement of flaves. In the room of thofe formalities, with which thefe enfranchifements were accompanied, he directed that the atteftation of a bifhop fhould, from that time forward, be deemed fufficient ; as if the proceedings and deci-

fions

fions were to be determined upon, like cafes
of confcience, or acts of penance.(*k*) Every
one recollects into how large a field this firft
encroachment began to fpread. All the different ways and means were immediately
fettled ; innumerable privileges were granted
to the clergy ; fuch as, a permiffion to receive legacies ; an exemption from all bur-
denfome offices, namely, the collection of
the taxes, municipal pofts, magiftracies,
guardianfhips, &c. fo exceffive were thefe
favours, that, intereft foon checking enthufiafm, it became neceffary to revoke them.
                                                    In

(*k*) One might reafonably fufpect *Conflantine* to
have been actuated by fome fecret motives, when he
made this regulation. A multitude of flaves, attracted
by that fpirit of equality, which reigned amongft the
Chriftians, prefented themfelves daily, and by embracing
their religion, broke loofe from the power of their
refpective mafters. Thefe deferters were, notwithftanding, to be given up, whenfoever they were demanded ;
but however flight the pretext for their enfranchifement might have been, the favour granted to the new
converts gave birth to decifions, fubverfive of the authority of the mafters. Now, it is probable, that, to
extend this favour, ftill farther, endeavours were ufed
to deprive the civil power of the privilege of carrying
on any procefs of this kind, and to render the atteftation of the bifhop, which might always be depended upon,
' fufficient of itfelf, without any other forms.

In fact, almoſt every one of the citizens, to ſecure his effects, turned eccleſiaſtic; and God was ſo well ſerved, that the ſtate no longer enjoyed either ſubjects,*(l)* or magiſtrates. Amongſt all princes, the intereſts of their treaſury or exchequer, have, as it were, fixed bounds to their faith : but, however unwilling *Conſtantine* might have been to give way to the clergy, in a point of ſuch importance, he was not afraid of ſacrificing to them the moſt ancient principles of the Roman government, by revoking the *lex Papia Poppæa.* By this law, the unmarried citizens were cut off from all collateral ſucceſſions; and the married citizens, who had no children, could only claim the half of

Y 4   ſuch

(l) Under *Conſtantine,* the number of the citizens was much diminiſhed, whilſt the number of ſlaves, and of foreigners, was conſiderably increaſed. It is not, therefore, extraordinary that the weight of taxes, and and all public charges bore hard upon each individual. The municipal employments were, in particular, ſuch heavy burdens, that, in the end, there remained neither landed property, nor perſonal property. All thoſe who, by their ſituation, were obliged to fill ſome public office, were called *Curiales.* Now, the rank of *Curialis,* and any eccleſiaſtical rank, were, by the principles of the church, deemed incompatible. See Bingham's antiquities of the church. b. 5. c. 3.

such of these successions, as might have fallen
to them; neither were they entitled to more
than the tenth part, of the effects of their
wives, in case of their decease. *Constantine*,
not contented with having extinguished these
respectable remains of Roman policy, encouraged celibacy, by every possible mean; and,
in particular, granted to such, as embraced
this state, the privilege of disposing of their
possessions, previous to the age required by
the laws.

But, whilst these exemptions were multiplied, in favour of the clergy, a new kind of
exorbitant taxes, spread the greatest conster-
nation amongst the people. Every fourth
year, the officers belonging to the emperor,
came, armed with whips and sticks, to collect a capitation, called *chrysargyrum*, because
it was paid, either in gold, or in silver. This
tax was levied with the most unparalelled
rigour. Even beggars and prostitutes were
forced to contribute their share; but the poor,
hunted from place to place, and lashed
about, like common beasts of burden, were
not the only individuals, who groaned under
these extortions; the rich apprehended them,
with an equal degree of terror; since accu-

fations of every kind, domeftic treachery, and public calumny, formed, as it were, the tarif, in which they were accuftomed to perceive them entered.

Zofimus, alfo, accufes *Conftantine*, of having waged war, againft the Pagan deities, only that he might be furnifhed with a pretence, for pillaging their temples ; but it would be unjuft to rely upon an author, who appears, by feveral paffages in his writings, to have been greatly prejudiced ; and particularly, when he imputes the converfion of *Conftantine*, to the remorfe with which the murder of his wife, and fon, afflicted him. According to this hiftorian, the emperor, having fought, to no purpofe, amongft the heathen priefts, for proper expiations, became a convert to the religion of the Chriftians, who were reported to have practifed a ceremony, of wafhing away all fins, in a myfterious water. But, however grofs the anachronifm may be, of referring the converfion of *Conftantine*, to an event, which happened fo long afterwards, it is, notwithftanding, very evident, that the crimes with which he had lately blackened his conduct, added to his inflexible perfecution, againft opinions generally

rally received, and a mode of worfhip, of fuch an ancient eftablifhment, had rendered him fo odious to his people, that he was obliged to quit Rome, and find out another afylum, where only the voice of flattery could be heard: upon which, I fhall beg leave to remark, that the ideas, relative to an exterior form of adoration, muft have had a terrible influence over morality; fince on one fide, the Chriftians have commended, even to the fkies, an emperor, who was guilty of the moft atrocious crimes; whilft, on the other fide, the *Romans*, who applaud-ed *Nero*, when he made his entry into their capital, after having put his mother to death, could not bear the fight of *Conftantine*, by whofe order, his own wife and fon were executed. It is thus, that an attachment to empty rites and ceremonies, perpetually pre-vails over that law, which nature hath en-graven on every human heart, but unfor-tunately, in characters too fuperficial, and too eafy to be obliterated.

We will not expatiate upon that abfurd error, which *Conftantine* committed, when he changed the metropolis of the empire. It is a circumftance too well known, and too fully

ac-

acknowledged, by all authors, not excepting
thofe authors, who have the moft commended this prince. We have already mentioned the reafons, which induced him to
take fo falfe a ftep; but we cannot avoid
adding, that no projeft could poffibly have
been conceived, more in the fpirit of pride,
or executed more in the fpirit of injuftice.
Whilft this oftentatious emperor is fo impatient to enjoy his palaces, that he doth not
allow his architects, even time to conftruct
them, in a manner fufficiently fubftantial;
and whilft he perceives his already mouldering
walls, threatening to fall on thofe walls,
which are yet rifing; he compels, by fevere
edicts, all the inhabitants of *Afia-Minor* to
erect expenfive edifices in the new capital.
A tyrannical law enacts, that all perfons, not
having an houfe at *Conftantinople*, fhould be
prohibited from tranfmitting any landed eftate
to their heirs: by fuch means doth he accelerate the building of this celebrated city, the
horofcope of which is caft, by his orders; and
the refult of this, is, a prophecy that it will
laft, during the fpace of fix hundred and
ninety-fix years.

The

The reader will, probably, be fomewhat
furprized to find, that fo excellent a divine,
as *Conftantine*, fhould have been induced to
confult the aftrologers ; but the character of
this prince appears, in no particular, fo inconfiftent, as in that particular, which hath
any the leaft relation to religion.   Equally
weak and vain, and as ready to preferve, as
to change his refolution, the imperfections
of his mind have accounted for the imperfections of his heart. Whether this prince
was an enthufiaft, or an hypocrite, is a queftion, which hath been often agitated.   One
party, ftricken with that frequently particular attention, which made him defcend
into all the *minutiæ* of ecclefiaftical matters ;
with that hatred which he had conceived
againft Paganifm ; and, above all, with the
devotion, which he difcovered, in the laft
moments of his life, have imagined that he
was more convinced, than enlightened ; and
that if the grace of God did not efteem it
fitting, to fupport him againft herefy, and
parricide, at leaft, it revealed to him, the
principal tenets of the faith.   The other
party, more attentive to his public conduct,
to the pretended miracles, with which he accompanied

companied his expeditions; and, especially,
to the advantages, which he drew from them,
seem inclined to believe, that he never had a
very lively faith, and that his religion was,
conftantly, kept dependant on his ambition.
As for me, I know not, if it arise from my
bearing a ftronger antipathy againft hypocrify, than againft any other vice; but I am
always averfe from fuppofing, that it can be
carried on to a certain degree: to act the part
of an hypocrite, feems to me, a tafk, at once,
fo painful, and fo difficult, that nothing but
the moft violent effort of patience and artifice, can fupport a long and fuccefsful performance of it. Let us always be fearful of
giving too much to the mind, by taking too
much away from the heart. If we enjoy
fome talents, wherewith we deceive others,
how many more talents do we not poffefs,
which feduce us to impofe upon ourfelves?
the willingnefs with which we are fo apt to
credit the fuppofed exertions of hypocrify,
may, perhaps, arife from the not having fufficiently reflected on the nature of the human
heart. All who have obferved the empire,
which our intereft maintains over our opinions, muft have met with ample reafon to
                                             be

be convinced, that its own fucceffes foon
prove the means of its deftruction. We lead
off, by difhoneftly affecting certain practices
and fentiments; and when this impofture
hath brought us within the reach of playing
fome great part; of commanding mankind,
and of receiving from them riches and confequence, we begin to repofe in it more truft;
and it, at length, happens that, by little and
little, our intereft attains to the power of
confolidating, in our mind, the bafis of our
authority. It is an old remark, that game-
fters begin by being dupes, and end by being
knaves: in matters of opinion, the cafe is
reverfed; and we begin by being knaves,
and end by being dupes. How often doth
the magiftrate, in paffing from one court
into another court, change his principles,
with his tribunal! at firft, his probity, or
rather the opinion which he hath conceived
of himfelf, becomes reftlefs and uneafy;
it, then, calls to its affiftance, fophiftry and
fubtlety; but, quickly duped by its own artifice, it no longer finds any thing to contend
with, and the man is rendered a convert to
vertue, through his own folly. It is thus,
that amongft the clergy, it hath fometimes
happened,

happened, that a fet of ecclefiaftics, entirely
abandoned to wordly views, and raifed to
dignities, either through favour or intrigue;
then, becoming the chiefs of a party,
and frequently conftrained to facrifice their
pleafures to their ambition, have ended by
adopting, as an article of their own belief,
fome portion of that which they would willingly have perfuaded others to believe. We
mention this to the honour of chriftianity,
the moral fyftem of which could never have
united itfelf to thofe atrocious crimes,
which *Conftantine* committed; and had God
Himfelf enlightened him; had He chofen to
have made ufe of him, any otherwife than
He made ufe of a Tiberius, or a Nero, who,
doubtlefs, were fubfervient to the accomplifhment of his purpofes, He would not
have expofed him to the difgrace of having
inceffantly difhonoured the faith, by his actions, and betrayed it, by his errors.

Conftantine, according to all appearances,
was induced to favour Chriftianity, by thofe
reafons, which we have explained, in a former
part of this chapter. But foon encouraged
by fuccefs; elated with pride, by the flattery, which he receiyed from the bifhops;
and,

and, above all, prompted by jealoufy, to
change the feat of the empire, he felt, at
length, a real zeal, in favour of thofe tenets,
which, at the opening, he had efpoufed,
from principles of intereft. It is eafy to trace
this conduct, in his mode of proceeding towards a general reformation. At firft, he
thought it enough to tolerate Chriftianity;
but he, foon afterwards, made Chriftianity
the reigning and exclufive religion. Although humble and fubmiffive to the bifhops, at the beginning, yet he did not wait
long, before he gave them leffons, in their
turn. We may perceive how his zeal daily
increafed, with his influence over ecclefiaftical affairs. No method, no rule actuated
his judgments; at one moment, a mode-
rator, and at another moment, a perfecutor;
now, he impofes filence on *Alexander*, and
on *Arius*; then he condemns *Arius*; then
abfolves him; then, condemns him again;
and after all this, concludes with adopting
his principles. I beg leave to infert the introduction of a letter, which he wrote, at
the fame time to *Alexander*, bifhop of *Alexandria*, and to *Arius*, who was then difputing
                                    againft

againſt him.*(m)* "Since you, *Alexander,* have required from your clergy their ſentiments concerning ſome particular paſſages of ſcripture, or rather concerning ſome empty and frivolous opinions ; and ſince you, *Arius,* have agitated queſtions, on which you ought never to have meditated, or meditating, to have remained ſilent, diſcord hath been ſtirred up amongſt you, &c. &c. .... Abandon, therefore, theſe ſubtleties in a matter which doth not admit either of a queſtion or of an anſwer." Now, theſe ſubtleties, theſe empty and frivolous queries, related to nothing leſs, than the conſubſtantiality of the word, on which occaſion an aſſembly was called, ſoon after the council of *Nice.*

Conſtantine was not more fortunate, in his treatiſes on the Chriſtian religion. Let ſuch, as have any curioſity, to perceive the height of extravagance and abſurdity, united to-

VOL. I.   Z   gether

(m) Cum enim tu, Alexander, a preſbiteris tuis requireres quid unuſquiſque eorum de quodam legis loco ſentiret, ſeu potius de quâdam inani queſtione eos interrogares; cumque tu, Ari, id quod nunquam cogitatum, vel ſanè cogitatum ſilentio premere deberes, imprudenter excitata inter vos diſcordia, &c....... Quidnam verò illud eſt ? nec interrogare de hujuſmodi rebus, nec interrogatum reſpondere, &c.

gether, perufe the eighteenth, nineteenth,
and twentieth chapters of his difcourfe, ad-
dreffed to the affembly of the faints, *(Oratio
ad SanEtorum coetum.)*   After having quoted
as authentic, an acroftic, by the pretended
Erythræan Sibyl, the initial letters of which,
form the words, *Jefus Chriftus Dei Filius, Servator*, as if God revealed the fecrets of fu-
turity, in quirks of wit, which barely deferve
a place amidft the common doggerel of a
news-paper, he feizes on *Virgil*, as an immenfe treafure of the cleareft prophecies, in
fupport of the Chriftian religion.   Amongft
other eclogues, he cites,

Sicelides Mufæ, paulò majora canamus.

Even *paulò majora*, (faith he) alludes to
many particulars.   But Virgil, then adds,

Ultima Cumæi venit jam carminis ætas.

Who doth not know that the *Cumæan Sibyl*
ceafed to prophefy, when the *Truth* himfelf
came into the world? but what anfwer can
be given to thefe verfes?

*Magnus ab integro fæclorum nafcitur ordo,
Jam redit et Virgo, redeunt Saturnia regna.*

Who

Who is this returning virgin, unlefs it be the Mother of God? doth not the poet himfelf fay?

Tu modo nafcenti puero, quo ferrea primùm
Definet, ac toto furget gens aurea mundo,
Cafta fave Lucina, &c.

Was not this, word for word, the Meffiah? *Doctè igitur hæc dicta funt, O Maro poetarum fapientiffime! . . . . . . &c. &c.*

Conftantine firmly believed that *Virgil* was a chriftian; but he imagined, that this celebrated poet was obliged to difguife his faith, and conceal his allufions behind the veil of allegory. *Eufebius*, who introduces the whole of this difcourfe, and without making any obfervations on it, feems to be of the fame opinion. What then muft have been the logic of the firft fages of the church, which made them confider *Mofes* and the *Sibyls, Ifaac* and *Virgil*, in the fame point of view? but as thefe reflexions are foreign to my fubject, I fhall immediately conclude with obferving, that *Conftantine*, having lived in the perpetration of guilt, and died an heretic, is unworthy of our encomiums, either as a *Man,* a *Prince,* or a *Chriftian.*

CHAP. V.

On the influence of Chriftianity over the happinefs
of the people. The fituation of mankind, from
the reign of Conftantine, to the deftruction of
the Weftern empire.

HAVING mentioned the eftablifhment
of the Chriftian religion; and having drawn,
with all the accuracy in our power, the picture of the fovereign, who imparted to it
fo fupreme an authority, throughout his extenfive dominions; it feems natural to examine,
in what manner the felicity of the people
was influenced by thefe important alterations.
And here, truth would not have prefumed to
raife her rigid voice, if the Apoftles of Chriftianity had ever pretended, that the temporary
                                    happinefs

happinefs of human life was the objeft to which the views of their religion were direfted. Idly would men alledge againft this religion, the deftruftion of thofe nations, who embraced it, and the downfal of the Roman empire, at a period fo little diftant from its converfion. The church, in her infancy, never extended her confiderations towards the glory and profperity of ftates. Humility poverty, penitence, and prayer, were all which the minifters of the gofpel thought themfelves commiffioned to inculcate; and far from endeavouring, like the Pagans, to affimilate the mode of worfhip, with the fyftem of polity, and to make each jointly confpire, in promoting the happinefs of nations, they gloried in a contempt of all vain grandeur, perfuaded as they were, that the theatre of the world muft fall, before the fcenes performing on it could find fufficient time to draw to a conclufion.

We have already fpoken of the error peculiar to the Millenarians; and fo common during the firft ages of the church. Whilft herefies, fpringing up with the primitive dogmas of the faith, tore the bofom of Chriftianity; whilft the moft orthodox emperors,

Z 3   governed

governed by their eunuchs, pufillanimoufly
deferted the defence of their frontiers; and
whilft the Barbarians, rufhing in from the
extremities of the univerfe, were fprinkling
with human blood, the provinces of the empire, the principal cities of which were frequently either fet on fire by the volcanos, or
demolifhed by earthquakes, the opinion generally propagated, that the world was going
to be deftroyed, was received with a ftill
greater degree of credit; and if the Pagans
continued obftinately bent on rejecting this
opinion, it was becaufe they had afcribed fo
many difafters to the defection from an ancient and reverenced fyftem of worfhip. At
this dreadful crifis, during thefe common la-
mentations, the defenders of Chriftianity
formed two divifions. The firft divifion confifted of thofe, who, above concealing the
miferies, with which they were laden; and
even ftriving to exaggerate the confequences,
drew from thefe events, frefh motives to enforce a more extenfive converfion. The fecond divifion, unwilling to make the leaft
allowance in favour of Paganifm, pretended
that the then impending evils were not more
calamitous, than the evils which afflicted the
                                        people,

people, during the ages of idolatry. To the invasions of the Barbarians, they oppofed the civil wars and the profcriptions; to the frequent deftructions, whether of *Antioch*, or *Edeffa*, or *Conftantinople*, &c. &c. they compared the remarkable eruption of *Vefuvius*, during the reign of *Titus*. *Saint Auguftin*, drawing all his arguments from his religion, wrote his elegant treatife, *de civitate Dei*, in which he proves, that the kingdom of God was not to be made manifeft in this world. *Paulus Orofius* alfo compofed his cold and tirefome chronicle, in which, however inaccurate his relation of the principal hiftorical facts may prove, he hath but too well fucceeded, in convincing us, that, of all creatures, human beings have conftantly been the moft unfortunate.

Every one, the leaft acquainted with hiftory, muft recollect, that no ages were more fertile in difafters, than the ages which filled up the intervals, between the firft invafion of the Barbarians, and their abfolute eftablifhment in the country which they had conquered. But it is eafy to perceive, that in order to follow the plan, which we have adopted, it is neceffary, that we fhould remove to a

diftance

diſtance from our obſervations, all phyſical events, ſuch as earthquakes, famine, contagions, &c. and the greater part of political incidents, ſuch as the unfortunate ſucceſſes of war, the miſconduct of generals, the want of diſcipline amongſt troops, &c. Indeed, there is every reaſon to believe that, whatſoever religion might have prevailed, throughout the Roman empire, the effeminacy of the people, the licentiouſneſs of the ſoldiers, and the deſpotiſm of the emperors, muſt ſooner, or later, have drawn it on towards its deſtruction. But, the power of religion, embracing, as it were, the majority of civil and moral actions, it may be aſked, whether, ſince the eſtabliſhment of Chriſtianity, mankind have been more vertuous, and more happy; whether ſovereigns have been leſs covetous, and leſs ſanguinary; whether the people have been more ſubmiſſive, and more quiet; whether crimes have been leſs numerous, and puniſhments leſs cruel; whether the progreſs of war hath been conducted with more humanity; and whether treaties have been more ſcrupulouſly obſerved?

We

We could wifh, not for the honour of Chriftianity, which doth not ftand in need of human confideration, but for our own fatiffaction, that we were able to anfwer in the affirmative; but the too ftriking appearances of truth, and the too authentic and univerfally known records of hiftory, rife up in abfolute oppofition to our defires.

In the bofom of the church, the errors of *Donatus* and *Arius* poifoned the firft feeds of the faith ; bifhops were in arms againft bifhops : the people efpoufed thefe quarrels, with a degree of fury ; the temples, and the bafilics were difputed, fword in hand, and fprinkled with the blood of the citizens ; odious accufations and atrocious calumnies were reciprocally fcattered abroad by the chiefs of each party, whilft thefe fanatics tore one another in pieces, with a ferocity, which, to borrow the expreffion of a contemporary author, furpaffed even the ferocity of wild beafts.(*n*) The firft emperor,(*o*) educated in the principles of Chriftianity, introduces

his

(*n*) Nullas infeftas hominibus beftias ut funt fibi ferales plerique Chriftianorum. Ammian. Marcellin. l. 22.

(*o*) *Conftantius.*

his reign with the murder of his uncle, and of his firſt couſin. He madly throws himſelf into the party of the *Arians*, whilſt, at one moment, a bloody perſecutor, and at another moment, an ignorant conciliator, he either deals out his orders for executions, or aſſembles councils. The biſhops, perpetually hurried, from place to place, abandon, for idle controverſies, the care of their flocks; whilſt the provinces, drained by the expences of theſe journies, become at length ſcarcely able to defray them.

The ſame iniquity, the ſame injuſtice prevailed throughout the civil adminiſtration. A jealouſy, equally extravagant and cruel, became the leading principle of the government. Informers infeſted the provinces, nor did their ſuperiors bluſh at having eſtabliſhed them as a body, and given them a particular rank.(*p*) The adminiſtration degenerated into a barbarous inquiſition; puniſhments were inflicted with additional cruelty; criminals were burnt for ſlight offences; the

faith

(*p*) Such were the Curioſi, a ſet of officers, who, in the quality of inſpectors, or ſpies, were ſent into all the provinces; their number is ſaid to have amounted to fifteen thouſand.

faith of treaties was no longer kept facred; kings were affaffinated in the very midft of peace, and even during the convivial joy, with which they celebrated their feftivals;(*q*) public morals became more and more corrupted; ennuchs, the vile inftruments of the moft abominable pleafures, were appointed generals and prime minifters; the expences of the table, and the luxury of the

court,

(*q*) *Valens*, by the bafeft act of treachery, accomplifhed the murder of an Armenian king, who had always been attached to the Romans. *Valentinian* ordered that *Gabinius*, king of the *Quadi*, fhould be affaffinated, at a feaft. *Valentinian* the fecond, jealous of the great increafe of the *Goths*, whom the emperor *Valens* had quartered, within the provinces of the empire, iffued a proclamation, to inform them that, if, on a certain day, they fhould affemble in the capital of their refpective provinces, each individual would receive a new diftribution of lands. Seduced by hopes, thefe unfortunate wretches did affemble, and were all put to the fword.

The barbarity of *Valens*, having been mentioned in the beginning of the note, it may not, here, be improper to introduce an example, at once ridiculous and dreadful, of thofe violent exceffes, to which the timid and ignorant fuperftition of this emperor was capable of driving him. An impudent impoftor, pretending to have difcovered, by his fkill in magic, that fome particular perfon, the two firft fyllables of whofe name,

were

court, were, at once, boundlefs and abfurd ;(r)
the laws,   by being multiplied without
end, were equal proofs of the depravity of
the government, and the wickednefs of the
people : in fhort, every thing was altered ;
every thing was corrupted ; even the difcipline of the armies, and the intrepidity of the
foldiers, were difordered and extinguifhed :
thus, the deftruction of whole generations,
became the only remedy againft the evils,
which afflicted the earth ; in like manner, as
the fetting fire to the thorns and briars,
which over-run neglected fields, proves the
fole mean of obtaining a new and advantageous harveft.

Whilft

---

were *Theod*, was deftined to be the next fucceffor to
the throne, Valens ordered all to be maffacred, whofe
appellations were introduced by thefe letters. The
reader may judge how general fuch a carnage muft have
been, when he hath recollected, that it was exceedingly common, during that and the two preceding centuries, for men to affume a name, fome
part of which alluded to the Greek word, fignifying
God. K.

 (r) It is well known that Julian, foon after he became emperor, concluded the barber, on his entrance
into the room, to be one of the great lords of his
court ; and being informed of the wages, which this
fervant received, he difcovered that they were fufficient to maintain more than an hundred perfons.

Whilft we are painting this melancholy picture, the affecting ftrokes of which are not heightened beyond reality, we anxioufly wifh to remove, from the reader, every occafion of fufpecting, that we have the fmalleft intention of attributing to chriftianity thofe diforders againft which we have exclaimed. Far from harbouring fuch an idea, our only aim is to prove, that the misfortunes of the times did not permit religion to procure, for mankind, an happier fituation in this life. Perhaps, even this very religion became a new fource of evils; for, as the pureft aliments are apt to grow corrupted, in bodies attacked by difeafes, fo the moft facred tenets of the faith are frequently converted into the inftruments of the moft fhocking difafters. Of all the enemies of human nature, the moft modern and the moft cruel enemy is intolerant perfecution, which, following religion in her progrefs, ftep by ftep, extended itfelf, as fhe extended, and unfheathed the fword wherefoever the voice of zeal had propagated the word.

If we fix this epoch at the origin of that empire, which the Chriftian religion hath maintained ever fince, it is not becaufe, in

the

the courſe of our reflections we had not
before obſerved ſome ſeeds of theſe dreadful
principles. A ſingle nation, amongſt the
multitude of nations, which have appeared
upon the ſurface of the globe, might be ſufficient to furniſh us with inſtances of the
moſt bloody acts ; if the Jewiſh people, who
conſidered their government in the light of
a perpetual inſpiration, could ſerve as an example, in the preſent caſe, where an intolerant ſpirit was exerted, ſolely, againſt ab-
ſtracted and fugitive dogmas.

It is more eaſy to comprehend, how naturally a people conclude themſelves obliged
to exterminate all thoſe, who worſhip ſuch
deities, as may have been ſet up, in oppoſition to their own God, than to explain how
the fire and the ſword can be employed to
compel perſons to expreſs the idea of *conſubſtantiality*, by a letter more, or a letter
leſs.*(s)* It is not, therefore, without reaſon,
that

(s) Ὁμοϐ́σιος, or Ὁμϐσιος.— ſo, probably from an
error in the preſs, are theſe words printed; whilſt
I write this note, the authorities to which I could wiſh
to refer, are not at hand ; but if I can truſt my memory, the two terms are Ὁμοϐ́σιος, which deſcribed
the conſubſtantiality of Chriſt with God, according to
the

that the origin of this intolerant fpirit, in matters of opinion, hath been fixed at the fame epoch, with the propagation of chriftianity, throughout the empire.

It may, perhaps, be objected, that the Pagan emperors were the firft emperors who afforded an example of perfecution; but when a madman, a furious wretch, like Nero, directed his tyranny againft the Chriftians, he could, at leaft, have pleaded in his vindication, that he confidered them in the light of innovators and as rebels, who refufed to fubmit to the ancient and eftablifhed laws; for, until that period, the mode of public worfhip had compofed a part of the legiflation; and the Jews, or the Chriftians, (Jews and Chriftians, being at that time, equally the fame to the heathens) were the firft who determined not to conform to the public rites. Any perfon, refufing to fwear by the Genius of the emperor, was deemed guilty of high treafon, and this is an article, which

the full meaning of the Unitarians, and Ὁμοιούσιος, a phrafe by which the Semi-Arians expreffed their opinion that the Son was indeed fimilar to the Father in his effence, yet not by nature, but by a peculiar privilege. K.

which fhould be thoroughly enquired into, if
we defire to become acquainted with every
circumftance, relative to the firft perfecutions. But, to inflict the moft horrid punifhments, in order to fix the decifion of queftions,
which were rather grammatical, than theological; to deftroy with fire and the fword,
thofe who invoked the fame Supreme Being,
who obferved the fame ceremonies, and reverenced the fame authority, befpeaks a
madnefs, till then unparalleled, and which
fprang, in the Roman empire, from the tyranny of the emperors, and the ambition of
the bifhops.

Let us be juft, and remove from the minifters of the gofpel a part of thofe reproaches, with which they have been af-
perfed. I affert it, with fatisfaction, and I
know not why the apologifts for chriftianity
have not afferted it before me; this barbarous and intolerant fpirit, thefe fcandalous
and atrocious difputes are indebted, for no
inconfiderable part of their origin, to the peculiar charaƈterftic of the *Greeks*, to that unhappy paffion, which this nation had introduced, for empty dialeƈtics, and frivolous
fophifms. Whatfoever may be the caufe,

it

it was not, until the Chriftian emperors began
to reign, until even the moft revered princes,
fuch as *Conftantine*, and *Theodofius* had af-
cended the throne, that the fentence of the
laws was, for the firft time, exprefled in
thefe terms: " if any perfon, whatfoever,
fhould dare to offer facrifices in the temple,
let him be exterminated by the avenging
fword......... We command all men,
upon pain of death, to believe, that one God-
head exifteth, in three Perfons, &c. &c."(*t*)

Thus, from the firft appearance of herefies,
that is from the æra, at which theology began
to fupply the place of morality, mankind,

VOL. I.   A a   already

(*t*) Placuit omnibus locis, atque urbibus univerfi
claudi templa..... Quod fi quis aliquid fortè hujusmodi perpetraverit, gladio ultore fternatur. Cod.
Teod. c. 10.

If, in the midft of fo much atrocious barbarity, any
thing ridiculous could extort a fmile, no words have
a better claim to it than the following, extracted from
a law made by *Conftantius*: ceffet fuperftitio........
&c. Nam qui contra legem divi parentis noftri, et
hanc noftræ manfuetudinis juffionem aufus fuerit facri-
ficium celebrare, competens in eum vindicta, et præfens
fententia exerceatur...... &c. It is as if he had
faid: if any fhould prefume to tranfgrefs the orders,
iffuing from our moft mild and moft benevolent
perfon, it is our will that he be immediately ftrangled.

already condemned to submit to the yoke of
unjuft mafters; laden with taxes; difturbed
in the enjoyment of their property; and harraffed by war, and all its attendant calamities,
perceived themfelves, on a fudden, expofed
to a new fpecies of tyranny, which, pene-
trating within the moft fecret receffes of the
human heart, fcatters through the faculties of
the foul, the fame diforders and afflictions,
which civil defpotifm fpreads through all our
exterior relations. Thus, from the meetings
of the *Nicene* council, down to the repeal of
the edict of *Nantes*, every dungeon was filled
with victims; fcaffolds were continually erected; and the blood flowed in ftreams, to con-
folidate, by the feeble efforts of humanity, the
work undertaken by the Son of God Himfelf.

Another inconvenience refulting from this
fanatic and exclufive fpirit, is the deftruction
of all critical inveftigation. This is abfolutely
to extinguifh the torch of hiftory. Truth
and certainty are the moft likely to be our
guides, when we direct our refearches up to
thofe ancient, but obfcure records of the paft
ages. In the place of *Xenophon*, of *Livy*, of
Polybius, and of *Tacitus*, refpectable citizens,
whofe bofoms glowed with the vertues of

every

every æra, and every country, we only find
a fet of party-writers, who relate facts, with
no view, but to fupport particular opinions.
The annals, even the calendars, are facrificed
to polemical difputes, and the memorials of
thefe miferable times are no more than fo
many infipid cafes.

Amongft a multitude of hiftorians, who
have been either the extravagant panegyrifts,
' or the bitter fatyrifts of their princes, according to their having merited commend-
ation, or invective, from their particular fects,
but two Pagan authors have prevailed over
the efforts, which were ufed to deftroy their
works. *Zofimus*, an hiftorian not much endued
with elegance or judgement, is fometimes
led away by that fpirit of party, which equally
animated the idolaters, againft their antago-
nifts; but his hiftory hath frequently ferved,
as a guide, to the difcovery of a great number
of facts, and the abridged and precife manner, fo confpicuous in his writings, leaves no
room to imagine, that his principal view was
to throw an odium upon the Chriftians. It
were to be wifhed, that our modern compilers,
who abide by his authority, in the other parts
of his work, were not fo ready to reject that

authority, whenfoever he condemns the conduct of thofe perfonages, whom they have
taken under their protection. *Theodofius*, indeed, the hero of the catholic authors, hath
met with no favour at his hands. He defcribed him as a prince, funk in luxury and
effeminacy; whilft the ecclefiaftical writers
fpeak of him, as uniting the character of a
great man, with the character of an illuftrious
faint.   But, although thefe laft hiftorians have
taken care to acquaint us, that he frequently
humbled himfelf before the clergy, and publicly afferted,   that *Ambrofius* had fully convinced him, *how fuperior a bifhop was to an
emperor*, yet they have not produced any negative proofs againft the imputations of
Zofimus.   That *Theodofius* waged war, with
intrepidity and fuccefs, cannot be denied:
but, hath the flattery of hiftorians been able
to conceal that exceffive indolence, which
made him fo long defer the moment of entering into action? and doth not this obfervation agree with that paffion for pleafure
and voluptuoufnefs, of which he is accufed
by *Zofimus?* May not, alfo, his behaviour to
Maximus, be taxed with diffimulation, or timidity? confidering this impoftor, as a rebel,
                                                    and

and a regicide, fhould he have admitted his
title of emperor, or have fuffered the ftatues
of fo flagitious a wretch, to be erected near
his own ftatues? if, on the contrary, *Theodofius* felt himfelf obliged by policy, to treat
as an emperor, the man whom armies and
fuccefs had crowned, ought he to have made
fecret and infidious preparations for attack-
ing him?(*u*) or, was it juft, after he became
the arbiter of his fate, to order that he fhould
be executed, as a rebel? again, when *Eugenius*, a new ufurper, a new accomplice of
another regicide,(*x*) fent ambaffadors to wait
upon him, fhould he have received them fo
gracioufly? fhould he have lavifhed fuch

A a 3   prefents

(*u*) *Theodofius*, to deceive Maximus, appeared bufied
in the equipment of a large naval force; Maximus fell
into the fnare, and, the more effectually to refift the
pretended attacks of Theodofius, embarked the greater
part of his troops. It was then, that *Theodofius* threw
afide the mafk; and marching towards Maximus, with
a powerful army, attacked and defeated him. It hath
been afferted, but how juftly is difficult to determine,
that *Theodofius*, touched with his misfortune, would have
fpared his life; and that the foldiers, who judged him
unworthy of fo much clemency, ftruck off his head. K.

(*x*) Arbogaftes, who caufed Valentinian to be ftrangled, and then faluted Eugenius, an obfcure wretch,
and once a fchoolmafter, with the title of emperor. K,

presents on them, at their departure, and
shortly afterwards, have marched against their
master, in compliance with the advice of
John the Solitary, and the commands of *Saint
Philip*, and *Saint John the Evangelist*, who,
although they had never borne arms, at any
period of their lives, did, notwithstanding,
make themselves known to him, by appear-
ing, like the *Dioscuri*, under the form of two
beautiful knights, caparisoned from head to
foot. I shall pass by the massacre of *Thessa-
lonica*, a massacre concerted with so much
barbarity, and executed by so detestable a
treachery:—we must not dwell on this atrocious circumstance. All historians unite in
describing it, as a fortunate event, since it
proved the occasion of presenting to the
Christian world a more consoling spectacle;
an emperor humbling himself in the presence
of a bishop:*(y)* but I cannot avoid observing,
that

(y) Ambrosius refusing to receive *Theodosius*, within
the pale of the church, until he had undergone a public
penance, and the contrite emperor implicitly submit-
ting to the injunctions of the bishop, must, undoubtedly, have proved a great occasion of triumph, amongst
the Christians; but comforting as the humiliating atone-
ments

that from the conflagration of *Rome*, as ordered by *Nero*, if *Nero* really was the author of that calamity, and the flaughter at *Alexandria*, under *Caracalla*, hiftory hath not furnifhed us with any inftance of a cruelty, at once fo odious, and fo criminal.

We have already fpoken concerning the judgement, which *Zofimus* hath paffed on *Conftantine*. Thefe two examples may account for the endeavours, which the ecclefiaftical authors have ufed, to weaken the credit of his writings.*(z)* True criticifm, more

A a 4   circumfpeft,

---

ments of fuch a tyrant might be thought, they were too dearly purchafed, with the deftruction of feven thoufand human creatures; for fo many, at leaft, were flaughtered at *Theffalonica.* K.

(z) That the reader may be the better enabled to judge, whether the cri·icifm of Zofimus be abfolutely contemptible, it may be proper to tranfcribe what he hath written, concerning the Monks. Speaking of the troubles excited at Conftantinople, on account of Saint John Chryfoftom, he faith: "the city was expofed to tumults, and the Chriftian church was already in the power of thofe, whom they call Monks. Thefe are men, who have renounced marriage; and who, inhabiting the country, and the cities, have given rife to a clafs of individuals, equally ufelefs, and unfit, either for war, or for any civil employment; whofe only occupation, is the grafping at, and amaffing of immenfe wealth,

ᵕcircumfpect, oppofes fuffrages to fuffrages, fcrutinizes all the interefts, and paffions of hiftorians, and wherefoever it doth not meet with impartiality, fufpends its judgement.

Ammianus Marcellinus hath been treated with more caution and refpect. This, indeed, was the beft expedient, to glofs over a diffent from an author, whofe character, whofe rank in the army, and whofe connections with the firft members of the ftate, are all known; a citizen, who relates his facts with perfpicuity, and that natural and ingenuous attachment, fo conftantly vifible, in the writings of thofe, who have taken fome part in the adminiftration of affairs; in fhort, a military man, whom we fhould, without hefitation, compare to *Mr. de Feuquieres,(a)*

if

wealth, under a pretence of affifting the poor, whilft they themfelves are the means of propagating mifery and beggary." Who doth not perceive from this paffage, how much Zofimus was blinded by prejudice, and what reafon there is to fufpect his judgement?

(a) The *Marquis de Feuquieres* was a lieutenant-general in the French army, during the reign of Lewis the fourteenth. His memoirs were written for the inftruction of his fon. Of thefe an Englifh tranflation was publifhed in 1737, forming two octavo volumes. They contain an account of the feveral operations of

the

if the erudition and the literature, which
have enriched his work, did not give him a
great advantage over the French author.
And yet this *Marcellinus*, from whom all the
hiftorians have borrowed materials, even for
the leaft detail, is, at once, neglected, whenfoever he hazards any favourable expreſſion,
in vindication of the Pagans, or of the emperor *Julian*.

The name of *Julian* is alone fufficient to
revive endlefs difputes.   This emperor, ap-
plauded

_____

the war, of the fieges which were undertaken, and the
battles fought from 1672, to 1710. The military merit of this officer may be called hereditary, and feems to
have defcended to him from his grandfather, and father,
Manaffes, and Ifaac de Pas, who were both defervedly
celebrated for their conduct and intrepidity. The martial genius of Anthony, the fubject of this note, hath
been honorably acknowledged, even by thofe compatriots whom he reviled. But whilft they did juftice
to his abilities, they were fo irritated by the feverity
with which he had attacked them, that it was hu-
moroufly obferved, that the Marquis muft be the braveft
man in Europe, who flept in the very midft of a hundred
thoufand enemies. His work contains a lift of the miftakes committed by the French generals. A propenfity
to cenfure hath fometimes feduced him into a mifrepre-
fentation of facts. Perhaps the lofs of a Marfhal's ftaff
occafioned fuch reprehenfible paffages in a performance
where fo much is to be admired. K.

plauded to the fkies, by the enemies of the
Chriftian faith, hath appeared fo meritorious
in the opinion of a celebrated modern, that
he took the pains to write his hiftory, wherein
he labours to rectify and afcertain the ideas,
which the reader ought to form of him.(b)
It will, doubtlefs, be expected by thofe,
who were offended at the liberty, with which
we have fpoken of *Conftantine*, that Julian, fo
ftriking a contraft to this prince, fhould be
complimented with our panegyrics; for the
fpirit of calumny is continually apt to fufpect
every motive; and its natural malignity eafily

(b) Unlefs I miftake, the modern alluded to, is Mr.
de V. who, in the third chapter of his " Melanges
Philofophiques," fpeaks of Julian, as inferior only to
a fingle individual, if not the greateft man, that ever
exifted. His affertion hath been attacked, and refuted
by *Gauchat*, *Soret*, and others. Were it impoffible for
one of the moft penetrating writers that hath enlightened any age, to be in the wrong; a fimilar paffage in
the " fpirit of laws" might give an irrefiftible weight
to the declaration of Mr. de V. but Montefquieu is not
without his errors, nor will all his readers conclude
him to be infallible, when they perufe this fentence.
" Il n'y a point eû après Julien de prince plus digne de
gouverner des hommes." ... l'Efprit des loix, l. 24.
c. 10, ... V. la vie de Julien par l'Abbé Blet-
terie. K.

fily fuggefts the artifice, which it fuppofes peculiar to the objects of its hatred. For once, at leaft, its conclufions will prove erroneous. Far from taking any fhare in this difpute, we cannot avoid agreeing that both parties have been influenced by a childifh obftinacy, lefs humiliating, however, to falfe zeal, than to philofophy; fince philofophy fhould never affift reafon with the arms of fanaticifm. Such eagernefs to *preconize(c)* an emperor, who ftiled himfelf a philofopher, feemed, if I may be allowed the expreffion, the youthful folly of philofophy. In fact, this averfion from prejudices, this fpringing forward towards the liberty of thinking, which comes, after fo many ages, prepared to enter its appeal againft fuch a multitude of received opinions, cannot, amongft us, be faid to boaft a very ancient origin; and with thefe firft efforts of reafon, paffion hath been frequently intermixed. It was, certainly, a crime to perfecute the Pagans, and

to

(c) *Preconnizare*, a term peculiar to the Roman Catholics, and alluding to the report ufually made in the Popes confiftory, that the party prefented to a benefice, is qualified for it. The expreffion, in this place, fignifies " to beftow exceffive praife." K.

to endeavour to fway their opinions, by the
feverity of punifhments; but was it not'an
equal crime to opprefs chriftianity ? were toleration, and liberty of confcience, the principles which actuated Julian, when he
drenched the empire with the blood of
victims; and when, a fanatic defender of
falfe deities, inftead of following, whilft he
was feated on the throne, the dictates of an
impartial philofophy, he prefented to the
world, in his own perfon, nothing more than
the pattern of a zealous heathen. I cannot
admire either the vertues, which are too
ftrongly tinged with imitation, or heroes
formed only after models. It is difficult to
determine, what character of the comedian
is the moft prevalent in the mind of Julian.
At one moment, it is Marcus Aurelius, at
another moment, Trajan, and then Alexander, whom he is fo eager to copy. This
effort is equally confpicuous in his vertues,
and his abilities. All his actions are concerted, all his defigns are borrowed from ancient examples, and all his compofitions are
grounded on the compofitions of his own
times. The *Myfopogon* is not the work of an
emperor, but the work of a fophift: his panegyrics

negyrics are not such as a *Cæsar* should have pronounced, but such as a Rhetorician would have written. During the war of the Gauls, he seems to have striven to copy Julius Cæsar; during the Persian war, he appears to have imitated the confidence and intrepidity of Trajan; but then, what consistency shall we discover in this medley of philosophy and devotion? in morals, he was a stoic, in the temple, an idolater, and in his closet, an unworthy platonist, who sought to corrupt the doctrine of this sect, by debasing it with the allay of magic.

But if we thus fearlessly treat with so much rigour one of the greatest princes, who adorned the lower empire, how justly, at the same time, ought we to exclaim against that bitterness, with which he hath been calumniated by the ecclesiastical historians? what dependance can we place on their judgment, when after having canonized Constantine, the murderer of his wife and son, they rail at Julian, with the most indecent fury, exerting every possible effort to fix upon his character an imputation of crimes, too atrocious to gain credit, even although they had been attributed to Caligula, and to Nero?

in

in this inftance, we perceive, how zeal over-
leaps all bounds, and to what blind and in-
confiderate exceffes the emotions of hatred
may be driven. Thefe, notwithftanding, are
the very authors who ferve us as guides in
ecclefiaftical matters, and whofe opinion we
ftill frequently follow in profane hiftory.
Having premifed this, it is not without apprehenfions, that we introduce the names of
Socrates, *Sozomenes*, and *Theodoret*; to thefe
writers are we indebted for a multitude of
exceedingly inftructive facts, the authority
of which might admit of a retrenchment of
fome part of that confidence, wherewith they
were received. And here, I muft beg leave
to remark, that thefe facts have, by a fingular
good fortune, maintained an higher decree of
credir, the more the authors who tranfmitted
them, have been neglected. The reafon of
this is very plain. It is impoffible to meet,
in the original, with any fact, or probable
event, which is not either preceded or followed by fuch abfurd tales, as foon deftroy
all that reliance which we might be fuppofed
to place on the teftimony of the author;
whereas in compilations, or in the modern
abridgements, great care hath been taken to
reject

reject whatfoever was fabulous, and to preferve only thofe details, in which the leaft
rifk feems to have been run, at the expence
of veracity. For example, the hiftorians
who have written, fince the time of *Ammianus
Marcellinus*, perceiving that he took notice of
an earthquake, which retarded the works,
carried on to accomplifh the rebuilding of the
temple of Jerufalem, have chofen from the
three authors, whom we have juft mentioned,
every credible circumftance, in the wonderful relation, which they have tranfmitted to
us; and having availed themfelves of thefe,
they thought proper to add, that they were
facts confirmed by *Ammianus Marcellinus*, a
Pagan writer. I muft confefs that there was
a time, when, relying on the credit of modern authors, I believed that *Ammianus Marcellinus* had afferted, that the emperor Julian,
having ordered the temple to be rebuilt, the
work was afterwards interrupted by the in-
terpofition of a miracle; and this appeared
to me the lefs extraordinary, as I know that
the ancients are not fparing of prodigies.
The original reading, fo conftantly neceffary
to enable us to form a judgement, relative to
the events of the paft ages, hath abfolutely

un-

undeceived me. This famous paſſage, ſo
often quoted, and yet ſo ſeldom delivered
with fidelity, runs thus: " although the emperor was much buſied in accelerating the
preparations for his expedition, *(againſt the
Perſians)* he notwithſtanding knew how to
divide his ſollicitude, and attention: neg-
lecting no circumſtance which might tend to
immortalize his reign, he prepared to re-
build a formerly much celebrated temple,
which had been deſtroyed during the continuance of the ſiege of *Jeruſalem*, begun by
Veſpaſian, and terminated by Titus. The
direction of this undertaking, to accompliſh
which immenſe ſums were neceſſary, had been
entruſted to *Alypius*, who formerly commanded in Britain. As this officer, aſſiſted
by the Prefect of the province, was ſuper-
intending and vigorouſly encouraging the
operations, dreadful flames frequently iſſuing
from the foundations, conſumed the workmen, and at length rendered theſe places in-
acceſſible. The irruptions continuing, all attempts to proceed were entirely given up."*(d)*
Here,

(d) Et licet accidentium varietatem ſollicita mente
præcipiens, multiplicatos expeditionis apparatus fla-
grantis

Here, feveral reflections naturally prefent themfelves : firſt, no circumſtance was leſs extraordinary, at that period, than the circumſtance of earthquakes attended by volcanos. At the fame æra, and in the fpace of a century, *Conſtantinople*, *Edeſſa*, *Antioch*, and the majority of the cities of *Aſia Minor*,

VOL. I.   B b   were

---

grantis ſtudio perurgeret, diligentiam tamen ubique dividens, imperiique fui memoriàm magnitudine operum geſtiens propagare, ambitiofum quondam apud. Hierofolymam templum, quod poſt multa et interne civa certamina obſiſtente Vefpaſiano, poſteaque Tito ægre eſt oppugnatum inſtaurare, fumptibus cogitabat immodicis ; negotiumque maturandum Alypio dederat Antiochenſi, qui olim Britannias curaverat pro præfectis. Cum itaque rei idem fortiter inſtaret Alypius, juvaretque provinciæ rector, metuendi globi flammarum prope fundamenta crebris aſſultibus erumpentes fecere locum exuſtis aliquoties operantibus in exceſſum hoc quo modo elemento deſtinatius repellente ceſſavit incertum. Ad verbum e lib. 23 Am. Marcel. fol. Bononiæ, 1517.

The truth of this miracle hath been denied, and aſferted with equal obſtinacy. The celebrated Bafnage endeavours to weaken its credibility in his " hiſtoire des Juifs, vol. 4. Againſt this unbelieving author, and his adherents, the over-bearing giant of literature, William, lord biſhop of Glouceſter, hath appeared within the liſts, and brandiſhing his unconquerable Julian in his hand, hath at leaſt ſilenced antagoniſts whom he could not convince. K.

were deftroyed by earthquakes. Hiftory makes mention of feveral earthquakes, which happened, even at Jerufalem. It is alfo well known, that this country abounds with bitumen, and that the conflagration of fo large a city, and fo rich a temple, muft have produced much fulphureous, and inflammable matter, which might take fire, at the flighteft communication with the air. Secondly, if this event was accompanied by miraculous circumftances, why did *Ammianus Marcellinus,* a lover of the marvellous, as all the ancients were, take fuch care to conceal them ? it will be anfwered that, nothing is more clearly to be accounted for : *Ammianus* was a Pagan, and fuch an event muft have proved a fubject of endlefs triumph, to the Chriftian religion. To this it may be replied, that it is very evident that no fuch effect was produced; and that fuppofing that our author, had not been free from all partiality, one of thefe two circumftances muft have been the cafe; he would either have entirely omitted the fact, or have endeavoured to give it a different interpretation; all which might have been very eafy, fince he could have oppofed a hundred reafons to one reafon. *" The Gods were ir-*
ritated

ritated at perceiving preparations, wherewith to erect a temple to the God of the Jews, a nation, over whom they had triumphed, with such signal success, under Titus. But Heaven would not suffer the treasures, and the labour of the people, to be sacrificed, during such calamitous times, to works, at once useless, and ostentatious." Do we not know that writers never seem to want reasons, wherewith to explain the causes of events? Ammianus did not, therefore, consider this event, as a prodigy, neither had any of his contemporaries embraced a different opinion, since he hath taken no pains to oppose it, nor even deigned to drop the smallest reflection on the subject. Now, I think that the indifference of one party, is, in general, the strongest evidence which can be produced, against the allegations of the other party; for, in short, with how little credit soever, the *convulsionnaires* might be received at present; no author will ever write the history of our times, without making some remarks on what happened at the church of *Saint Medard*, and even the fanatic performance of M**** hath been honoured with some refutations. But *Sozomenes* and *Theodoret* are reputable authors; and they enter into a full

B b 2   detail

detail of this fact.   Be it fo; but if the teftimony of Sozomenes prove of fuch great
weight, we muft, then, believe in forcerers,
we muft imagine that magicians were able to
make the·demons appear before them, and
to command the oracles.*(e)*   We muft alfo
fuppofe that Julian, the leaft fanguinary of
all the princes, ordered the bodies of the
women to be ripped up, that he might confult their entrails; we muft ·be convinced
that the Sibyls have evidently mentioned the
myftery of the redemption, and alluded to
it in this line.

" O felix lignum in quo Deus ipfe pependit."

Neither

(e) It is to Sozomenes that we are obliged for the
childifh ftory of Julian, who is faid to have been introduced into a cave, in order to confult the demons, and
to have made, on his becoming frightened, the fign of
the crofs, which occafioned them to difappear.   This
author quotes a number of oracles, in favour of the
Chriftians; and yet it hath been well known, at leaft,
ever fince the appearance of that famous differtation,
compofed by Mr. Vandale, and the excellent abridge-
ment of it by Mr. de Fontenelle, that the oracles never
were infpired by the demons; and that this whole af-
fair was nothing more than an impofition, carried on
by the deteftable knavery of the priefts,

(*f*) Neither is it to be doubted, that in Judæa, a luminous crofs appeared, which covered half the fky; and that another crofs appeared, during the rebuilding of the temple of *Jerufalem*; and that the habits of the labourers were covered with little ftars, which abfolutely remained fixed thereon, and feemed as if they had been worked into the ftuff.(*g*) If the reader fhould prefer *Theodoret*, he will find that *Julian*, when he quitted *Gaul*, in order to give battle to *Conftantius*, paffed by a vine, the grapes of which had been already gathered, and yet found it loaden with frefh green bunches, having an infinite number of little croffes, imprinted by the drops of dew, upon their berries. It will be no great trouble to open *Socrates*, who hath advanced the fame fact; and from whofe writings thefe authors

B b 3   have

(*f*) See his ecclefiaftical hiftory. b. 11. c. 5.

(*g*) The Chriftians of this period, were poffeffed, even to a degree of frenzy, with a notion that they faw croffes, in every place. When *Theodofius* ordered the temple of *Serapis* to be pulled down, it was reported that in demolifhing the walls, croffes were difcovered, engraven on the greater part of the ftones: but, on a clofer examination, it appeared that thefe engravings reprefented the Phallus. It is well known that the Phallus was a reprefentation of the mark of virility.

have probably copied. The only difference between *Socrates* and Sozomenes, is, that the one afferts that the miracle wrought at Jerufalem, converted all the Jews ; whilft the other affirms, that not one of thofe Jews was either ftricken with thefe prodigies, or difpofed to embrace the religion of the Chriftians.

We fhall conclude this article with a reflection, which feems to have efcaped the notice of the preceding critics ; namely, that whether it arofe from the frauds practifed by the people, who were enemies to drudgery, and labour, or whether it proceeded from that fuperftition, peculiar to unpolifhed minds, in whofe ideas, the great and the marvellous are fo eafily confounded, it frequently happened that important enterprifes were interrupted by prodigies. I fhall only produce one inftance taken from Dion. This author relates, that whilft Nero was attempting to divide the *Ifthmus* of *Corinth*, feveral phantoms appeared, and intimidated the workmen. Thefe phantoms were, in fact, no other than the phantoms of fatigue, and impatience, but the writers of thofe times, were cautious of making fuch a confeffion, for then, a prodigy was of more confequence,

and

and in higher eftimation, than any natural, or probable circumftance whatfoever.*(b)* As to the reft, it would furnifh fuch little occafion of triumph to the Chriftian religion, whether this miracle happened, or not, that we cannot reafonably be taxed with any ill intentions, in the courfe of this inveftigation. We are not, in the prefent inftance, more criminal than many refpectable writers, who have called in queftion, the relation of the miracles of the *Theban Legion*, and the *Labarum*, whatever honour they might have reflected on Chriftianity. Judicious and difcerning criticifms will always redound to the advantage of truth; they will increafe its luftre, either by throwing it into its genuine and moft brilliant light, or by feparating it from all impure allay.

B b 4 We

(b) How many ftories of apparitions, have rifen out of the inventions of lazy, or felf-interefted domeftics? even amongft the troops, fuch relations have been known to gain credit, and abfolutely elude the vigilance, and difcernment of the chief officers. It hath frequently happened that the foldiers fatigued and harraffed with having mounted guard, at fome inconvenient poft, have, at length, feduced others into a perfuafion that it was haunted by a fpirit, and fo, concluded the farce, by deferting their ftations.

We ſhall not enter into the particulars of
thoſe times, which fill up the interval, from
the death of *Conſtantine*, to the deſtruction of
the Weſtern empire. The ravages of deſpotiſm, ſuperſtition, and war, preyed equally
on the conquerors, and the conquered. The
ancient ſtates were driven to the laſt ſtage of
calamity. New nations, or rather *Barbarians*,
as yet ferocious, as yet wandering through
the darkneſs of ignorance; without a country,
and without property; now warriors, and now
travellers; at one moment crowned with victory, and at another moment ſunk in ſlavery;
always agitated, and as conſtantly, either
laden with adverſity, or intoxicated with
ſlaughter, were, then, more aſtoniſhed at,
than charmed with their ſucceſs. No enjoyment followed their acquiſitions, whilſt their
only happy hours were the hours of victory.
All the *Barbarian* princes, except *Genſeric*,
fell by the hands of one another, and periſhed
miſerably.

The motives for war, were, at that period,
the moſt reaſonable, which could have been
ſuggeſted in its juſtification: and theſe motives were, on the one hand, the defence of
their country; and on the other hand, the
neceſſity

neceſſity of procuring a ſubſiſtence, and the deſire of enjoying an happier life, within a milder climate. But this war became more ſanguinary than ever; religion far from diminiſhing the horrors of it, had only given a keener edge to the inveterate exertions of hatred ; ſuch was the ſpirit of party; ſo intimately was it blended with ambition, and all the ſcourges of humanity.

It is not a little ſingular that this æra of guilt and madneſs ſhould have given birth to excellent civil laws.(i) We may perceive, that ſome of the wiſeſt of thoſe laws were inſtituted by princes, who reigned in the very midſt of theſe troubles, and whoſe reigns were alſo but of ſhort duration.(k)

When

(i) Valentinian the firſt introduced a toleration act within his dominions; we read in " l'hiſtoire du bas empire," that this prince, after having long meditated on the part which might be the propereſt for him to take, at length, gave the preference to the worſt part. This book hath been written, ſince the beginning of this century.

(k) Valentinian, who ſucceeded the emperor Julian, in February, 364, and died, in conſequence of the burſting of a vein, during a fit of paſſion, in November 375, did not reign quite twelve years. This prince, perceiving the ſordid habits of the ambaſſadors of the
Quadi,

When the perpetration of abuſes was confined to no limits, ſuch regulations became neceſſary. Thus, amidſt epidemical diſorders, the ſcience of phyſic acquires a greater degree of perfection; and thus, amongſt armies, the knowledge of ſurgery is rendered more unerring, and extenſive. The power of the clergy was, at different times, made ſubject to particular reſtrictions: the boldneſs, and the inſolence of the monks were ſomewhat curbed by the *Chalcedonian council*,(*l*) and the unmarried women were forbidden to take the vows, until they had attained

---

Quadi, a people too poor to purchaſe apparèl, and too unpoliſhed to underſtand the propriety of dreſs, ridiculouſly imagined that their garbs had been aſſumed, with an intention to inſult him, and thus ſacrificed his life to the violence of rage. Valens, his brother and aſſociate in the empire, had only reached the fifteenth year of his reign, when taking refuge after his defeat within a neighbouring houſe, he was ſurrounded by the Goths, who, with the building, reduced the body of their enemy to aſhes. K.

(*l*) They were made ſubject to the juriſdiction of the ordinary, and forbidden to intermeddle in civil affairs, and particularly in matters relating to the finances. " Hiſt. du bas emp. l. 33.

tained to the age of forty.*(m)* Each city was allowed its tribunes, or protectors, who, under the title of *defenfores*, undertook to plead the caufes of the poor and oppreffed citizens. *(n)* The emperors, alarmed at the readinefs, with which they granted favours, and privileges, directed that their conduct fhould be fubmitted to the examination of the magiftrates, and commanded thefe laft to pay no regard to their orders, whenfoever they did not appear ftrictly conformable to the eftablifhed laws. But fuch precautions which ftill fubfift amongft the French, and are ufeful under an abfolute form of government,*(o)* difcover an imperfection in the main

spring

(m) This law was inftituted by Majorian, who made a ridiculous decree, obliging all widows who had no children, either to marry again, or to give up the half of their effects, to their next heirs. ibid. l. 34.

(n) Under Valentinian, and Valens.

(o) An ordinance paffed, during the reign of Lewis the twelfth, forbidding the magiftrates to pay the leaft regard to the " lettres de juffion," *(letters containing orders from the chancellor, &c.)* whenfoever they fhould be found contrary to the laws of the monarchy, and the public welfare.

With this edict, no unpleafing earneft of the fubfequent felicity of his people, Lewis opened a reign, which,

fpring of the political machine, a defect in
the conftitution. Republics are ftrangers to
any thing like this: and it were perhaps
better that authority fhould reftrain its powers
of adminiftration, within certain bounds,
than that the difobedience of the magiftrates
fhould be connived at. The emperors alfo
concerted meafures, to render travelling more
eafy. The roads were repaired; places of
accommodation were erected, at convenient
diftances, and relays were always kept in
readinefs, at the expence of the provinces.

At

---

which, could we throw a veil over his mercenary dif-
pofal of preferments, his unworthy protection of Alexander the fixth, the worft Pope, and the worft man,
and his defertion of his allies, the Swifs, approached
nearer than moft other reigns to the government of an
excellent father, over his fortunate children. In fpite
of fome difagreeable fhades, his picture, as drawn by
the rough pencil of *Saint Gelais*, is certainly a juft refemblance. " *Il ne courut oncques du regne de nul des au-
tres fi bon tems qu'il a fait durant le fien.*" It is fcarcely
poffible for an Englifhman, who perceives even in a
rival ftate fuch multitudes deferving of a better lot, to
clofe this note, before he hath remarked, with equal
indignation and concern, that had the ordinance of
Lewis fubfifted in its full force, during the prefent period, every *lettre de juffion* would have proved as infignificant, as are the murmurs of the meaneft peafant,
who languifhes under its oppreffions. K.

At this period, mankind had no idea of the very interefting fcience of finances and commerce. The neceffity of erecting an impaffable wall, around the frontiers, to prevent the circulation of the national fpecies, through foreign countries, was, then, univerfally affented to: and this opinion hath prevailed, even till within thefe fifty years. *Conftantius* proclaimed a law, declaring that commerce fhould be carried on, folely, by barter. It provided that all foreign negociators, on their arrival, within the empire, fhould be obliged to declare what fums of money, they brought with them, in order that means might be taken to prevent them, from adding to thofe fums, previous to their return. The fame law prohibited an exchange of the money of the empire, for the money of any other nation. It was not, at that time, known that merchandize can command fpecies, and that without liberty, neither commerce, nor riches can exift.

As to the *Barbarians*, no fooner did they acquire a degree of ftability, before they turned their thoughts towards a neceffary legiflation. They feem to have fucceeded even better than the emperors, whofe too compli-

cated

cated laws were fomewhat infected with the fubtlety of the Greeks. The *Theodorician* code was during a long time in force, in Spain, and it may, in part, be difcovered in the capitulars of *Charlemagne*. But this is a fubject, on which we muft expatiate more largely, in the courfe of the following chapters, where fociety will affume a different afpect, and where we fhall find a new order of things, a new political, and moral fyftem. In fact, the very expreffion, *feodal law*, of itfelf fufficiently announces the greateft revolution, which hath ever been effected upon earth, and at once reveals to us the fcources of all modern governments. It is time, therefore, that we take our leave of this celebrated people, to whofe fway the univerfe fubmitted and whofe ftate we have prefumed to make the fubject of our obfervations. After having feen them laborioufly extend themfelves through the little territory of the *Romagna*, free themfelves from the *yoke* of kings, reduce nations under their own yoke, become intoxicated with glory and fuccefs, fall into that imbecility which fucceeds a delirium, then, wear frefh chains, grow fhortly more mean, and abject, than they were once

haughty,

haughty, and oftentatious; and, to fill up the meafure of infamy, yield to *Barbarians*, the empire of arms, and to effeminate Greeks, the empire of opinion, we, at length, find them, fubmitting to the power of a *Goth*, and an *Herulian*.(p)

Before we turn our eyes afide from this prodigious ruin, we muft lament, not that fuch a feries of good fortune fhould have been eclipfed, to leave behind it, only the moft melancholy traces; but that a period of near twelve centuries affords no æra, at which fo powerful a nation hath attempted to clofe the wounds of humanity, by cherifhing the exiftence of public welfare and profperity. We are not apprehenfive of afferting, that all the long and brilliant career of the *Roman* empire, cannot, to a philofopher, be worth the times, which have elapfed in England, from the revolution, to the prefent period; but of this, we muft treat more fully in the courfe of our work. We fhall, however, obferve, that as in the celeftial revolutions, the planets are confined to their particular motions, fo, in political revolutions,

the

(p) Odoacer, and Theodoric.

the capitals, the great cities are fubject, alfo,
to their deftiny, their peculiar fortune, which
either accelerates, or retards their deftruction,
which either overthrows, or fupports them.
But farther; this particular chain of circumftances is, according to all appearance, more
frequently advantageous, than detrimental to
them.   Experience proves that, during thofe
unhappy times, when military defpotifm rofe
upon the wreck of government, the great
cities always maintained a kind of liberty.
The reafon is, becaufe, however fpecious the
mafk which policy may have affumed, force
alone preferves the privilege of governing ;
becaufe a great number of men, ftrictly
united, become refpectable ; and becaufe the
multitude, or common people are always to
be dreaded ; efpecially, when deprived of re-
prefentatives, and protectors, they exprefs
their meaning only by tumultuous fhouts,
and act but by fome fudden, and wild affault.
Even Rome was not reduced to this laft ftage
of power.   She always enjoyed the fame order
of magiftrates ; and the credit of names, is
to a degenerated people, what the credit of
the magiftracy itfelf, is to a vertuous people.
Some remains of Ariftocracy maintained their
ground,

ground, in this metropolis of the world; and
to thefe remains Paganifm was conftantly attached; all which fully confirms what hath
been before advanced, relative to the union
of this religion, with the Roman ariftocracy.
The *Symmachi* and the *Pretextati* revived the
memory of *Cato*, and of *Cincinnatus*. As to
the people, if they retained the leaft traces of
their ancient liberty, they were vifible in the
indifference with which they frequently treated the moft formidable emperors. The dif-
guft, which the furious Dioclefian conceived
at their behaviour, is well known. When
Conftantius, all covered with the blood of his
fubjects, made his triumphal entry into *Rome*,
low tauntings, and ridiculous jefts were, according to the ancient cuftom, levelled at
him, with impunity. This fplendid city was
yet filled with riches, when the Barbarians
pillaged it, for the firft time. Several authors
affert, that many citizens were in poffeffion
of a revenue of above four millions; and
that fuch as were worth no more than a million, or a million and an half, were placed
only in the fecond clafs of citizens. Thefe
indolent and opulent men imagined that the
enjoyment of pleafure was the fole end of

VOL. I.   C c   their

their creation; and were contented to remain as idle fpectators of the events of war, as they were of the events of the Circus; with this difference only, that in thefe laft events, they feemed to feel themfelves more interefted. Even the emperors had, during a long time, accuftomed them to this luxurious effeminacy. *I go* (faid *Aurelius* to them, in one of his edicts) *to fight the enemy: and I will take care that the Romans fhall not fuffer the flighteft un-eafinefs. Attend to your games. Frequent your Circus. It is our part to conduct the public bufinefs. But you fhould be entirely devoted to pleafure.(q)* It is eafy to conceive that in the midft of fo much luxury, and effeminacy, the public morals were daily degenerating. *Petronius* and *Lucian* have made us fufficiently acquainted with the parade and extravagance, peculiar to the entertainments, which were given in their times: but as *Ammianus Marcellinus* hath taken the pains to defcribe the manners of the Romans, during a lefs diftant period, namely, the age in which he lived, the reader will, probably, be pleafed

---

(q) Ego efficiam ne fit aliqua follicitudo Romana. Vacate ludis, vacate Circenfibus; nos publicae neceffitates teneant, vos occupent voluptates. (Vopifcus.)

pleafed if we prefent him with the whole
paffage, as related in the fixth chapter of the
fourteenth book.

Were you, on your arrival at Rome, to be in-
troduced, as a reputable foreigner, to an opulent,
or in other words, a very oftentatious man, your
firft reception would be accompanied with every
mark of politenefs; after having been over-
powered by queftions, to which it will be the
moft frequently neceffary to anfwer, by relating
fome extravagant ftories, you will become afto-
nifhed to find, that a perfon of fuch diftinction,
fhould treat a fimple individual with fo re-
fpectful an attention: nay, you will even be ready
to condemn yourfelf for not having vifited fo
charming a city, ten years fooner. But if, en-
couraged by this obliging welcome, you fhould re-
turn on the morrow, to pay your compliments,
a ftranger, dropped from the clouds, could not
be more ftared at. Who is he? and, whence
comes he? would be circulated in ill-bred whif-
pers round the room. At length, however,
you will attain to the honour of being known,
and admitted on a familiar footing; but yet, if,
after three years of affiduous attendance, you
were to abfent yourfelf, for the fame fpace of

C c 2 *time,*

time, you would not, on your return, be either asked how you had been employed, or even told that the loss of your company was perceived. This absurdity is carried still farther, for, previous to the giving of those entertainments, which are so long, and so detrimental to health, it is a matter of tedious deliberation, whether, exclusive of such guests, as are entitled to invitations, any strangers shall also be asked: and if, after a full hearing, and on mature reflection, this point be carried in the affirmative, then the great adepts in all the laws of public games, who never fail to mount guard at the houses of the charioteers belonging to the Circus, *or persons the most instructed in the science, and the tricks of play, are the only strangers destined to be admitted. As to the men of learning, and vertue, they are shunned, as the tiresome and useless disturbers of festive mirth: nor doth it once employ their thoughts that the* Nomenclatores, *accustomed to sell the favours of their masters, take care to invite to the feast, and the distributions, only the most obscure and inferiour individuals, from whom they can extort more money, than from the others. I shall pass slightly over that sumptuous profusion, in their entertainments, and particularly those voluptuous refinements*

ments lately introduced, to take notice of the ridiculous cavalcades, attending on our oftentatious, rich men, who amufing themfelves with running poft, up and down the ftreets, at the rifk of breaking their necks, on the pavement, are followed by fuch a numerous train of domeftics, that, to borrow the expreffion of a comic writer, they do not even leave the fool behind, to keep houfe: however abfurd this diverfion be, the very matrons are not afhamed to follow it, but hurry through every quarter of the town, in open litters. In thefe pompous proceffions, nothing is neglected, and as the expert general, who marfhals his army, in a proper order of battle, places his heavy infantry in the front line, his light infantry in the fecond line, and his bowmen in the rear, fo the mafter of the ceremonies, bearing a wand in his hand, fingles out all thofe who are to have the honour of walking before the triumphal car, and conftantly obliges the black troop of cooks, fcullions, &c. to fall back into the hinder ranks. Thefe, again, are followed by the remaining number of footmen, and by the Commenfales: *the proceffion is then clofed by the eunuchs, a deformed multitude, who teach us to execrate the memory of* Semiramis, *that barbarous queen, who, firft violating the*

laws

laws of nature, filled this tender, but imprudent mother, with regret, for having too early shewn, in the generations which were scarce begun, the hope of future generations. In such a state of manners, it will easily be supposed, that the few houses, in which the sciences were formerly cultivated, are now only the receptacles of vain and frivolous pleasures: so that in the place of orators, and philosophers, nothing is heard from morning till night, except the sound of flutes, and the airs of the musicians. As to the libraries, they are more shut up and more abandoned than the sepulchres: dances, accompanied by wind instruments are substituted in their room: nay, to so shameful a length have these indignities been carried, that when the famine had rendered it necessary, to send all foreigners out of the city, the law was rigorously put in execution against every one of those useful men, who were the instructors in liberal arts; whilst mimics, stage players, and even three thousand female dancers, with their whole band of musicians and singers, were suffered to remain within the capital. Wheresoever you turn your eyes, you will, also, perceive the women painted, and ridiculously dressed; these tire you more by their continual dancing, than they fatigue themselves;

felves ; *and thefe, had they been married to honeft men, might have fupplied the ftate with an ufeful army of citizens. Rome was once a fure afylum to every individual, who introduced the arts and induftry ; but now, a foolifh and unaccountable vanity efteems every thing vile, and abject, which comes from beyond the* Pomærium. *I muft, however, except the unmarried men, and fuch as have no heirs. Thefe are loaden with refpect and complaifance ; although another felfifh refinement makes us avoid even the tendereft duties of humanity ; for the moft terrible difeafes, raging within this capital of the world, have occafioned a ftrict prohibition of the leaft communication with thofe unhappy wretches, who are infected with them : and it is now cnftomary, not only to think it fufficient, if fome domeftics be fent to thefe perfons, to enquire of them any particular news, but to oblige the meffenger to go through long ablutions before he can be admitted, to deliver the anfwer. How delicate thefe men are ! and yet, if you invite them to a feaft, or offer them money, they will run for you, even to* Spoletum. *Such are the manners of the nobility : as to the common people, they generally fpend the night in drinking houfes, or even in the theatres, under thofe*

booths,

booths, the invention of which we owe to Ca-
tulus, *who firſt introduced at* Rome *theſe far-
fetched commodities, which might better have
become* Capua, *than the city of* Romulus. *Multitudes are intoxicated with a paſſion for gaming.
Others expoſe themſelves, during whole days,
to the heat, and the rain, to be the umpires
amongſt the charioteers, and decide on the events
of the* Circus. *Amidſt ſuch frivolous engagements,
is it poſſible that the* Romans *can ever be reaſonably employed?* &c. &c.

END OF THE FIRST VOLUME.

APPENDIX.

ADDITIONAL NOTES.

SECTION I. CHAPTER I. page 33. line 7. Thefe pyramids, in vain intended to efcape the rage of time, are now mouldering into ruin. " When the monarchs of Egypt erected fuch ftupendous maffes, for no other ufe but to record their names, they little fufpected that a weed growing by the Nile would one day be converted into more durable regifters of fame, than quarries of marble, and granite." I am indebted for this remark to Mr. Horace Walpole, one of thofe un-common writers in whofe hands the pen of hiftory amufes the imagination, whilft it enlightens the under-ftanding.

SECTION I. CHAPTER II. page 54. note (i). " Diodorus Siculus affigns three millions of inhabitants to Egypt ; a fmall number ; but then he makes the number of their cities amount to eighteen thoufand : an evident contradiction." See Hume's effay on the populoufnefs of ancient nations. vol. 2. 8vo. p. 224.

SECTION I. CHAPTER II. page 57. note (l). I flatter myfelf that the reader who hath no opportunity of con-fulting the works of that celebrated political arithme-tician, Sir William Petty, will not think me tref-paffing upon his time, whilft I prefent him with a quo-tation, the fingularity of which may atone for its length. " Here, I beg leave, among the feveral matters which I intend for ferious, to interpofe a jocular, and perhaps whimfical digreffion, and which I indeed defire men to look upon rather as a dream, or refverie, than a rati-onal propofition, the which is, that if all the moveables, and people of Ireland, and of the highlands of Scotland, were tranfported into the reft of Great Britain, that then the king, and his fubjects would thereby become more rich, and ftrong, both offenfively, and defenfively, than now they are."

a

" It

" It is true that I have heard many wife men fay when they were bewailing the vaft loffes of the Englifh in preventing, and fuppreffing rebellions in Ireland, and confidering how little profit hath returned either to the king, or fubjects of England, for their five hundred years doing, or fuffering in that country, I fay, I have heard wife men, in fuch their melancolies, wifh that the people of Ireland being faved, that ifland were funk under water. Now, it troubles me that the diftemper of my own mind in this point, carries me to dream that the benefit of thofe wifhes may be obtained practically, without finking that vaft mountainous ifland under water, which I take to be fomewhat difficult; for although Dutch engineers may drain its bogs, yet I know no artifts that could fink its mountains. If ingenious, and learned men, amongft whom I reckon fir Thomas More, and Des-Cartes, have difputed that we, who think ourfelves waking, are, or may be really in a dream; and fince the greateft abfurdities of dreams are but a prepofterous, and tumultuary contexture of realities, I will crave the umbrage of thefe great men laft named, to fay fomething for this wild conception, with fubmiffion to the better judgment of all thofe that can prove themfelves awake."

" If there were but one man living in England, then the benefit of the whole territory could be but the livelihood of that one man: but if another man were added, the rent, or benefit of the fame would be double, if two, triple; and fo forward until fo many men were planted in it, as the whole territory could afford food unto: For if a man would know what any land is worth, the true, and natural queftion muft be, how many men are there to be fed? but to fpeak more practically, land of the fame quantity, and quality in England is generally worth four, or five times as much as in Ireland, and but $\frac{1}{4}$ or $\frac{1}{3}$ of what it is worth in Holland; becaufe England is four or five times better peopled than Ireland, and but $\frac{1}{4}$ fo well as Holland. And moreover, where the rent of land is advanced by reafon of a multitude of people, there the number of years purchafe, for which the inheritance may be fold, is alfo advanced, though perhaps not in the very fame proportion; for 20s. per annum in Ire-

land

land may be worth but 8l. and in England, where titles are very sure, above 20l. in Holland, above 30l."

I suppose that in Ireland, and the Highlands in Scotland, there may be about 1800000 people, or about $\frac{1}{5}$ part of what is in all the three kingdoms. Wherefore the first question will be whether England, Wales, and the lowlands of Scotland cannot afford food, that is to say, corn, fish, flesh, and fowl to $\frac{1}{5}$ part more people than are at present planted upon it, with the same labour that the said $\frac{1}{5}$ part do now take where they are? for if so, then what is propounded, is naturally possible. 2. It is to be enquired what the value of the immoveables which upon such removal must be left behind, are worth? for if they be worth less than the advancement of the price of land in England will amount unto, then the proposal is to be considered. 3. If the deserted lands, and the immoveables left behind upon them may be sold for money, or if no other nation shall dare meddle with them, without paying well for them: and if the nation who shall be admitted shall be less able to prejudice, and annoy the transplantees into England, than before; then I conceive that the whole proposal will be a pleasant, and a profitable dream indeed.

"As to the first point, whether England, and the lowlands of Scotland can maintain $\frac{1}{5}$ part more people than they now do, that is to say, nine millions of souls in all? for answer thereunto, I first say that the said territories of England, and the lowlands of Scotland contain about 36 millions of acres, that is four acres for every head, man, woman, and child; but the United provinces do not allow above 1 acre and $\frac{1}{2}$; and England itself rescinding Wales, hath but 3 acres to every head, according to the present state of tillage, and husbandry. Now, if we consider that England having but three acres to every head as aforesaid, doth so abound in victuals, as that it maketh laws against the importation of cattle, flesh, and fish, from abroad; and that the draining of fens, improving of forests, inclosing of commons, sowing of Saint-foin and clover-grass be grumbled against by landlords, as the way to depress the price of victuals, then it plainly follows that less than three acres improved as it may be, will serve the turn, and consequently that four will suffice

abundantly. I could here fet down the very number
of acres that would bear bread, and drink corn, together with flefh, butter, and cheefe, fufficient to
victual 9 millions of perfons, as they are victualled in
fhips, and regular families: but fhall only fay in general that twelve millions of acres, viz. $\frac{1}{3}$ of thirty-fix
millions, will do it, fuppofing that roots, fruits, fowl,
and fifh, and the ordinary profit of lead, tin, iron
mines, and woods would piece up any defect that may
be feared."

" As to the fecond, I fay that the land, and houfing in
Ireland, and the Highlands of Scotland, at the prefent
market rates are not worth 13 millions of money ; nor
would the actual charge of making the tranfplantation
propofed, amount to 4 millions more: fo then the
queftion will be, whether the benefit expected from
this tranfplantation will exceed 17 millions." " To
which I fay, that the advantage will probably be near
4 times the laft mentioned fum, or about 69300000l.
For if the rent of all England, and Wales, and the
Lowlands of Scotland be about 9 millions per annum,
and if the fifth part of the people be fuperadded unto
the prefent inhabitants of thofe countries, then the rent
will amount unto 10,800,000l. and the number of
years purchafe will rife from $17\frac{1}{2}$ to $\frac{1}{5}$ more, which is 21.
So as the land which is now worth but 9 millions per
annum, at $17\frac{1}{2}$ years purchafe, making 157 millions
and $\frac{1}{2}$, will then be worth 10800000l. at 21 years purchafe, viz. 226,800000l. that is 69,300000l. more
than it was before."

" And if any prince willing to enlarge his territories,
will give any thing more than $6\frac{1}{2}$ millions, or half the
prefent value for the faid relinquifhed lands, which are
eftimated to be worth 13 millions, then the whole profit
will be above 75,800,600l. or above four times the lofs,
as the fame was above computed. But if any man
fhall object that it will be dangerous unto England,
that Ireland fhould be in the hands of any other nation.
I anfwer in fhort, that that nation, whoever fhall purchafe it, being divided by means of the faid purchafe,
fhall not be more able to annoy England, than now in
its united condition: nor is Ireland nearer England,
than France, or Flanders.

" Now

" Now if any man fhall defire a more clear explanation, how, and by what means the rents of lands fhall
rife by this clofer cohabitation of people above defcribed ? I anfwer, that the advantage will arife in
tranfplanting about 1800000 people from the poor,
and miferable trade of hufbandry, to more beneficial
handicrafts ; for when the fuperaddition is made, a
very little addition of hufbandry to the fame lands will
produce ⅟₄ more of food, and confequently the additional hands, earning but 40s. per annum, (as they
may very well do, nay to 8l. per annum) at fome other
trade, the fuperlucration will be above 3,600000l. per
annum, which at 20 years purchafe, is 70 millions.
Moreover, as the inhabitants of cities, and towns,
fpend more commodities, and make greater confump-
tions than thofe who live in wild, thin-peopled countries ; fo when England fhall be thicker peopled in the
fame manner above defcribed, the very fame people
fhall then fpend more, than when they lived more for-
didly, and more inurbanely, and farther afunder, and
more out of fight, obfervation, and emulation of each
other; every man defiring to put on better apparel
when he appears in company, than when he has no occafion to be feen."

" I further add that the charge of the government,
civil, military, and ecclefiaftical would be more cheap,
fafe, and effectual in this condition of clofer cohabitation, than otherwife, as not only reafon, but the example of the United provinces doth demonftrate."

With what juftice Sir William drew thefe obfervations from the compleétion of affairs, towards the clofe
of the laft century, and whether they can in any manner
be applicable to the prefent times, the intelligent politician muft determine.

SECTION I. CHAPTER V. Page 151. Note (a) The
commentaries on Polybius are ample teftimonies of the
military experience of the chevalier de Folard, an able
and intrepid officer. He had the honour of inftructing
Marfhal de Saxe, and frequently foretold the luftre
which fo particularly diftinguifhed the riper years of
that hero. Such a pupil is the beft panegyric on the
mafter. The materials of his work are more excellent,
than the form, into which they are thrown, is pleafing,

The

The ſtile is negligent, the reflections are too detached, and the digreſſions often long and needlefs. Yet his talents were as eminent as his vertues. It is a melancholy circumſtance, that integrity and knowledge, which ſhould be the moſt invincible ſecurities againſt the abſurdities of ſuperſtition, are not conſtantly ſufficient to guard us from it. Folard enliſted amongſt the partiſans for the miracles of the Abbé de Paris, and therefore, the cardinal de Fleury, who perſecuted, when he ſhould have pitied, prevented his advancement. The other works of this writer are " Nouvelles decouvertes ſur la guerre." " Traité de la défenſe des places." " Traité du metier de Partiſan." He died at Avignon in 1751.

Section I. Concluſion of the fifth chapter. note (f). Paulus Æmilius addreſſed the Romans in words to this effect. " The conviction that ſuch an honour was neceſſary to my views, induced me to ſollicit the elevation to my firſt conſulſhip: that I am again choſen to fill this important ſtation, muſt have proceeded from your being ſenſible how much you wanted the ſervices of ſuch a general. For this reaſon, I cannot imagine that I owe you any thanks : if it be your opinion that the operations of the war may be more advantageouſly conducted by another, than by me, I will chearfully reſign my poſt. If, on the contrary, you confide in my abilities, remember that I will not ſuffer you to interfere with me, in the execution of my office. It is not your province to preſcribe the meaſures which I am to purſue, but in ſubmiſſive ſilence to furniſh me with all the means which may be wanting to the accompliſhment of my deſigns. By an endeavour to govern me, whom you have exalted to the chief command, you muſt unavoidably render this expedition as ridiculous as the former expedition."

Section I. Chapter VI. Page 178. Line 17. Polieuctes, a character in a tragedy of that name; written by Corneille.

Section I. Chapter VI. page 194. note (r). This period of the Roman hiſtory is caſt within ſo marvellous a mold, that every leſs exaggerated fable, when put in competition with ſuch abſurd romances, aſſumes the face of ſober truth. When Florus obſerves

that

that " tum illa Romana prodigia, atque miracula Horatius, Mucius, Clelia, quæ nisi in annalibus forent,
hodie fabulæ viderentur," he seems, however, credu-.
lous himself, to authorise our doubts. The extraordinary anecdote of Horatius is indeed supported by the
testimonies of Livy, Dionysius Halicarnaffius, and
Plutarch, who mention his having plunged into the
Tyber, and rejoined his fellow soldiers ; but it is remarkable that Polybius, a writer of no inconfiderable.
weight, hath afferted that Horatius perished in the
river. " Ο δι Κοκλης ριψας εαυτον εις τον ποταμον εν τοις
οπλοις κατα προαιρεσιν, μετηλλαξε τον βιον." lib. 6. To
the remark which the ingenious author of this work
hath made, concerning the filence of Dionysius, on
the fubject of Mutius Scævola, having reduced his hand
to ashes, may be added the circumstance of his being
conftantly ftiled by that hiftorian, Cordus, and not
Scævola. The account of Clelia is equally involved in
obfcurity, and varioufly related by Livy, Dionyfius,
and Plutarch. The latter obferves that it is not certain
that this valiant female paffed the river on horfeback.
Why, therefore, was she honoured with an equeftrian
ftatue ? but Dionyfius only calls it a ftatue of Bronze,
and Plutarch doubts whether it was erected to Clelia,
or to Valeria, the daughter of the conful. Such is the
conformity peculiar to the hiftorians of the five firft
centuries of Rome ! though truths were mingled in thefe
varieties of defcription, it would be difficult to feparate
them from the falfities with which they are fo frequently interwoven.

I have never feen the differtation by Mr, de Pouilly ;
a book, with a fimilar title was publifhed abroad in
1738; its author was fuppofed to be Mr. de Beaufort,
who fome few years fince favoured the world with
" la republique Romaine, ou plan general de l'ancien
gouvernement de Rome." To his former work, " differtation fur l'incertitude des cinq premiers fiecles de
l'hiftoire Romaine," I acknowledge myfelf entirely
indebted for the materials of this note. They deliver
the fentiments of an ingenious, and learned writer, as
accurately as they could be collected during the fhort
opportunity, which an accidental perufal once afforded
me: The champion, who, in fupport of the *certainties*
of the Roman hiftory, entered the lifts againft Mr. de

Pouilly,

Pouilly, was Abbé Sallier, whose pleafing elegance of ftile hath fometimes difguifed the weaknefs of his arguments. His moft violent attacks are directed againft the leaft defenfible conclufions of his antagonift, who is faid to have filled feveral pages which fhould have been enriched by the exertions of his own abilities, with inferences drawn from the parallels foifted into the works of Plutarch, and long fince acknow-ledged as the productions of an obfcure author in the tenth century.

SECTION I. Conclufion of the 6th chapter. note *(a)*. l. 10. "Nemo ferè faltat fobrius, nifi fortè infanit: neque in folitudine, neque in convivio honefto. Intempeftivi convivii, amœni loci, multarum deliciarum comes eft extrema, faltatio." Cic. orat. pro Muræna.

SECTION I. CHAPTER VIII. page 240. note(*m*) "Quid aliud exitio Lacædemoniis, et Athenienfibus fuit, quamquam armis pollerent, nifi quod victos pro alienigenis arcebant?"

SECTION I. CHAPTER VIII. page 250. note *(u)*. "Magna vero quondam fterilitate, ac difficili remedio, cum venalitias et laniftarum familias, peregrinofque omnes, exceptis medicis, et præceptoribus, partemque fervitiorum urbe expuliffet: ut tandem annona convaluit, impetum fe cepiffe fcribit, frumentationes publicas in perpetuum abolendi, quod earum fiducia cultura agrorum ceffaret: neque tamen perfeveraffe quia certum haberet, poffe per ambitionem quandoque reftitui. Atque ita poft hanc rem temperavit, ut non minorem aratorum, ac negotiantium, quam populi rationem deduceret." Suet. vit. Augufti. c. 42.

SECTION II. CHAPTER II. page 294. l. 10. "Flora, cum magnas opes ex arte meretricia quæfiviffet, populum fcripfit hæredem, certamque pecuniam reliquit, cujus ex annuo fœnore fuus natalis dies celebrareretur, editione ludorum quos appellant Floralia. Quod quia fenatui flagitiofum videbatur, ab ipfo nomine argumentum fumi placuit, ut pudendæ rei quædam dignitas adderetur, deam finxerunt effe, quæ floribus præfit, eamque oportere placari, ut fruges cum arboribus, aut vitibus benè, profperèque florefcerent." Lactant. inft. l. 1. c. 20.

It

It is fcarcely neceffary to obferve, that the above relation is imagined to be the invention of the writer. Lactantius is the more liable to be fufpected, as he produces no authority to fupport his affertion. Flora was the Chloris of the Greeks. "Chloris eram quæ Flora vocor." Ovid. She was afterwards received as a divinity by the Sabines, and then acknowledged by the Romans. The indecencies which prevailed at the celebration of her rites, might, however, naturally have fuggefted to the pious father an idea that this goddefs, like her fifter-deities, was no better than a ftrumpet. If the reader chufes to examine the paffages which weaken the evidence of Lactantius, he may refer to Varro; Ennius. Ovid. faft. 195, &c. and Græv. præfat. ad. 1. tom. thefaur. A. R.

SECTION II. CHAPTER III. page 304. note *(x)*. "The difciples were called Chriftians firft in Antioch." Acts, c. 11. v. 26 Until that period, they were ftiled by the Jews, Nazarenes; or Galileans; and by each other, difciples, believers, brethren, faints. I have no opportunity of confulting Bingham's antiquities of the church," to which my learned author refers the reader, but fuppofe that by the appellations, ικλικτοι, γνοστικοι, are meant the different fects, which, like the Therapeutæ, and a multitude of others, diffatisfied with the fimplicity of the Chriftian religion, attempted to eftablifh a mode of worfhip, drawn from the abfurd licentioufnefs of their own imaginations. The Eclectics, whilft they refufed their attachment to any particular fchool, pretended to felect from all, fuch tenets only as they deemed rational. The Gnoftics, bewildered in a ridiculous maze of errors, and affecting to have received extraordinary illuminations, approached nearer, in their fyftems of faith, to ideots, than the reft of their contemporary heretics. They maintained the exiftence of eight different heavens, each governed by its refpective prince. Sabaoth, their prince of the feventh heaven, created the heavens, and the earth, the fix heavens below him, and an innumerable hoft of angels. Barbelo, fometimes the father, and fometimes the mother of the univerfe, was placed in the eighth heaven. God, and the creator of the world were two diftinct beings. Chrift was not born of the virgin Mary, and when fent to redeem man, did
not

not affume real flefh, nor fuffer but in appearance. Re-
furrection, and a future judgment were difbelieved by
the Gnoftics, who imagined that their followers would
return into the world, and enter into the bodies of
hogs, and other animals. The gratification of their
appetites was afferted to be at once legal, and commendable ; to this article of their creed, they were attached with an undeviating bigotry. Their apocry-
phal books, of which they had many, were not calculated to prevent them from being diffolute. If Epi-
phanius may be credited, their " prophecy of Batfuba,"
" Gofpel of perfection," and, " Mary's queftions, and
lying in," were filled with the moft contemptible ob-
fcenities. The Therapeutæ were melancholy, mifguided enthufiafts ; their tenets were lefs fanciful, and
more harmlefs than the tenets of the Gnoftics. They
were lovers of folitude, filence, and contemplation ;
yet could mingle amongft their own difciples, fing fuch
hymns as they had compofed, and fometimes dance together during the whole night. It is not certain that
they were a branch of the Effenes ; nor, probably, were
they, as hath been fuppofed, either Chriftians, or
Egyptians. Stiling themfelves, the true difciples of
Mofes, and vain of fuch a title, it is natural to imagine that they were Jews.

SECTION II. CHAPTER III. Page 309. Note (f)
Claude Fleury, prior of Argenteuil, was chofen, by
the duke of Orleans, confeffor to Lewis the fifteenth.
Abbé Dorfanne obferves that when he was advanced to
this office, an age of feventy-five years was the fole objection which could be found againft him. He felt that
it was infuperable, and refigned his employment in
1722. In fome months afterwards, and when he was
eighty-three, an apoplexy put a period to his life. His
capital work is the ecclefiaftical hiftory, unlefs we except the preliminary difcourfes affixed to it, which ex-
ceed in elegance, purity, precifion, and force, the generality of his other writings, where negligence, a tame
monotony of ftile, and fome pedantry frequently occur.

SECTION II. Chapter III. page 309. l. 17. Οἱ απο Ιεδαιων
εις τον Ιησεν πιςευοντες ε καταλελοιπασι τον πατριον νομον, βιεσι
γαρ κατ' αυτον επωνιμοι της κατα την εκδοχην πλωχειας τε νομε
γεγενημενοι. Εβιων τε γαρ ο πλωχος παρα Ιεδαι ις καλειται, και
Εβιωναιοι χρηματιζεσιν οι απο Ιεδαιων τον Ιησεν ως Χριςον πα-
ραδεξαμενοι. Και ο Πετρος δε μεχρι πολλε φαινεται τα κατα
τον Μωϋσεως νομον Ιεδαικα εθη τετηρηκεναι, &c. Και αυτος ο
Παυλος τοις Ιεδαιοις Ιεδαιος εγινετο, ινα Ιεδαιες κερδηση.

Judæi qui in Jefum crediderunt non defciverunt a pa-
triis legibus; vivunt enim juxta eas, paupertati fuæ
legis cognomines. Nam Ebion pauper Judaicâ lingua
vocatur, et Ebionæi dicuntur a ceteris Judæis qui Jefum pro Chrifto receperunt. Quin et Petrus videtur
longo tempore juxta Mofis legem obfervaffe ritus Ju-
daicos, &c. Et ipfe Paulus Judæis Judæus factus eft,
ut Judæos lucraretur. V. Origen contra Celfum. l. 2.
Edit. Cantab. 1658.

SECTION II. CHAPTER III. page 311. end of note (i).
"An enquiry into the prefent ftate of the feptuagint verfion of the Old Teftament," written by Doctor Owen,
will furnifh the reader with a very comprehenfive view of
the defigned, and accidental corruptions which have
crept into the fcriptures. Much learned information
may alfo be gathered from the work of Mr. Lami.
This author hath been attacked for the harmlefs fingularity of his affertions, with all the violence of controverfy; the diviner parts of religion, her inimitable
precepts could neither acquire a confirmation, nor
fuffer a diminution of their excellent propriety, becaufe Lami maintained that John the Baptift was twice
a prifoner; the firft time, in purfuance of an order
from the Priefts, and Pharifees; the fecond time, at
the command of Herod; that our Saviour did not eat of
the Pafchal lamb, at the laft fupper; that the true
Pafchal lamb was crucified, whilft the Jews facrificed
the typical lamb; and that the two Marys, and Mary
Magdalene were one, and the fame perfon. It is not
from that vivacity of genius, which feduced him into
fanciful fuppofitions, that we are to expect a juft picture of Lami. The honeft tenor of his life, and the
particularity of his death, are proofs of fuch a ftriking
attachment to Chriftianity, as rendered him incapable
of furviving the defertion of it, in another. A young
man,

man, whom his writings had extricated from a ſtate of
hereſy, became his pupil, and for ſome time, made
quick advances in piety, and ſcience. He had conceived the moſt extravagant hopes of his new convert,
when he diſcovered that he was again an infidel, and
had plunged deeper into error than ever. The ſhock
was fatal to Lami. He was ſeized with a ſettled melancholy ; his health became immediately impaired ; and
a vomiting of blood ſoon put a period to his days.

Section II. Chap. III. page 324. note(q). l. 6. Ουχ οτι
αλλοτρια εϛι τα Πλατωνος διδαγματα τω Χριϛω, αλλ οτι ωκ εϛι
πολυ τη ομοια. Non equidem quod alienæ ſint a Chriſto
Platonis doctrinæ, ſed quod ſibi ipſis non omnino con-
ſtent. Juſtin. Ap. 1. p. 51. folio. Pariſiis, 1636.

Section II. Chap. III. page 325. note (q). l. 28. Εϛι
των οντων εκαϛω, δι ων την επιϛημην ανωγκη παραγιγνεϲαι τρια,
τεταρτον δε αυτη, πεμπτον δ' αυτο τιθεναι δει, ο δη γνωϛον τε
και αληθες εϛιν ; ων εν μεν, ονομα, δευτερον δε λογος, το δε τριτον,
ειδωλον, το τεταρτον δε επιϛημη : και κατα ταυτα δε ειποιμεν αν
οτι φωνη μεν βοωντος εν τη ερημω ειϛηκλαι ο Ιωαννης προς τω Ιηϲω,
αναλογον τω Πλατωνι ονοματι, δευτερος δε μετα τον Ιωαννην δει-
κνυμενος υπ' αυτω ο Ιηϲες, ω εφαρμοζει το, ο λογος ϲαρξ εγενετο,
αναλογον ον τω παρα Πλατωνι λογω. Πλατων μεν ων το τριτον
φηϲιν ειδωλον, ημεις δε το ονομα τω ειδωλω επ αλλω ταὶτοντες
τρανοτερον φηϲομεν εν τη ψυχη γινομενον μετα τον λογον των τραυ-
ματων τυπον τωτον ε῏ναι εν εκαϛω Χριϛον, απο Χριϛω λογω, ει
δε και αναλογον εϛι τω τεταρτω οντι επιϛημη, η εν τοις καθ ημας
τελειαις ϲοφια ο Χριϛος.

Section II. Chapter III. page 326. note(q). l. 47.
The only compoſition by Origen, which I have an opportunity of conſulting, is his defence againſt Celſus. In
this, I do not find the reaſons to which my learned author alludes, when he deſcribes that writer, as denying
his adoration to the angels, whom he ſuppoſes to be
endued with a portion of the divinity. Many paſſages
in the fifth book expreſsly forbid the worſhipping of
angels, and enforce the prohibition by quotations from
the ſcriptures. Perhaps I have examined the defence
with too little attention. Perhaps, this aſſertion of
Origen is to be met with in another work. I would
not be underſtood to level the moſt diſtant inſinuation
againſt the French writer, who ſeems too candid to
miſrepreſent, and too accurate to be miſtaken.

Section

SECTION II. CHAPTER IV. page 340. note (a) l. 1.
γν ταχα μεν αλλα λεγοντος, η ραδιον γη αποδεξαϑαι. Quod si
quidem, &c.

SECTION II. CHAPTER IV. page 342. l. 11. "Praise be
to God," the favourite expreffion of thofe religious
perfecutors, who judged the maffacre of his heretical
creatures to be the moft acceptable facrifice to the
Creator, was the fignal, at which their predeceffors
the Circoncelliones rufhed on to flaughter. They were
a favage, illiterate, bloody multitude, inflexibly attached to the Donatifts, and, of courfe, the murderers
of the followers of Cæcilian. Their leader affumed
the title of " Chief of the faints." They difclaimed
agriculture, and affected continence: in the firft inftance, the fincerity of their profeffions, cherifhed by
an obftinate difpofition to idlenefs, ftood continually
unimpeached; in the fecond inftance, they were lefs
fcrupulous. Their female companions, whom they
dignified with the appellation of facred virgins, were
inflamed with wine, and generally pregnant. As the
Circoncelliones ftiled themfelves the adminiftrators of
juftice, and the guardians of the oppreffed, they re-
leafed debtors, and affaffinated thofe creditors who refufed to annul their bonds.: they dragged the mafters
from their chariots, and made them run before their
flaves, who were feated in their places. God having
forbidden Peter to ufe the fword, they were for fome
time too devout to meddle with it; and, until they
had recourfe to arms of every kind, they fought with
fticks, which they emphatically called " the clubs of
Ifrael." When they attacked a miferable apoftate
from Donatifm, with thefe, they exhibited fuch fpeci-
mens of dexterity, as would have done honour to an
executioner of the inquifition: without killing the
fufferer on the fpot, they broke all his bones, and
left him to languifh during feveral days, before he ex-
pired. When they were foftened into a fit of mercy,
they deftroyed the fortunate objeĉt of it, at once.
When they were driven into the more favourite exceffes
of barbarity, they formed lime, and vinegar into a pafte,
with which they fmeared the eyes of thofe, whom they
before had crufhed, and wounded. Satiated with the
blood of others, they turned at length upon themfelves;
and with the moft frantic refolution, fought all the

dreadful

dreadful varieties of death; multitudes committing their bodies to the flames, plunging into the sea, and casting themselves headlong from the tops of precipices.

SECTION II. CHAPTER IV. page 347. l. 13. The elegant author of this work, must permit me to observe, that his remark at the 193 page, in the original, is probably a mistake; in this part of his masterly character of Constantine, his words are; "il oublie de se faire baptiser, et meurt hérétique." Constantine was baptised at Nicomedia, by Eusebius; this ceremony appears to have been one of the last incidents of his life. Whether this delay arose from too feeble a conviction of the divinity of the Christian religion, or from a secret dislike to the profession of the gospel; is difficult to determine. Some allowances will, however, be made in his favour, when it is recollected that he himself declared that it was his intention to have been baptized in the river Jordan, whither the sick and infirm were wont to resort, and bathe, during the Epiphany. It was, besides, a custom amongst many who lived in the fourth century, to defer the office of baptism to their last hour, from a supposition, that as this rite conferred a remission of sins, so they who received it immediately before their departure, ascended in a spotless state to heaven.

SECTION II. CHAPTER IV. page 369. note (m). Ὅτι γὰρ σὺ Ἀλέξανδρε παρα τῶν πρεσβυτερῶν ἐξήτεις, τι δὲ ποτε αυτῶν ἱκάστος; ὑπερ τινος τοπω τῶν εν τω νομω γεγραμμενῶν, μαλλον δ' ὑπερ μα ταιω τινος ζητησεως μερης επυνθανω. συ τε ο. Αρεις τωθ οπερ η μητε την αρχην ενθυμηθηναι; η ενθυμηθεντα σιωπη παραωθναι προσηκον ην, απροοπλως εντεθεικας οθεν της εν υμιν διχρoιας εγεηθησης ; . . . . τι δε τετο σ[ιν; ετε ερωταν υπερ τῶν τοιετων, ιξ αρχης προσηκον ην, ητε ερωτωμενον αποκρινεσθαι. Cum enim tu, Alexander, a presbiteris tuis requireres quid quisque eorum de quodam legis loco sentiret, seu potius de quadam parte inanis quaestionis eos interrogares; cumque tu, Ari, id quod vel nunquam cogitare, vel sane cogitatum silentio premere debueras, imprudenter protulisses, excitata inter vos discordia, &c. quidnam vero illud est? nec interrogare de hujusmodi rebus principio decebat, nec interrogatum respondere, &c.

Section II. Chapter IV. Page 370. l. 15.

Σικελιδες Μυσαι, μεγαλην φατιν υμνησωμεν
τι τυτυ φανερωτερον; προςιθησι γαρ
Ηλυθε Κυμαιε μαντευματος; εις τελος ομφη

Κυμαιαν αινιτιομενος; δηλαδη την Σιβυλλαν, και ουκ ηρκεσθη τυτοις
αλλα περαιτερω προεχωρησεν, ως της χρειας την αιτυ μαρτυριαν
επιτοθυσης. τι λεγων αυθις;

Ουτος αρ αιωνων ιερος; στιχος ωρευται ημιν
Ηκει παρθενος αυθις, αγυς ιρατον βασιλεια.

τις ουν αρα ειη παρθενος η επαινεσα; αρ ουχ η πληρης τι και
εγκυος γενομενη τε θιυ πνευματος. και προσιθησιν ο ποιητης,

Τον δε νεωςι πυ τεχθεντα Φαεσφορε μνη
Αντι σιδηρειης χρυσην γενεμην ο πασαντα,
Προσκυνει

πεπαιδευμενως δε ω σοφωτατε
ποιητα Μαρων.

Sicelides Mufæ paulo majora canamus.
Quid hoc apertius? addit enim
Ultima Cumæi venit jam carminis ætas.
Cumæam fcilicet Sybyllam intelligens. Nec his con-
tentus ulterius progreffus eft, quafi neceffitas ipfa
teftimonium ejus requireret. Quid igitur dicit?
Magnus ab integro fæclorum nafcitur ordo,
Jam redit et virgo: redeunt Saturnia regna.
Quænam ergo eft illa virgo quæ redit? nonne illa quæ
plena, et gravida fuit Spiritu fancto? Sic enim addit
poeta.
Tu modo nafcenti puero quo ferrea primum
Definet, ac toto furget gens aurea mundo
Cafta fave Lucina!
Docè igitur hæc a te dicta funt, O Maro! poetarum
fapientiffime!
Conft. orat. ad fanct. coet. c. 19 & 20.
The reader will eafily perceive in many parts of the
Greek tranflation, how much the fenfe of the lines
from Virgil hath been tortured, to fupport the favourite
hypothefis of Conftantine. The expreffion "Saturnia
regna" is not the only expreffion which is quite loft in
this unwarrantable paraphrafe.

Section II. Chap. V. page 404. note (e). l. 9. The
"differtations fur les oracles des Paiens," written by
Anthony Vandale, concealed under a languid, and difgufting

gufting ftile, a fund of learning and penetration.
When fuch rough, but valuable materials were polifhed
by the fkilful touch of Fontenelle, it was no wonder
that they joined the livelinefs of amufement, with the
folidity of inftruction ; and the precifion of method,
with the ftrength of argument. The philofophers, and
the men of tafle were equally warm in their commendations of this work. Fontenelle was, notwithflanding,
attacked by Baltus the Jefuit, to whom he made no reply. His filence did not proceed from a conviction
that his antagonift had defeated him, but from his extreme diflike to literary difputes. He would rather have
chofen (to ufe his own expreffion) that the devil fhould
have paffed for a prophet, than have entered into a difcuffion which might not have terminated in his perfonal
fafety. It muft be truly an enlightened age, in which
no fecret enemy would confpire againft an author, who
fhould be daring enough to explode the oracles for human impofture. Fontenelle felt that he had been concerned in a fervice of fome danger; and it was imagined
that "le Tellier," the confeffor of Lewis the fourteenth, had inveighed fo ftrongly againft the fuppofed
impieties of the differtation, that the Marquis d' Ar-
genfon, in endeavouring to prevent the ftorms of religious perfecution from burfting over the head of his
friend, was obliged to exert his intereft with the fovereign, to its utmoft length.

Corrections neceffary in the French edition.

Introduction, p. 5. l. 15. inftead of "fuit fes fembla-
bles," read fuit fes femblables.
Introduction, p. 6. l. 3. inftead of "il doit en etre de
même," read il en eft de même.
Chap. 2. p. 18. note 1. l. 3. inftead of "fept" read
trois.
Page 22. note 1. l. 1. inftead of "heavealy offspring"
read offspring of heaven !
Page 25. l. 10. inftead of "propolace" read populace.
Page 26. note 3. l. 1. inftead of "m'empêcha" read
n'empecha.
Page 34. note 10. l. 11. inftead of "cauffam habere"
read caufam belli habere.
Page 34. note 10. l. 12. inftead of "in imperio" read
in maximo imperio.

Page

(17)

Page 37. l. 14. inſtead of " Tout etoit" read car tout
etoit.
Page 44. l. 16. inſtead of " et tandis que" read tandis
que.
Page 49. l. 9 inſtead of " ſur un million" read pour
un million.
Page 58. l. 10. inſtead of " le mot" read ce mot.
Page 65. l. 6. inſtead of " qui eſt" read il eſt.
Page 71. l. 12. inſtead of " ſous" read qui ſous.
Page 75. note 8. l. 8. inſtead of " bello Gallos" read
gloriâ belli Gallos.
Page 76. note 9. l. 3. inſtead of " fuimus" read ſumus.
Page 79. l. 25. inſtead of " torpeur" read langueur.
Page 104. note 11. l. 10. inſtead of " cauſſa" read
cauſa.
Page 106. l. 31. inſtead of " de la liberté qui eſt" read
de la liberté ; qui eſt.
Page 107. l. 1. inſtead of " attachée" read attaché.
Page 109. l. 4. inſtead of " des Gracques" read dans
l'hiſtoire des Gracques.
Page 116. l. 16. inſtead of " l'empire, Ottoman telles"
read l'empire Ottoman, telles.
Page 119. l. 28. inſtead of " autorité" read auſterité.
Page 121. note 3. l. 1. inſtead of " omnipotentes" read
impotentes.
Page 132. note 5. l. 25. and 26. inſtead of " recidere
aggrediar" read recipere adgrediar.
Page 153. l. 17. inſtead of " puiſqu'il impoſſible" read
puiſqu'il eſt impoſſible.
Page 159. l. 28. inſtead of " decidé" read obſtiné.
Page 162. note 10. inſtead of " Inſtit. liv. 4." read In-
ſtit liv. 1.
Page 173. l. 12. inſtead of " docet" read docebit.
Page 173. note 15. l. 9. and 10. inſtead of "repoſitum"
read repoſitus. inſtead of " ſtatutum" read ſtatutus.
Page 182. note 21. inſtead of " inſtit. liv. 4." read
Inſtit. liv. 1. c. 6. l. 4. C. 6. 9. l. 6. c. 25.
Page 183. note 25. l. 14. inſtead of " Miltiade" read
Melchiade.
Page 189. note 2. l. 3. inſtead of " XXXVIII" read
XXVIII.
Page 193. note 6. l. 2. inſtead of " LXVI" read LXV.

b   When

When I had concluded the tranflation of this firft
volume, and committed it, with the additional notes,
to the prefs, the particular attention which I was obliged to pay to my own private affairs, detained me,
during feveral months, from the profecution of an undertaking, to which, I greatly fear, I may have proved
unequal. This half of my tafk was fcarcely finifhed,
when a fortunate accident gave rife to my acquaintance
with the French author, Monfieur le Chevalier de
Chatellur, Brigadier of the armies of his Chriftian
Majefty, and late Colonel of the regiment of Guienne.
On his abilities as a writer, his book is a more elegant
panegyric, than any which I could poffibly compofe.
The qualities which he poffeffes as a foldier, and the
vertues which he hath difplayed in the more exalted
character of a citizen of the world, are as public as his
writings. Furnifhed as I am, with information from
thofe who long have known him, it is with pleafure,
that I could expatiate on thefe accomplifhments, if a
defire of fhewing my own gratitude, in return to thofe
friendly marks of intimacy with which he fince hath
honoured me, would let me difobey his modeft orders
that I fhould be filent. I muft now proceed to the execution of his other commands, after having obferved,
that in how favourable a point of view foever he may
have feen my note, relative to Rollin, it fhould not have
appeared, had there been a poffibility of erafing it : but
the firft volume of the tranflation was printed off, before I had the happinefs of being acquainted with the
Chevalier. He bids me, in his name, befpeak the indulgence of the public, to the errors of the French
edition. Thefe will be confidered as unavoidable in-
conveniencies, when the works of an author are printed
at fuch a diftance from his refidence, that he cannot examine the proofs ; and I am much miftaken, if the candid reader will not rather be furprifed, that fo few in-
accuracies have occurred, than offended with fuch as
he may meet with. Whilft the Chevalier was engaged
in this work, he frequently fhifted his abode, and was
alfo obliged to attend his regiment, during four months
of the year : at thefe times, he could only have recourfe
to fuch books, as were at hand ; many of which were
tranflations, and but a fmall number originals. This
circumftance will apologize for the unavoidable neceffity
which

which he was under, when citing the Greek authors, of quoting at one moment from the text, and at another moment from the verſion. In the courſe of this tranſlation of the firſt volume, I endeavoured, as much as it was in my power, to inſert copies from the originals; but confined to an obſcure ſpot, at an inſurmountable diſtance from the capital; and far, very far from any intercourſe with a man of learning, I muſt lament in ſolitude, that want of books, of which my more eccentric friend ſo feelingly complains. Whilſt but an inconſiderable number of the claſſics, and ſcarcely one of all the fathers, are found within my humble library, it is with diſappointment, and concern, that I perceive the ſtudies of the neighbouring clergy, as naked as my own. The Euſebius, from which I have quoted, is imperfect, and the original reading of the paſſage in the fourth chapter of the ſecond ſection, in this tranſlation, beginning with "itaque cum omnes, &c." is torn out. It were ridiculous to mention this deficiency; but as an excuſe to the Chevalier, for not obeying his requeſt, and to the reader, for not ſupplying him, as in ſome other places, with the Greek text. The alterations, and the materials of the notes which follow, have been tranſmitted to me by the author.

SECTION I CHAPTER V. page 113. note(q). Several editions of "principi di ſcienza nuova intorno alla commune nature delle nazioni" have been printed at Naples. The author Giam-Baptiſta Vico, a celebrated Italian lawyer, hath been dead ſome years. Many particulars of his life are in the firſt volume of "Racolta di opuſculi ſcientifici, e filologici del Angelo Calogera." Venezia, 1728.

SECTION I. CHAPTER V. page 121. note(s). l. 26. The Chevalier with the moſt commendable ſincerity acknowledges a miſtake in his explanation of the term "major natu quidam," which ſignified, amongſt the Romans, the age, and not the rank, or precedence to which an individual was intitled by his birth. All the conſequence, therefore, which he had drawn from the paſſage in Livy, falls to the ground. A new ſheet was printed off, and inſerted in the copies which remained at Paris, in order to rectify what was imagined to be ſo capital an error. The reader is deſired to paſs over all

the

the remainder of the note, from the words of the fourteenth line, " n'a jamais exifté a Rome," to the end.
What follows is intended to fupply the place of the can-
celled lines.

" Il eft fur que quelque modification qu'ait reçu
l'efclavage chez les anciens, jamais les efclaves n'ont
eté regardés comme peuple, comme partie integrante de
l'etat. On peut voir dans Athenée des recherches affés
curieufes fur cet objet : il diftingue plufieurs fortes
d'efclavage, comme lors qu'une nation fe foumet en-
tierement a une autre ; l'orfqu'un peuple emigrant de-
mande des terres à cultiver ; ou lorfqu'un peuple vain-
queur les abandonne aux vaincus, à certaines conditions
onereufes ; ce qui fe rapproche affés de la fervitude
feodale : mais il ne parte nulle part de cette demi-fer-
vitude, de cet etat mitoyen entre la liberté, et l'efclavage, qu'on fuppofe avoir exifté dans les deux premiers fiecles de la republique." V. Deip. l. 6. ch. 7.

The miftake is adopted in the tranflation, where it
might probably have remained, an inftance of my
inability to amend it, unlefs I had been favoured with
the foregoing correction. The paffage after the words
" never exifted at Rome" (l. 19. note(*) is to be omitted,
and thefe lines muft be inferted in its place.

It is evident that whatfoever modification flavery
might have received amongft the ancients, the flaves
were not confidered as a people, as a conftituent part of
the ftate. Some curious enquiries into this fubject, may
be feen in Athenæus, who hath diftinguifhed flavery
into feveral kinds ; as, when one nation fubmits entirely to another nation ; when a body of emigrants afk
for an allotment of lands, that they may cultivate them ;
or when the territories acquired by conqueft, are abandoned, under certain burthenfome ftipulations, to the
conquered ; the which approaches nearly to the feodal
fervitude. But Athenæus no where mentions that kind
of half-flavery, that middle ftate between freedom and
fervitude, which is fuppofed to have exifted in the two
firft centuries of the republic.

V. Athenæi deipnofophiftarum, l. 6. c. 7.

Section I. Chapter VI. page 178. l. 16. Seide. See
the Mahomet of Voltaire.

SECTION I. CHAPTER VI. page 123. note(*k*). The author of "l'hiſtoire politique du gouvernement Romain"
is a young eccleſiaſtic, named l'abbé Bignon.

SECTION I. CHAPTER VI. page 194. note(*r*). l. 12. The
"diſſertation ſur l'incertitude des quatres premiers ſiecles
de Rome," written by Mr. de Pouilly, is in the "me-
moires de l'academie des belles lettres." To this elegant
author, France is indebted for "Remarques ſur la chro-
nologie de Newton," and "la Theorie des ſentimens
agreables." The third edition of this laſt work, was
printed in 1749. To have thrown a valuable preſent
into the treaſury of learning, was in Mr. de Pouilly,
only a ſecondary merit. The city of Rheims feels a
pleaſing conviction, that the benefactor who ſupplied
her inhabitants with wholeſome fountains, in the place
of putrid wells, who founded public ſchools, embelliſhed
walks, and concerted, during the laſt moments of his
life, a plan for raiſing magazines of corn, left ſtronger
claims upon the approbation of his fellow-citizens,
than any which the mere abilities of the moſt poliſhed
author could have ſupported. The manuſcripts of
Monſieur de Pouilly, which fill twelve folio volumes,
are in the poſſeſſion of his brother Mr. de Burigny, a
gentleman whoſe extenſive erudition, and aſſiduous labours, ſtill continue to embelliſh the French literature.
Mr. de Pouilly, the ſon, is lieutenant-general within
the bailiwic of Rheims, and hath acquired no inconſiderable reputation by his life of the chancellor de
l'Hopital, publiſhed about the year 1765.

SECTION I. CHAPTER VIII. page 248. note (*s*).
Mr. Dutens, the ingenious author of "Recherches
ſur l'origine de decouvertes attribuées aux modernes,"
2 vol. 8vo. Paris, 1766, is a gentleman of French ex-
traction, and a miniſter of the church of England.
He attended earl Percy on his tour through Italy, and
was ſome time ſecretary to our embaſſador at Turin.
A zealous advocate for the ſuperiority of the ancients,
over the moderns, muſt peruſe this work with unlimited approbation : but the reader, who hath embraced
a contrary opinion, will probably imagine that the
learned writer, notwithſtanding the new and ſolid information with which he hath enriched ſome paſſages
of his production, is more the partial admirer, than the
candid

candid judge. How will the warm lover of the philofophy of a later period bear even the infinuation that
Locke, Berkley, Leibnitz, Galileo, Newton, Harvey,
and Buffon; poor in the midſt of imaginary difcoveries,
and without one fyftem which they could truly call
their own, are plunged in debt to Ariftotle, Protago-
ras, Sextus Empiricus, Lucretius, Plato, Hippocrates,
and Plautinus?

SECTION II. CHAPTER I. page 266. note (d). The
author of " l'Introduction a l'Hiftoire de Dannemarc,"
is Mr. Mallet, who wrote " hiftoire de Heffe," and
whofe abilities are too well known to render any enco-
mium neceſſary. It would be a kind of literary injuftice, to mention the former work, without obferving
that the tranflator of it into our language, hath inferted
feveral valuable additions, together with the Latin verfion, by Goranfon, of the Edda, or fyftem of Runic
Mythology.

SECTION II. CHAPTER IV. page 189. l. 11. original. Inftead of " c'eft qu 'Origene," read c'eft que
Lactance.

SECTION II. CHAPTER IV. p. 340. l. 3. tranflation.
Inftead of " Origen," read Lactantius.

SECTION II. CHAPTER V. page 403. l. 23. Abbé de
Paris, after having furrendered all his eftate to his
brother, devoted himfelf to folitude, and remained a
voluntary prifoner within his own houfe. Here, he
employed his time in prayer, the feverities of penitence,
and the labour of his hands. To the poor, he frequently prefented ftockings of his own weaving. Some-
time after his deceafe, his brother erected a monument
over his grave, at Saint Medard; and hither, the
ftaunch admirers of the pious Janfenift repaired in multitudes. It was pretended that miraculous cures were
wrought at his tomb; and the ridiculous enthufiafts
who furrounded it, were feized with a religious frenzy,
during the continuance of which they danced, jumped,
and threw their bodies into ftrange contortions. Hence
they received the name of *Convulfionnaires*. The
court, at length, imagined it neceſſary to interfere,
and in January 1732, gave orders that the monument
fhould be inclofed, fo as to prevent all poffible accefs to
it,

it. The *Convulfionnaires* then removed the fcene of
their farce, and performed it in their own apartments.
They ftill continue to appear at Paris, though not fo
frequently as ufual. The lieutenants de police, contented with obferving their motions, without proceeding againft them, have funk them into a contempt,
from which the violence of perfecution might probably
have fheltered them. The fanatical production, to
which the Chevalier alludes, is written by Mr. Montgeron, a counfellor of the parliament of Paris; it is
entitled, "La verité des miracles opérés par l'inter-
ceffion de M. Paris," and was prefented by its author,
to the king, at Verfailles. Montgeron fell a martyr to
Janfenifm: he was, at firft, committed to the Baftille,
then, confined within an abbey of the Benedictins, in
the diocefe of Avignon, and afterwards, removed to
the citadel of Valence, where he died, in 1750. Punifhment nourifhed his enthufiafm, and quickened his
perfuafions : in prifon, he added two more volumes to
his work, and left a manufcript full of bitter invectives
againft the incredulous.

www.ingramcontent.com/pod-product-compliance
Lightning Source LLC
Chambersburg PA
CBHW031823270326
41932CB00008B/529